About the author

Before becoming a writer, Sue Hepworth worked as a research psychologist, a social researcher, a full-time mother and various combinations of these. She has been a frequent contributor to *The Times* and has been published in *The Guardian, The Observer* and *The Independent.* Her fourth novel, *But I Told You Last Year That I Loved You,* was named by the National Autistic Society as one of their favourite novels about autism. Sue lives in the Derbyshire Peak District with her husband. Her blog, *Fragments of a Writer's Life,* can be found at www.suehepworth.com

Days are where we live

by

Sue Hepworth

Novels by Sue Hepworth

Zuzu's Petals

But I Told You Last Year That I Loved You

Even When They Know You

Novels written with Jane Linfoot

Plotting for Beginners

Plotting for Grown-ups

Days are where we live

by

Sue Hepworth

Dedicated with love to all my blog readers

These are the readers whose names I know:

Alanna	Lois
Ana	Manjit
Anita	Marilyn
Chris G	Marmee
Chris O	Natalie
Chris S	Pete
Chrissie	Rosemary
Donna	Sally
Gill	Shafia
Helen	Sushma
Jan	Thea
Jenetta	The family
Karen	member who
Kath	declines to be
Kay	named
Kristine	Valerie
Liz	Wendy

Introduction

I began writing my blog in 2006 as a simple web presence after the publication of my first novel *Plotting for Beginners* (written with Jane Linfoot.) By mid-2008 it had developed into something else – a place to share my thoughts and amusements, my daily life, and sometimes my feelings.

In deciding how to edit the last ten years of my blog for publication in book form, I was faced with a tough decision: should I choose posts that are representative of everything that has been on my mind, and thus attempt a kind of 'self-portrait' of my life from 60 to 70? Or should I make it a book of entertainment, comfort, humour and friendliness? I chose the latter.

Even before Covid-19 arrived, I found the world in 2020 increasingly disturbing and dark. And although I engage with it and try to contribute to making it better, sometimes I need to retreat and escape. This was clear when in July 2019 I was asked what my comfort reading was and I gave the interviewer not just one book title but a huge long list.

Comfort reading has its place and is not to be sneered at. It can be a case of *reculer pour mieux sauter*. Sometimes we don't want to read an 'important' book - we want a book that is intelligent, yet undemanding, to keep us company.

Lately on my blog there has been a tension between comfort and harsh reality. It has been growing since Israel's devastating bombing of Gaza in 2014, and since 2015 when the crisis facing millions of refugees erupted. And in the UK, millions of people have been suffering under the crushing austerity programme begun by the government in 2010.

But although I talk about life and death in this collection, you will be hard pushed to find any politics, even though politics is there online. It is a strand I would have included if this collection had been 'blog as self-portrait.'

The unedited blog and the many photographs which couldn't be included here can be found online at

www.suehepworth.com

and you will find a link at the right-hand side to a post containing photographs of many of the people mentioned in this collection.

This book is dedicated with affection to my blog readers, some of whom have become friends, even though we have never met. Many readers have commented on the blog online, and these comments have been important to me, as well as to other blog readers, but I haven't been able to find room for them in this collection. I have included just one, which you will find in February 2016.

I hope you enjoy the posts I have chosen.

Glossary

Dave	Husband
Zoe	Daughter
Isaac	Elder son in the USA
The family member who declines to be named	The family member who declines to be named
Wendy	Daughter-in-law in the USA
Lux	Granddaughter in the USA
Cecilia/Cece	Granddaughter in the USA
Jaine	Daughter-in-law
Kath	Elder sister
Pete	Elder brother
Jen	Younger sister
Jonty	Younger brother who lives in Wensleydale
Rachel	Jonty's wife
Karen/ Aging Hippie	Friend in California

Chrissie	A crime writer friend
Liz	Friend
Het	Friend who lives in London
Mel	My saxophone teacher
Bakewell	Small market town 3 miles away
Monsal Trail	A local disused railway line - now used as a bridleway - in the Derbyshire Peak District
Wensleydale	My parents lived here in the Yorkshire Dales
Crokinole	A traditional Canadian board game that involves flicking wooden counters
Rammel	Assorted small junk, usually chaotically stored
Slackline	A tensioned band suspended above ground between two fixed posts, to walk along while balancing. This is not easy.

JANUARY

January 4th 2010

Kitchen conversation

Me (observing Dave's idiosyncratic way of making milky coffee): "I have to tell you that I'm going to give some of your interesting characteristics to a rather unpleasant character in my next book."

Dave: "I know you find some of my habits odd."

Me: "Well, you were the hero in my first three novels. You can't expect to be the hero *every* time."

Dave: "Of course. It would be too exhausting."

January 5th 2010

Perfect Timing

There are certain times of day when I miss my mother – a lot. I often used to ring her at teatime. I sometimes try to fill the gap, sort of, by ringing up one of my sisters.

We often say to each other "I wanted to ring Ma, so I'm ringing you." No-one is offended. We all feel her lack. And it's not as if we don't ring each other at other times, times when we are *not* thinking that the person who is forever out of earshot is the one we really want to ring.

Yesterday at half past six I yearned to ring her, and I sat down to write about that feeling, and then the phone rang.

It was my son in California, ringing his mother.

January 8th 2010

That damn patchwork

Last night I dreamed I had a baby, and I wasn't pleased. Come on – I've done it three times, that's enough for anybody. I realise now why I had that dream. It's because I'd been thinking about making another patchwork.

All this staying inside because of the dratted snow, all this enforced separation from my slackline, a woman can write only so much, a woman can play only so much sax before she is sick of the sound of *Misty*. And that's how it happened that a little voice said - "Wouldn't it be nice to make another patchwork...all those lovely fabrics, all those vibrant colours that aren't like that stuff outside — WHITE."

I've said here before that making a patchwork is like having a baby. You forget just how awful those sleepless nights and midnight feeds and tantrums were, how boring were those wet afternoons with a toddler who isn't well enough for playgroup and yet is well enough to want you to play at fire rescue (actually, what am I saying? – I *love* pretend play...OK

3

I am getting distracted now). The point is that however delightful babies and children are, there is an awful lot of tedium in bringing them up, and that's how it is with patchwork. The last time I completed one, I said – NEVER AGAIN. And I expect that that is exactly what I am going to say when I have finished the one I have just begun.

January 9th 2010

School Milk

Sometimes, when you wake up ridiculously early (4.50 a.m.) and you foolishly talk to your partner for half an hour (foolishly, because this makes you fully awake) and you're desperate for a cuppa, and before you get out of bed you have to put on two jumpers over your pyjamas because it's so cold, and then when you get back into bed with your tea and your laptop, you find an email from your sister about a website of the village where you grew up, and you look at the photographs of yourself and your brothers and sisters at the lovely village school, and you read all about a classmate's memories, and you remember the way the school milk popped out of the tops of the tiny bottles when it froze and how the teacher used to defrost it in front of the classroom coal fire, and how you took your best friend Christine Cook's milk home for her when she was ill, and how Perfect Person (Miss Brown) taught you beautiful italic script and how Miss Coggan took you on nature walks and let you pick brambles for the dinner ladies to use for pudding for school dinner, you are

4

overwhelmed and burst into tears, and you wonder why life isn't simple and sweet any more.

And you snuggle under the bedclothes again, and all you want is for your mother to be downstairs in the kitchen cooking bacon for your breakfast, and for the smell of it to be wafting upstairs, and for your brother to be groaning in the next bedroom about how cold it is, and how there's frost on the inside of his window. Sometimes, when all of this happens, all you can do to cheer yourself up is to ditch your usual sensible porridge, and make yourself pancakes for breakfast.

January 10th 2010

School Milk Redux

On the other hand, I am very, very, very, lucky to have a big warm bed and someone to share it with and NO ice on the inside of my window panes, and there are definite advantages to being grown up and free to decide I'm going to stay in bed an extra hour with *Victoria Wood* on my laptop to make me laugh, and eat my deux pains au chocolat, which I bought the day before as a prophylactic against early morning angst.

And anyway, I did always think that the school milk looked odd when it froze and popped out of the bottles in those little columns, so I didn't fancy drinking it, and nor did I like sitting cross-legged on the floor in infant class at story-time behind that boy who got his hankie out and wrapped it round his index finger and then licked it and spent the whole of Little Red Riding Hood picking the scab on his knee.

Who *was* that boy?

January 15th 2010

Sensory Deprivation

I've been living like a hermit (with Dave) for what seems like three months (but when I count it up it's only two and a half weeks – *what?*) and I've not been anywhere but the village shop, the village dairy, the Bakewell Co-op and Quaker Meeting (OK, not like a hermit, but I have *felt* like a hermit) so when I got on a train yesterday alongside people *I didn't know* (except for - by chance - my crime writer friend, similarly starved of excitement, but who always has interesting things to say, such as "Did you know that Amazon sells a bullet-proof memory stick?") and then I got off the train 15 minutes later in Sheffield and saw hundreds of people *I didn't know* all walking about unimpeded on snow-free streets – well, it was sensationally stimulating. **WOW!**

And I am sitting here now in bare feet typing this because it isn't cold anymore, and outside the window it's raining and thawing, which has cheered me up as much as going to the pictures yesterday to see Meryl Streep's new film, *It's Complicated,* which was good fun, if flawed, not least because neither of the male leads was anything to write home about. I mean – Alec Baldwin and Steve Martin as romantic leads?

Come on…why didn't they have someone yummy like Gabriel Byrne…or George Clooney? (or even that chap who played the father in the remake of *The Parent Trap*?...)

Yes, you're right. Yesterday's excitement has gone to my head and affected the style of this post. Normal service will be resumed as soon as possible.

January 27th 2010

Bunged up

When you have a filthy cold and your nose is dripping snot on your keyboard, you don't feel much like blogging.

FEBRUARY

February 3rd 2010

Freaking Scales!

I actually made it to a sax lesson yesterday, after missing 2 weeks for Mel's Christmas hols, 2 weeks for snow, 1 week because Mel was ill, and 1 week because I was ill. Mel could really see my progress. She said she was speechless at my rendition of *Misty*, and I stood there glowing. And then I asked her to help me add frilly bits to it.

Oh my God.

Up until yesterday I was thinking I could get away with learning major and minor scales and that would see me through. Now I realise that if I want to improvise there are all kinds of frigging scales I have to learn, scales I didn't even know existed – Dorian scales, Mixolydian scales, Phrygian scales, Pentatonic scales, and now Dave has walked in and told me not to forget the Blues scales. AAARRRGGGHHH.

And all these scales fit together in a really weird way. For example, a Dorian scale in G is really a Gm7 but if you look at the signature on the stave it has one flat which makes it look like F Major. How the hell am I supposed to get my head around all of this? I have stumbled into a nightmare world that is an impenetrable matrix of incomprehensible musical meta-theory. It makes multivariate statistical analysis (that I did in my former life) look as simple as counting on my fingers. And all because I heard that man playing *Misty* on the sax outside the Co-op in Bakewell. That man has a lot to answer for. I shall track him down and give him what for.

February 17th 2010

Still Cheerful

There is freezing fog outside the window and all the trees are white again. Am I downhearted? No. But I am far too busy to blog, so I thought you might enjoy this piece I had in *The Times* one February, some years ago.

What did you say spring cleaning was, exactly?

At the beginning of January, as I helped my mother take down her Christmas decorations I asked her what she would like me to do on my next visit, in a few weeks time. "The spring cleaning, please."

Hadn't she seen the correspondence in *The Times* in December, where readers were asking whether the grass they were cutting was the last of the autumn or the first of the spring? Didn't she realise that as global warming is blurring the seasons into one, spring cleaning can be classed as an outmoded practice, and moved from the conceptual broom cupboard to the conceptual attic?

When I told my husband – a man raised with a lavatory brush in one hand and a bottle of Windolene in the other – that my mother had asked me to do her spring cleaning, he turned the colour of his rubber gloves. He knows I am still working in Key Stage One in dusting the bookshelves. And he blames my mother.

Funny that, because I blame his mother for giving him unreasonable expectations. She would spend all morning every morning, cleaning the house from top to bottom, and on Tuesdays and Thursdays would have a cleaning lady round to mop up the speck she had missed. Hers was the only house I have been where, if you dropped a biscuit under the bed, you could pick it up and eat it without first checking it for fluff.

My mother, on the other hand, had her priorities right. For her, reading the paper, helping us furnish our dolls houses, making us cowboy suits on her sewing machine, or taking us out to fly our kites, were all activities preferable to cleaning. She would clear the kitchen floor not to wash it, but so that we had space for roller skating.

Now she is 84 she has no children to entertain, but she has trophies for bridge, and she is the only granny we know whose bedtime reading includes Stephen Hawking, J.K.Rowling, and Matthew Parris. She is still, like me, a slattern, but she is a wonderful conversationalist.

Slatterns fulfil a socially useful role: they allow others to feel superior, even other slatterns. ("My cooker may need cleaning, but you should see the state of her fridge.") I get immense pleasure from eyeing my mother's bathroom with disgust, and getting out the Jif to clean the washbasin. Similarly, my daughter loves to come home and chide me about the state of my dishcloth.

Admittedly, some of my mother's housekeeping habits were beyond the pale. Her most memorable misdemeanour was the time she was making breakfast and dropped a bacon rasher on the kitchen floor. She picked it up, dunked it in the washing up water and slung it back in the pan, and then pooh-poohed our protests with "A bit of dirt will build up your resistance." Recent research lends weight to her view (though that specific practice remains dubious.)

But all this chat does not get the skirting boards washed. However warm the winter, you cannot escape the fact that at this time of year the sun shines low in the sky to expose dirty windows and grimy walls. But how can I do my mother's spring cleaning when she has never shown me how?

I asked my husband to explain the process. Through gritted teeth he spelt out the major rules: everything moveable in the house must be moved; everything must be cleaned; and it is vital you start at the top of the house and work your way down. Also, you throw out a lot of clutter. It sounds to me like a load of old Feng Shui.

In the last few years, parenting classes have become de rigeur for people struggling with a task that earlier generations launched into without a whimper. Perhaps the next thing to catch on will be courses in housework, with a specialist module in bottoming the bedrooms, and an advanced one in spring cleaning?

Maybe not. Those eccentric people who see housework as the new sex won't need classes in it, and the rest of us won't want to waste time and money on learning to do something we hate. Personally, I shall rely on the global warming excuse, and take my mother to the library instead.

February 19th 2010

The bloody weather

I hope the winter ends soon, if only because Dave can't get out on his bike in the snow, which means that when his interesting indoor activities pale, he has taken to feverishly washing clothes. He thinks that if there is something in the laundry basket, it has to be washed ASAP, that if the laundry basket is approaching a quarter full, the world will end.

I think that one should build up a decent load and then stick it in the washer. He cleared all the washing yesterday and has just ironed it all – thank you, Dave – but now there are two pairs of pants in the basket and two pairs of socks and I just heard him lift the basket lid and dither – to wash or not to wash. I am going to start hiding dirty clothes and then we can have a house that is clear from either wet washing hanging up to dry, or a clothes horse filled with ironing that is airing.

He says he likes to see wicker at the bottom of the basket. This, however, does not apply to desks. If there is a clear spare inch on his desk it is covered in thick dust. Mine, however, is clean and dusted and virtuous – like its owner.

February 22nd 2010

My latest crush

It's a jolly good job I'm not taking exams in my quest to learn the sax. At my lesson two weeks ago, Mel said: "I think you're ready for *Rachel and the Boys*." This is a bluesy piece and it's on the syllabus for Grade 4. Grade 4! I was so chuffed that she thought I could play a Grade 4 piece after only 5 months, that I brought it home and practised it obsessively.

The piece was interesting, annoying, attractive, and like nothing I had come across before (a bit like the heroes in my novels.) I played nothing but *Rachel and the Boys* for a whole week and managed to get it note perfect *once*. The rest of the time it was good enough to pass muster. Dave cheered me on and told me how great it sounded. "You're going to wow Mel," he said.

When I arrived at my next lesson, I was all keyed up, anxious to show Mel what I could do. But in front of her, my fingers turned to al dente spaghetti and I *couldn't play it*. I was mortified. I was crestfallen. All that hard work, all my determined practising, and I was useless.

Mel was sweet, as always, and got me to play it with her "as if you are drunk and going for a rambling walk in the park." But I could still only botch the wretched piece. When I got home, I couldn't face *Rachel and the* bloody *Boys*, and opened my Gershwin book to cheer myself up. And I fell into the arms of another song - *But not for me*. I think I'm in love with this piece now.

February 24ᵗʰ 2010

Potential suicide note

We have had more snow, and I am as disconsolate as a disconsolate sheep. The snow has even had a deleterious effect on my similes.

Yes, yes, I know that this long winter is *NOT* unprecedented. I know we had a similar one in 1979. And yes, yes, I have heard all about the glorious spring we are due for – with everything bursting out all at once, etc. etc. but I am still fed up. That is the polite version. I am still sick to the back teeth of snow and ice and leaden skies. And for all of you who are reading this who have long winters every year, you have to understand that the winters here are *NOT* snowy white, bright and clear and sunny. They are freezing and dull and grey. And when I say grey, I mean GREY. Occasionally we will get a bright white day when everything looks beautiful but that is rare.

Two months ago, I arranged to go up to my mother's house for a long weekend with my two sisters, at the end of February, thinking it highly unlikely we'd be worrying about snow and ice on the roads. Looking forward to seeing them all, and seeing Wensleydale, and our brother who lives there, is one of the things that has got me through this dreary winter. So if the winter weather now gets in the way of our weekend together, I'm going to throw myself under a gritting lorry.

If you don't hear from me, you will know that it is either because

a/ I am having a great time in Wensleydale, in a house with no internet, or

b/ I have met my death under aforementioned gritting lorry.

MARCH

March 2nd 2010

Love conquers all

I've seen some blogs where every post is chirpy, and they read like an exercise in counting blessings. Blogs like that get on my nerves. On a personal basis, cheerfulness is attractive. Upbeat people are a joy. But unrelenting cheerfulness in a diary is dull. I can't take the cheesiness. And it sounds so fake. What is this person NOT telling me?

A weekend away for three sisters in their mother's empty house (empty of their much-loved mother) had the potential not for cheese, but for immense discomfort, when the purpose of the weekend was to prettify the house on a tiny budget, and with odds and ends from home, so that buyers could see its potential, and be willing to take on the modernisation required. Three women with different tastes engaged on a joint venture of domestic chic is bad enough. If those three women are straight talking, with very definite views, and are also picky, it doesn't bear thinking about.

Other conditions were not propitious. We arrived in fog so thick we couldn't see the hills; the house was freezing cold (despite the fact that Jonty had turned up the heating and also lit the fire for us – what a peach!) because a cottage with three foot thick stone walls takes a lot of warming up. The weather was cold and grey, with rain and sleet. We were too busy to enjoy the dale, apart from a brief walk to Aysgarth Falls, and an evening out with Jonty and Rachel, who cooked us a fantastic dinner.

As for the mission…there was a spat over whether a leather suitcase on the dresser looked old-lady-ish or *Country Living*–ish, a disappointment over a framed poster that one sister wanted to hang and the others hated. One sister's cushions were banished to the boot of her car because they were the wrong colour, and there were tussles over the exact position of a vase of flowers on the windowsill, and oh yes – a chair which one wanted in one corner and the other wanted "Here! To cover up this stain!" There was also a last minute overruling that the basket in the porch was an affectation, and looked twee.

But the mission was accomplished: with new curtains, new bedspreads, new cushions, different pictures and lots of hard work and careful thought, the house looks lighter and prettier.

And we had lots of teasing, lots of laughs, lots of cosy chats in bed with mugs of tea. We loved being together.

Love really does conquer all.

(And you'll just have to forgive the cheese.)

March 4th 2010

Dinosaurs and Zen Buddhism

Yesterday afternoon, I went to play with my 3-year-old grandson. We played a weird and hilarious game we concocted together. He wanted to have his dinosaurs dancing round his plastic volcano to the tune of *Here We Go Round the Mulberry Bush*. So I supplied a doctored version of the song, and we danced the dinosaurs round. Then he pressed a switch, which made the volcano erupt and throw off rocks, and this knocked over and injured several dinosaurs (though none fatally, I'm happy to say.) So then we had to get the dinosaur ambulance and wheelchairs and stretchers and take them to the dinosaur hospital. When the patients were settled on makeshift beds, we left the doctor examining them, and started the whole process again with more dinosaurs. It was completely absorbing, and wildly funny.

Later on, at teatime with my friends, we ate sausage and mash, and talked about a variety of things:

astrology;

the latest Marilynne Robinson book and whether narrative drive is essential to one's enjoyment of a novel;

a daughter's recent childbirth experience;

whether or not if you say that someone looks after their own needs in a relationship it therefore means they are selfish;

17

Zen Buddhism;

the slowness of the Co-op check-out staff;

Taoism;

and how vital it is at our age not to put down a novel you are reading, because if you do, you forget what has happened and have to go back to the beginning and start again.

When I look back on these evenings I always remember the laughing and the jokes and the way we tease each other, and yet I always come away with a lot to think about…Zen Buddhism, for example. Living in the moment is a very appealing notion. Driving home, I realised that when I am playing with my grandsons, or laughing with my friends, I cannot think of anything else. I am utterly absorbed. I am living in the moment. I am completely happy.

March 10th 2010

Doolally

It's all very well having to write tasks down so you remember them. It's all very well having to write tasks down on post-its and stick them on the inside of the front door so you remember them, because you always forget to look in your diary. But when you come down in the morning and see one such post-it and you read it and you don't know what the hell it means, it may be time to get a minder.

I found a post-it yesterday that said "Ring re bin." What did it mean? What bin? Ring who? Did I write the post-it? I examined the writing carefully. It had to be mine, because Dave doesn't use pink heart post-its. Every time I passed the note, I puzzled over what it meant. "Ring re bin"?????

An hour later I remembered. *Ring Jonty in Wensleydale and ask him to put out Ma's wheelie-bin on bin day.* I was in Wensleydale the day before. I had seen Jonty the day before. That wasn't so very hard, was it? Apparently so.

March 12th 2010

A map of grief

In the last year I have progressed from intense grief for the loss of my mother, to a place on the map that is not so bleak. I miss my mother and think of her often, but now when I go to stay at her house with brothers or sisters, I enjoy the visit. Eleven months ago, I felt differently and wrote this…

Losing my mother

Sometimes, it's a comfort having my mother's things around me - her Austrian jug on the windowsill, her mahogany chest in the bedroom, her Piers Browne painting on the wall. Sometimes I hate to look at them.

Sometimes I like to see her photograph – her smiling, strong, straightforward face. Sometimes I can't abide it on my desk. I never had her photo on display before she died, so if I have it here now, she must be dead. And I don't want her dead. I don't like the new dispensation.

We have been clearing out her house in monthly weekend bursts, ever since she died at the end of last October. It's April now, and I've just spent a weekend there. The weather was achingly beautiful – clear blue skies and sunshine, the full bright light of early spring skies, lambs in the fields, daffodils in the gardens and on the verges - and a brother and sister to keep me company.

Over the months we've been denuding the house of personal, sentimental and valuable items, and now it's like the holiday cottage it was when our parents bought it, 50 years ago. It no longer feels like our mother's home, but like a cottage we all feel comfortable in. We know how everything works – that there are two immersion heater switches, and both of them must be on for the heater to work, that the draught for the fire points to the right, that you have to thump the washing machine in the middle of the door at the top to get it going. But it does not feel like the place where I took my babies, my children, my teenagers, to visit their grandparents, and latterly went on my own to visit my mother.

We have a lovely photo of her, taken 6 weeks before she died. When we visit the house, we take it out from behind the bookshelf curtain and stand it on the shelf, and see her wise, healthy, loving face, and when we drink our wine at meals we toast her.

It was good to be with my brother and sister at the weekend, comforting to have a hug and a laugh, to share memories and to miss our mother together. But the only time I got that rush of the safe, the cosy, the familiar, was when I was standing at my mother's sink, washing up. At that moment, she might have been still alive, sitting in front of the fire, doing the codewords puzzle from the Telegraph, turning on the radio for a cricket update.

When Peter and Jen set off on the Sunday morning for their long drive south, I waved them off, and sat under the front wall on the bench that Ma put there (to catch the last of the setting sun) and I looked at the house.

Behind me on the road, two hikers were walking down the lane and when they saw the estate agent's sign, the woman said, "I could live there," and her partner agreed.

"It's a tidy garden."

"A very tidy garden."

"And look, it's big – there's an extension at the back."

They walked out of earshot.

I didn't feel sad at the thought of someone else living there, or outraged at the thought of someone talking about my mother's house as if it was on the open market – after all, it was! I ached because she wasn't there. No matter how many times I go up to stay with a brother or sister, she won't be there. It wasn't a chore to visit her, a woman in her nineties. She was vivacious, alert and chatty and she had a great sense of humour, a ready laugh. She was good company, and easy. And she was a rock.

Not one of my siblings – and I love them all – is a substitute for her. She wasn't there on that bright spring day and she won't be there in May for my nephew's wedding, when the May blossom is out and the verges are thick with sweet cicely and cow parsley. She won't be there to smell the Arthur Bell roses in June, or the lavender in July. She won't be there to enjoy the colours of Crocosmia Lucifer in August, or the Michaelmas daisies in September.

I have to get used to losing her. To having her missing from my life. To have her gone, out of reach, unavailable for hugs or chats or encouragement, to live without that unfailing love that made the world feel safe.

March 19th 2010

Pet hates

When we were playing Scrabble last night I asked Dave about my pet hates, and he said that I have so many they would fill a book. But he was confusing pet hates with pet preferences. e.g. I would prefer him not to whistle the first few phrases of *Rachel and the Boys* over and over and over again, all the way through a game of Scrabble.

I hate…

1/ ringing up a business at 10.30 a.m. and getting an answering machine message that tells me "Our opening hours are 9 a.m. to 6 p.m."

2/ shop assistants who carry on a conversation with a colleague all the time they are serving me and don't even flash me one second's eye contact.

3/ people in call centres who pick up the phone and say "How are you today?" as if they know me, as if they care, as if it is at all relevant to the call. The Co-op Bank staff get ten gold stars on this count as they say "How can I help you today?" and proceed to be helpful and friendly and human, without that inane question at the outset.

4/ people who put their hiking boots on in the kitchen and don't notice when they stand up that all the dried bits of mud fall out of their soles, all over the floor. You know who you are.

There – four pet hates – that wasn't so very many, was it, Dave?

March 29th 2010

Foxed

So there you are. It is a Sunday teatime. You have waved goodbye to your sister, with whom you have just spent a great weekend in your mother's house. You have packed your car to drive the 100 miles home. You go round the house one last time to check that everything is in order, because the house is on the market and the estate agent has a viewing later in the week.

You pull the front door to, and the door handle breaks off in your hand. You are not a practical woman - you find wheelbarrows complicated – what do you do?

You ring up Dave. He was born with a screwdriver in one hand and a chisel in the other. He is practicality personified.

It should, *in theory*, have been possible for him to talk me through what I should do about the door knob, the fused circuit and the dodgy light fitting (neither of which I mentioned to you) but as T.S.Eliot would say – *Between the idea and the reality falls the shadow.* When Dave and I are talking about practical matters, all communication fails. I do not understand him and he does not understand me. (As Wendy from *Plotting for Beginners* would say - it's because I have Mercury – the planet of communication - in Libra, and he has Mercury in Cancer, and they are in hard aspect.) Oh yes, we span the literary universe on this blog – from Eliot to Hepworth & Linfoot.

So Dave said... "Make sure the front door is locked and I will drive up on Tuesday and fix everything."

My hero.

p.s. I can sew, knit, patchwork, cook, garden, write books, balance on a slackline and play the sax, and I have tried and tried to become accomplished in DIY, but to no avail. So don't start telling me I am a pathetic loser. I have a fluffy brain and there is no doing anything about it.

MAY

May 10th 2010

Constrained

Imaginary play is not *always* unbridled fun. If you are invited to steal the treasure from the dungeon of a castle, and there is a shark in the moat, a portcullis, a fire-breathing dragon at the top of the slope, and the walls are defended by deathly light sabres, cannons and a row of "intelligent parrots" ready to peck you to death, you kind of get a bit disheartened. My playmates couldn't relate to my discouragement, although when I protested, my younger grandson did eventually hand over the shark as a sop.

May 30th 2010

Break a leg, why don't you?

That is the last time I let a 16-year-old loose on my slackline. Michelle and Mac dropped in a couple of days ago, and while Michelle and I had a cuppa and a chat, Mac worked his way from complete novice status to being able to walk half way along the line. I can't do that, and I've had the line since October. What's that about?

JUNE

June 5th 2010

Perfect happiness

I've just been baking a coffee cake while listening to a saxophone playing Gershwin songs. It's warm enough to have bare feet on the wooden kitchen floor, to have the front door open, to sit outside and lick the bowl, to smell the peonies on my windowsill as I sit and write this post.

June 7th 2010

A quarter to six in the morning

I am sitting in bed. There is a pearl grey sky behind the May blossom, and the copper beech is heavy with rain. The clock in the hall has just chimed the half hour (it's slow), the cat has just climbed in the spare room window (yes – upstairs! - where Dave sits with his computer) and come in to see me. She didn't have wet feet so she didn't leave muddy footprints on my newly washed patchwork quilt, which is what she did last week, and which is why the quilt is newly washed. There is a pheasant in the garden, making that awful scratchy croaking sound, and in the distance, a pigeon is cooing.

A moment ago the air was still and muggy. Now a faint breeze is coming in through the window and the leaves on the lime trees across the road are swishing.

My son in California rang last night – as he always does on a Sunday. I miss him. His (and Wendy's) first baby is due next month and I long to see them both now, and then immediately the baby is born. But my ticket is booked for September. I shall have to wait.

June 17th 2010

Five Quakers injured in slackline fiasco…

The slackline is back in my life. I had a breakthrough yesterday. When Mackenzie was here he said that walking backwards on it was easier that walking forwards. So I had a go and realised that the reason is because you bend your knees. When I tried to walk forwards on the line with my knees bent, I did much better. And it's hot today and set fair, so I shall be out there practising, knees bent, as soon as the sun falls on the line.

The other thing that happened is that my friend Ella sent me a link to a master class in tight rope walking with Philippe Petit. It's in August in Brooklyn and she suggested I went to stay with her and go to the class. Wow.

And the third slackline strand is that Viv, a friend from Quaker Meeting, came to have a go on it and suggested that the Spiritual Exploration group should have a meeting here, using walking the slackline as a metaphor for life.

When I mentioned it to Dave, he said that if you were using walking the line as a metaphor for life, there should be broken glass on the lawn, someone jumping out of the hedge with a flamethrower, and someone at the end of the line, hacking at it with a blunt Swiss army knife. Also, he has not a scintilla of admiration for Philippe Petit.

Everyone has their problems.

June 28th 2010

In praise of sisters

Sisters are great. You can have a laugh with them, talk for hours with them, or sit in silence, drinking wine and watching the sun go down...

They'll tell you when you're being daft, give you a hug when you're sad, and when you want to buy *a voluminous floral smock trimmed with satin ribbon* in Jigsaw - which looks lovely on the petite and pretty dark-haired twenty-something assistant – they'll suggest that if you buy it, you might regret it when you get home. And then when you've resisted and left the shop without said smock – which was obscenely expensive anyway, and three times as much as you would normally spend on a blouse - they will tell you it made you look like Grayson Perry.

28

June 29th 2010

The last word on sisters

And they also buy you cashmere cardigans in your favourite colour because "It was reduced to £19 in M&S, and I couldn't just leave it there, could I?"

JULY

July 1st 2010

Life won't wait

You turn your back for one minute (sloping off to the seaside for a couple of days with your sister) and when you get back the convolvulus has taken over your back garden. But then so many wonderful things have happened, too. The roses are blooming as if their life depended on it, the fragrance of the honeysuckle and orange blossom makes you swoon, and the climbing rose is out.

And finally, that funny buddleia - that you've had for four years and was just about to pull up because it refused to produce anything but leaves – has produced odd little yellow flower balls.

And then there are the strawberries. I've just been out in the quiet morning garden, to pick this morning's crop.

It was balmy. It was heaven. Such a morning as this makes up for the four months of grey cold winter we get here every year. The birds have been at the strawberries. They think I don't know. I used to have a net on the strawberry patch, but one day I found a dead blackbird caught in it, so I threw the net away. There are plenty of strawberries - enough for us to share. Which is a good job, because as well as the birds and the slugs, there are other creatures who like my fruit...frogs.

If I die today, I won't mind. I have had a fabulous week, away with Jen, and back here at home in my summer garden.

July 8th 2010

Less is more

The other evening, my brother Pete and I looked through a suitcase of papers I'd brought back from Wensleydale last year. Most of the stuff in there was to do with Pa. There were records of the prizes his cows won at the Dairy Show, appreciative letters from his employers, the 1958 brochure for the dispersal sale of the prize-winning herd he'd built up, and so on and so on.

We found some things we had never seen before – such as a letter awarding him a scholarship, a photograph of him in a school play, and one doing the long jump (mid-flight), and a photograph of him, clutching a Dairy Show trophy. I don't remember him looking like this - I was only 3 at the time.

To begin with it was interesting and fun to look through the papers in the suitcase. I was curious, and then enthralled, and we plundered on, and then suddenly I had had enough, overcome with a heavy sad weariness at the weight of it all…the memories, the sadness of his huge successes reduced by a corporate decision to sell the farm, the transience of everything, the loss of our childhood, the fact that we would rather have our father back than *any* kind of treasure trove.

July 13th 2010

Home

I have just got in from the garden. I've been picking strawberries in my nightie and dressing gown and wellington boots. It's good to be home.

Yes, it's good to be home. There is no comfort in my mother's house any more. Aristotle asked - when you are eating an apple, when does it cease to be an apple? Is it after the first bite? Or the second? Is it when you get down to the core?

We have stripped the house of everything that was uniquely my mother and father – except for the cloth thing with pockets that hangs at the bottom of the stairs and is stuffed full of knitted gloves and scarves and a rolled up, yellow kagoule.

When Kath and I wanted to sit down, to read the paper, or to eat our dinner, we sat in the sunny porch on Kath's garden chairs, not in the cheerless house. Oh, there's an old tapestry cushion made by my mother still in the porch, and a piece of faded floral linen (so archetypical of her taste) on one of the garden chairs.

It's all but finished, now. We took down the ancient airing rack from the kitchen ceiling for Kath's daughter. She will have the cutlery, too. Every one of the eleven grandchildren has taken something, which is a wonderful testament not just to their upbringing of re-using old things, but more because they have such happy memories of staying at Gran and Grandpa's house, and they want a little bit of them somewhere in their own homes. Someone has the milking stool, someone the sewing machine, someone will have the fire irons.

How lucky I was to share the task with my cheerful, positive, hard-working, big sister Kath. And how lucky I was to be able to drive down the M1 and arrive at Zoë's house in Sheffield where part of the future of the family – my elder grandson – was having his sixth birthday. He is dinosaur crazy, and knows the names of them all, every last syllable. He even knows what it means when a fossil is labelled the Cretaceous period. He wants to be a palaeontologist when he grows up – "Actually," he said, "I am a palaeontologist now."

Here's to the future (she said, trying to buck herself up.)

July 21st 2010

The Bunny Club – a late night posting

Do you remember I said we had a mouse in the kitchen and the cat wasn't interested because she just wants to catch rabbits these days? Well…

… there I was in the dining room at 7.45 pm, eating a late tea of fish and chips and drinking a glass of Oyster Bay Sauvignon Blanc, trying to recover from some bad news I'd just received via a phone call, when Dave came in from the kitchen and said, "It's not a mouse in the kitchen, it's a rat. And it's hiding under the dresser. I'm getting my boiler suit on and my wellies, and I'm going to deal with it." Then he retreated.

Five minutes later he came back and said, "It's not a rat, it's a rabbit. Can you come and help?"

I finished my tea and went into the kitchen, to find him climbing behind the washing machine.

"I thought it was under the dresser," I said.

"It ran out when I poked it. It was too quick to catch."

We don't have a big kitchen. We don't have a fancy kitchen. Half an hour later we still had not found the dratted rabbit. Had it escaped through the open window while his back was turned? Who bloody knows? We've left the cat in there, and I'm telling you now, Dave can go in there first in the morning.

The phone caller with the bad news had left a message with Dave for me to call her back when I got in at 7. "I hope that doesn't spoil your dinner plans," she said.

Dinner plans? Fish and chips for one, while the only other person at home dismantles the kitchen in search of a fugitive rabbit?

July 22nd 2010

The Bunny Club episode 2: Outed

I wrote the last post late at night because I couldn't sleep (on account of the bad news – of which more later). I sat here in my study writing. The house was silent, and I was just about to go and make some cocoa, when I heard a sudden skirmish behind the kitchen door. I froze. I didn't want to stumble on a scene of carnage. So I went to bed, cocoa-less. When your kitchen -the ultimate altar to domesticity - becomes a place of creepiness and possible death, it's deeply uncomfortable.

What was hiding in there behind the units? When four mousetraps had not caught it, but were contemptuously tossed across the kitchen by the quarry, you worry. When the demon is lurking out of sight, just sneaking out occasionally to snatch fragments of chocolate digestive lodged on said mousetraps ("Sorry, Ben," (the painter), "the rabbit has finished the chocolate biscuits, you'll have to have shortbread fingers") - somehow the intruder assumes the proportions of a monster. I mean – Dave said he saw a rabbit, but was it really a rabbit? It could have been a rat. He has been known to be wrong. He is a man. He just came in the bedroom saying he was freezing cold and had been waiting for me to wake up before coming in for clothes, and I pointed out that he has a heap of discarded jeans and jumpers in his study. If he can miss those, he could surely confuse a rabbit and a rat…

Thankfully, in the morning, the kitchen floor wasn't strewn with bloody lapine entrails nor garnished with a headless corpse. We hadn't *really* wanted the cat to kill the intruder, but we'd gone to bed fed up, and it seemed the natural thing to say to her - "You brought it home, you flush it out!"

When we opened the door, she bolted from the kitchen, as if desperate to get away from something. *Was* it a rat?

Later she deposited a gutted bird on the doorstep, an apology for failing us.

"Right," said Dave, after breakfast. "We can lure it out with lettuce, or consider force majeure." He began to dismantle the kitchen again.

"I think it must be behind the fridge," I said.

Dave pooh-poohed the idea: "There isn't room."

He pulled out the washer, the cooker and the dishwasher and cleaned their tops, their sides and the floor behind them. Then he took the kickboards off the units and swept out the droppings underneath. "Where the hell is it?" he said.

"I think it's behind the fridge," I said.

35

More pooh-poohing: "There isn't room."

He poked between the units and the wall with a long stick. Nothing.

"I think it's behind the fridge," I said.

Finally, he pulled out the fridge, and yes! It *was* a rabbit! Thank God! It wasn't injured, and it didn't have a stray mousetrap clipped to its ear. But then it rushed into the boxing around the pipes. So Dave unscrewed the boxing.

He put it on the back lawn and the harmless, cuddly bunny hopped jauntily away.

Our kitchen hasn't been this clean for years.

Dave is a star.

July 27th 2010

Sue Hepworth is a ratbag

I am a ratbag. It's official. I chew people up on the phone. And I don't mean people selling double glazing or trying to entice me back to BT, or someone from the subscription department of *The Times*, with a great, great offer.

I chew people up who I like. I chew them up when I'm stressed. I chew them up when I'm waiting impatiently for a particular call and the wrong person rings.

On Saturday morning a friend got it. She was due to come over with her boys, and after speaking to me, she changed her mind. (Who could blame her? Even I didn't like me much on Saturday.) The boys were looking forward to seeing me, so she tried to bribe them to go paddling in Padley Gorge instead. They chose me. She told them I was a ratbag. They still wanted to come. She told them she'd buy them an ice cream. But they wanted to see me more. I apologised profusely on the phone to her, and begged her to come. She relented, bless her. She forgave me.

So…I may not have a publisher for my novel, but it is a *delicately nuanced* novel.

I may be a ratbag, but some children like me more than ice cream.

No-one is perfect. And I am especially not perfect, but the people who matter still love me. So everything is OK.

And here is an official apology to everyone I have ever chewed up. I'm really sorry.

July 30th 2010

Waiting

It's a still quiet morning here, at 5.42 a.m. The dawn was red and yellow and deep dark grey – beautiful. I am up and awake because I am waiting for news of the baby. The Little Red Hen went into labour 13 hours ago and all through last evening we got updates and now there is no response to my texts, and Isaac's last tweet said "update: no update." San Francisco is an awfully long way away, and 13 hours is a long time to be in labour, although I know it's not been heavy going all that time, because on Isaac's first call he said Wendy was having contractions every four minutes and eating cereal in between. Several hours later, his text read "Wendy is eating a burrito." But that was a whole English night ago. What is she eating, now?

10 a.m. I am still waiting. Poor Wendy. I don't think she'll be eating anything.

AUGUST

August 1st 2010

My darling new and first American grand-daughter arrived in the world on Saturday after a long long labour, and then a Caesarean. She's called Lux.

I can't wait to meet her in September.

August 3rd 2010

An ending and a beginning

While little Lux, latest addition to the family tree, was settling on her twig, and while the Little Red Hen was recovering from 44 hours of labour – actually, while we were ALL recovering from her 44 hours of labour – I was doing a final sweep of Ma's house with my big sister, Kath.

We have a buyer, we think it will go through, and this was our final weekend. Jen was there the weekend before, taking down curtains and dispatching remnant furniture to a sale, and she'd left us three mugs (one each, and one for Jonty, when he called), two dishes, a kettle and a pan. We had garden chairs and a card table, and we slept on a mattress on the floor.

It didn't feel as awful, or as raw as it did last time. I don't know why.

Jonty was there on Saturday afternoon helping us, when a cousin and his wife rolled up. They live 100 miles away, but happened to be driving through the dales, and thus Ma's village, on their way to a holiday cottage, and Janey thought they should make a quick detour down the lane to say goodbye to Ma's house.

"And there were three cousins standing in the road!" she said.

We sat on the lawn, with three of the party drinking tea (remember – only three mugs), and we remarked on how pleased Ma would be to see us there together in the sunshine on that last historic visit.

On Sunday, Kath and I locked up for our last time. There was nothing left of Ma, except a vase on the windowsill (for Jonty) and a photograph of Ma, aged 90, sitting in the garden talking to some local children. Kath hid it in a quiet corner for the new owners to find.

August 13ᵗʰ 2010

Restraint

You may be looking for a new post, but you need to be thankful I'm not peppering my blog with pictures of my new granddaughter and her parents. Don't you think I am being restrained?

August 19ᵗʰ 2010

Dialogue

Sue: 'When you sit at your computer, you lean forwards and peer at the screen like an old man.'

Dave: 'Well, we're getting old.'

Sue: 'At least you're fit. It's pretty good still being able to cycle 35 miles.'

Dave: 'That's true. (Pause.) 'Though I can't always remember where I've been.'

August 20ᵗʰ 2010

Unable (at the moment) to go with the flow

It's the middle of my night and I am lying awake, worrying that the people who have just bought my mother's house won't realise that in order to get hot water, you have to turn on the immersion switch upstairs *and* the one downstairs.

I spent yesterday with an empty feeling that felt like hunger, but I knew that eating something wouldn't make me feel any better.

I told my good friend about it, and she emailed about her own experience - "the sale of my mother's house was uniquely upsetting and I wonder if that was when I really understood that she wasn't coming back."

That may be it.

When I was little and I got in a tantrum my parents said I was "having a swee." When they laughed about it later, they never mentioned my brothers and sisters having a swee, it was just Sue who had swees.

There is a three-year-old here – right here - and she is stamping her foot, and shouting:

I didn't want to lose Pa in 2002!

I didn't want to lose Ma in 2008!

And I don't want to lose the house now! I don't! I don't!

Just like in olden times, my reasonable (and lovable) brothers and sisters are getting on with their lives, and being sensible, and I am having a swee.

And it's hard to sleep when you're having a swee.

SEPTEMBER

September 8th 2010

Apologies

I'm sorry, you guys, but I'm not in a bloggy kind of mood at the moment. I am writing, paying my sax, gardening, and making lists for my trip to see Lux and family next week. Yay!

Today I have to go and buy some dollars while trying not to pay too much attention to the appalling exchange rate.

In the meantime, you might be amused by the following piece I had in *The Times* some time ago.

Every couple needs one

Just as every newly married couple should have a shed on their wedding list if they want their marriage to survive, so there is something every older couple needs, and I know what it is.

It's not just retired people who need it, such as those poor wives whose husbands – bereft of work - follow them around all day asking "What are you doing? What are you doing *now*? Where are you going? What time will you be back?"

It can also be couples who work from home, like my husband and I, who have a room and a computer each and who have, you would think, no need to argue.

Our problem is our different styles of working. He works in short bursts, sharp and efficient, sure footed and sound. He cuts through work like a man with a machete hacking through brambles.

I am slow and woolly headed. I need to go to my room and shut the door and be left alone for hours at a time. I am like the author who, when she was asked if there were words she tended to overuse, said "Yes - two words: go away."

But machete man does half an hour here, and gets up for a drink; half an hour there, and gets up to stroke the cat. Then as he's on his feet he will come and ask if I remembered to ring the plumber. He'll do ten minute's writing, then look outside the door to see if there's enough blue sky to make a sailor a pair of trousers, so he can go out cycling later. But then as there's only enough blue sky for one leg, he will come and ask if I think it's going to rain. Then it's fifteen minutes on the phone, and a shout to ask where his stapler is. He does half an hour of planning, then feels peckish and slopes into the kitchen for a bowl of yoghurt, and while he's there he may as well listen to the headlines. Then he comes up to rage about what he's just heard. Aarghh!

This was all true until a month ago. That's when he bought the router, which (for the uninitiated) is a power tool used for precise cutting and shaping of timber.

Routers are wonderful. Every couple should have one. The router has revolutionised our lives, which I now divide up into BR and AR (Before Router and After Router). Now, in the AR epoch, I have no excuse not to get on with my work, because he sits in his room as if nailed to his chair until all of his work is done: the sooner it's done, the sooner he can play with his router.

He started with picture frames. Everything in the house that's vaguely rectangular has now been framed. Luckily, a router isn't just useful for framing. It can do decorative edging for shelves, cupboard doors, engraved wooden signs, etched patterns and pictures, dovetails – anything in wood that needs shaping or grooving, cutting or profiling.

And in the evening when his back aches from bending over the workbench, and his fingers are numb with vibration, he sits and flicks through his catalogues of router attachments and cutters. All is quiet except for occasional exclamations, such as "I'm going to get some pronged teenuts. They're a joy." Or he may read one of his routing magazines - the sort of publication that features in the missing words round on *Have I got news for you* - with headlines like "Power up!" or "Beautiful Beast! The new big Bosch router is here."

It's not just my husband who is besotted with his router. Believe me, there is a routing fraternity, with ramifications way beyond woodwork. Last week my brother (who has a "tasty" Elu router) asked my husband's view on some abstruse etymological question and on hearing the reply said "Yes, of course. Anyone with a router talks sense."

As well as improving domestic harmony, the router has solved the Christmas present problem: from now on I'll buy presents for his router. There is an infinite variety of cutters: no man could live long enough to try them all. I've just been down to get his catalogue to count them, but my husband had gone, and on his study door was a new wooden sign "Gone routing."

September 17th 2010

Here at last

I am here in San Francisco - at last - where the sky is blue, the sun is hot, and the babies are beautiful.

I am sitting here in my pyjamas nursing Lux. Her parents are asleep next door. She came in to play, to kick, to crow, to wave her hands around. She has long fluttering fingers that are never still: she is like a tiny sea anemone, but one with intense dark eyes, a cupid's bow mouth, a pointy chin and a very serious expression. I am 5,000 miles from home, but I'm never alone with a grandchild, even when she's asleep.

September 19th 2010

I am living in a children's picture book

My American family live in the Mission district of San Francisco. I love it - when you walk down the street it feels like you're in the pages of a Richard Scarry book. There is a saloon car on the corner with a cop leaning on each side of it, one talking through the window to the driver, their cop car parked behind; there is a man with an ice cream trolley; a big, shiny, and very long, San Francisco Fire Dept truck gliding down the street, a big blue and yellow cement mixer truck, mixing cement; a nail boutique, an ice cream parlour, a café, a shop that cashes your cheques, one that buys gold for cash, a deli, a hairdresser, a garage that will fix your brakes, a nursery. But I have not yet spotted Lowly Worm.

September 20th 2010

Things I don't understand

Things I don't understand:

1/ why I can't get images to fit on my blog any more

2/ what there is to eat on a grilled artichoke

3/ why Marks and Spencer no longer make good quality knickers. I bought some new ones to bring on the trip but left them at home to return later, because they were so hopeless, so thin and so flimsy. So Wendy took me to Victoria's Secret (where, not being into shopping, I have never been before) and I bought some knickers like M&S used to make. They're such great quality, I am going to stock up. When I told Zoë this on the phone, she said "Oh, so you're going to become a transatlantic knicker mule."

September 28th 2010

What I'll miss when I get home

Isaac and Lux

Hanging out with Wendy

Drinking a margarita in the sunshine. I never drink margaritas in England, and we all know how often the sun shines there. Dave has just emailed to say that "Yesterday it was damp and grey, and this morning, peering out into the dark, it is damper and greyer. The morning looks like a run-over squirrel. There is fog licking the windows." Has he forgotten who the writer is in this family?

OCTOBER

October 30th 2010

She was a cracker

It is two years ago today that my mother died. We were so lucky to have her as head of our family, and for so long, too. We miss her badly.

I started to write a post about her, but a list of all the things I valued about her would be so long, that I would still be sitting here writing in my pyjamas at dinner time; and anyway, you have your own mothers to think about. I hope you are/were as fortunate as me.

Here is her obituary, which appeared in the *Darlington and Stockton Times:*

Helen Willis 1917- 2008

Helen Willis was a well-known resident of Wensleydale, whose life was not marked by outstanding professional achievements, but whose influence was profound. She was like countless people who live quiet, modest lives but whose loving nature and strength of character are appreciated by their family and many beyond.

She was a long-time member of Leyburn Quaker Meeting, serving the meeting in a number of different offices. In 2003, aged 85, she attended a peace demonstration against the Iraq war. For her 90th birthday, she held a garden party to raise money for the Yorkshire Air Ambulance.

She was a prize-winning bridge player and a talented craftswoman. Her intellectual curiosity was insatiable and wide-ranging, and included nuclear physics, mathematics, engineering, astronomy, education, code-breaking and architecture. In her early eighties she went on a 24 hour winter trip into the arctic circle to see the Northern Lights. In her late eighties, she learned to use email to correspond with her large, far-flung family.

Born near Bedale, Helen Barron was an identical twin and was educated at Ackworth Quaker School, where she combined mental acuity with extraordinary physical vigour, qualities that she maintained throughout her life. She captained both the hockey and cricket teams, and gained a 1st class Instructors Certificate of the Royal Lifesaving Society. She was also Head Girl.

She then graduated from the Rachel MacMillan Training College for Nursery Education. She played hockey for Kent while at college, and later played for Lancashire.

She was called up a month early to her first teaching post at Hunslet Nursery School in Leeds in August 1939, to help evacuate the school to Bramham Park, the home of Lord Bingley. For the first few weeks, the children and teachers lived, worked, played and slept in the ballroom. She was on duty 24 hours a day, seven days a week.

She worked as a nursery teacher until her marriage in 1944 to Fred Willis, whom she first met at school. They set up home in a farming community of conscientious objectors at Holton Beckering in Lincolnshire. After 18 months, the couple moved to north Lincolnshire, on Fred's appointment as a Farms Manager. There they brought up five children.

After a spell in Derby, the couple moved to Aysgarth in 1972, and played a full part in village life, with Helen particularly making sure to welcome newcomers and include them in local activities.

Mrs Willis laughed easily and bore difficulties with casual fortitude, refusing to be cowed by any adversity. She was self-effacing and talked little of her considerable achievements, but was ambitious for others, giving encouragement, support and praise in equal measure.

She was an indefatigable maker, producing craftwork of grace and vigour until shortly before her death. Her making was carefully matched to the tastes and interests of the delighted recipient, who recognised not only her skill, but the love which had gone into the making.

Mrs Willis died on 30th October, after a brief illness borne stoically, with her usual dismissive disdain for her ailments.

November 14th 2010

Strung out

I am in lying in 'bed' in my study but am so tired I can't go to sleep. My head has been a maelstrom of people and cooking and conversation, and I have been lying here gazing at my music stand and wishing I could play my sax to calm myself down. But it's midnight, everyone is in bed, and the sound of the sax travels as far as the end of our lane.

The only thing I have found to chill me out is to flick through a TOAST catalogue. I love the things in TOAST but they are so ridiculously expensive that I only ever buy T shirts in the second round of the sale. The current catalogue contains Christmas presents, such as a pair of silk velvet lavender bags for £14.50. Oh, come on! A Christmas tree decoration for £9.95. Are you kidding?

But I have done some serious ogling of the silk velvet dressing gown in kingfisher blue on page 67 – a "mere" £175.

Now I'm going to creep into the kitchen and make some cocoa. Why am I sleeping on my study floor? Because with the American wing of the family staying, and an English member of the family who declines to be named occupying the spare room, Dave and I decided that Lux and her tired parents should have our room, and that Dave should sleep on his study floor, and I should sleep on mine. Yesterday we had an email conversation from our respective studies at half past five in the morning. It was fun. We may be provincial but we know how to party.

November 25th 2010

There is no such thing as a free lunch

The narrowboat we were on last week was advertised as a "premium" boat, but when we got on it we wondered why. We kept saying to each other "But it *was* very cheap, and it's fine for just a week, isn't it?" We had fun, despite the gearbox packing up half way through the trip, making us come home early.

From my journal-

Sunday November 21st 2010, 7 a.m. The Llangollen Canal

In bed under 3 duvets, and on top of the seat cushion from the dinette, which itself is on top of the mattress to give the bed a smidge of

*springiness, and I am wearing pyjamas, bed socks, a thick Aran
sweater, greasy hair and varifocals. The engine is loud and throbbing,
and the whole boat vibrates: we have it turned on right now to make
the heating work. It is dark outside. I have just finished off my packet
of pork scratchings, which I gave up eating last night because in the
quiet of the cabin on the silent canal, the crunching was too loud. It's
pretty awful to be eating pork scratchings first thing in the morning,
but this barge lowers one's standards. There is a putrid stench in the
bathroom, which the owners know about because they have left a
vapona in there to combat the smell. It does not combat the smell.
When you are playing Scrabble, waiting for your tea to cook and the
hopeless cooker secretly cuts out, so that when you have totted up
your final score and gloated because you got 600 points between you
(a minor gloating because 700 would be so much better) you take
your cheese and lentil savoury and baked potato out of the oven and
find them uncooked and lukewarm. I have been reading the Grapes of
Wrath about poverty and hardship in Dust Bowl Oklahoma and
migrant life in California in the 30's. If there had been a narrowboat
in the Grapes of Wrath it would be like the one we are on.*

November 29ᵗʰ 2010

There is no such thing as a free lunch (continued)

My brother Pete rang yesterday and asked about our
narrowboat holiday. He thought - from my blog post - that it
had been awful. But it hadn't. It hadn't been awful. We had a
great time.

There is more to narrowboating than the quality of the boat. I love being so close to the open country, waking up and stepping out on deck and being part of the still morning, seeing the mist rising from the quiet canal, the sun coming over the horizon through the bare trees, the pure reflections on the water as we travel along, the slowness of the journey so I can soak up every last view of the landscape before it changes, the simplicity of the life – the choosing of where to moor, and the way a walk to an unknown village in search of milk and papers and little unexpected treats – like the best pork scratchings in the world that I found at the village store in Wrenbury - that such a simple trip becomes an adventure.

I lead a sheltered life. I hardly see a packet of pork scratchings from one year's end to the next. And now I have finished the last of the packets I bought in Wrenbury, my life is drab.

DECEMBER

December 2nd 2010

The ubiquitous white stuff (snow)

Well, here I am sitting in bed typing again, but this time I have the huge white blinding SAD light sitting on the blanket chest facing me. Dave says the light beaming out from the room is like that scene in Ally McBeal where she meets the unicorn. I hope this thing works and stops me from getting seriously fed up like I did last winter when the snow and ice and fog went on and on and on.

Meanwhile, 16 miles away, my daughter in Sheffield (the third largest city in England) says that after 24 hours of snow, the roads have not been cleared at all, and her local shops have run out of bread and milk and eggs, because delivery trucks cannot get into town. We Brits have really got to get our act together if this is going to be our new winter climate.

Meanwhile, Dave – who two days ago was saying he wanted snow as high as the dry stone walls like we had 30 years ago – is now saying the snow is a bit claustrophobic. We went for a lovely walk yesterday morning, but when we emerged in the afternoon, the snow plough had been and turned the road into a treacherous sheet of ice, so we gave up and came home.

The snow gets in the way of my life. On Tuesday the snow made me miss my saxophone lesson, on Wednesday I missed a meeting in Bakewell, and today I will miss my trip to the cinema to see *The Kids Are All Right* – a film I am desperate to see. It is probably my last chance before it disappears from the schedules.

UPDATE at 10.29

OK, *now* it's getting exciting. The drifts on our lane are waist-deep in places. We are officially snowed in. It's getting interesting. We have flour, but the best before date on the yeast packet is September 2007. Will it work?

December 11th 2010

Liberation

Yesterday we woke to a landscape that looked like a lino-cut, and a house so warm we didn't need slippers. Yay!

And I got to do exciting things like leave the house in a car that I was driving myself, and go to Sainsbury's in Matlock for food, and get stuck in traffic jams of people saying to each other "I haven't seen you in ages! Hasn't it been awful?" The world and his wife and his granny were there, and everyone was cheerful, despite the long queues at the checkouts. Everyone was so delighted to be OUT.

And then in the afternoon I had to go to the post office with Christmas mail and had to stand in a queue for half an hour, and it didn't demolish my good mood. Me! The most impatient woman in Derbyshire! That is what a week of incarceration does to me. I'd go crazy in prison.

December 16th 2010

Bliss

I am sitting here in bed at 9.06 a.m. The house is empty. The house is silent. My SAD light has been on since I woke and sat up in bed. Now, finally, it is light outside, and I can see the bare trees disturbed by the wind, the telephone line from our house stretching to the pole on the road is bouncing up and down, and a sudden gust of wind rushes round the house. But now it is silent again. I have not been in the oasis of an empty house for over a month. I love my family, but to be here – just me – for eight whole hours – and know I am free with my thoughts, my plans, my sax, my writing, it is bliss. An ocean of quiet in the air, and a lake of inner calm inside my head.

Update. I have just told my daughter on the phone about the bliss of my empty house and she - a woman with two small boys – knew the treat of it, the significance of it. She said: "What are you going to do with your empty day?" and I immediately hit a block. One of the joys of the empty house and the empty day is not having to tell anyone what you are doing or what you are planning. I explained this to her and she understood. Now I am going to live it.

December 21st 2010

Awesome

I had a bad, sad day yesterday and I decided that my mood might improve if I got more sleep. "I think I've been getting up too early," I said. "I'm going to resolve not to get up before 6 o clock."

So there I was this morning, dying for a pee from 5.25 onwards, and not wanting to get out of bed because it was cold. I stayed under the covers and opened *Try Anything Twice* by Jan Struther. Three pages later Dave (who had been up since 4) came in and said he was going to drive up Longstone Edge and watch the lunar eclipse. "It's the first one on the winter solstice since 1638!" he said, with the same unbridled excitement and enthusiasm as if he were Sol in *But I Told You Last Year That I Loved You.*

How could I not go with him? Pah to resolutions about staying in bed.

I took the camera, but forgot the zoom that Isaac gave me (I was barely awake.) We watched the earth's shadow move over the moon and it filled me with awe. I took 47 photographs, and none of the big ones worked. Now I have another resolution - to learn how to use this camera properly.

Dave was standing looking through the binoculars when a friendly farmer drove up and asked what he was up to.

"Are you from Longstone?" he said.

"Yes," said Dave.

"Are you the vicar?" said the farmer.

When he had driven off, we laughed. "Why would he think I was the vicar?" said Dave.

"Because only a vicar would be daft enough to be standing in the freezing cold before dawn, staring at the moon?" I said.

December 24th 2010

My Christmas Eve Edition

This is for all my new readers who know nothing about the ON/OFF Christmas concept. Enjoy, whether you are new or old. And happy holidays, whether your Christmas is on or off.

Christmas in the Shed

Are you and your partner at odds as to how to celebrate Christmas? Does one of you want to go and sit by a peat fire in a bothy in the Outer Hebrides, while the other wants to stay in the thick of things and party every night?

Although we have tried to find the perfect Christmas compromise, for us there is no middle ground. It was somehow not a problem when we were first married. As impoverished students we both thought it fun to have a second hand Christmas tree and to make baubles out of painted eggshells. Now – forty years and three children later – we disagree.

You may need some background. I come from a meat eating, sub-Walton family of five children, with a history of jolly Christmases - not extravagant, there was no money for extravagance - but certainly festive. I don't ask for incessant parties, or for spending overkill. For me there is nothing more heart warming than having the house packed with people I love, sharing good food, conversation and games, and to have decorations and a tree.

For my teetotal, vegetarian, atheist husband, who is an only child, and who is not one of life's natural celebrants, an empty, quiet house is the ideal. He is allergic to visitors, cards, tree, seasonal food and tinsel, and his idea of jolly activity is a spot of DIY, whilst his only concession to over indulgence is an extra carton of natural yoghurt.

Last Christmas I tried to be selfless and to accede to his puritan yearnings by having no decorations and by giving up the tree. This was painful. Admittedly we missed out on the annual row about where to place it (the issue for him), and whether or not it was perfectly vertical (the issue for me), but still I was bereft. I lasted out till Christmas Eve, but failed to go cold turkey, and resorted to assembling all my over-wintering geraniums in the dining room, and stringing the fairy lights on them. It was sad, but it was better than nothing.

This year he floated the idea of the Christmas Shed. I was suspicious, because we already have a potting shed, a storage shed and a workshop shed, and I know he harbours an evil imperialist plan to have the garden covered with a vast shed complex. But actually his idea has promise.

Firstly, we would alternate a Christmas ON year with a Christmas OFF year. In an OFF year (his year) we would have no visitors and the house would be declared a festivity free zone. I would decorate the Christmas Shed to my taste, with a tree, cards, holly and tinsel, and there would be a stash of Christmas goodies in there, and a radio for Christmas music. If friends or family visit I would entertain them in the Shed. If no-one calls (and who would blame them?) and if the sitting room is not available for a surreptitious screening of *It's a Wonderful Life*, I could seek refuge from the monastic desert and go out to the Shed for a mince pie and an invigorating blast of *Jingle Bells*.

In an ON year, the house would be mine to fill with whoever and whatever I liked. My husband could slink off to the Christmas Shed with a bowl of yoghurt and sit in a deck chair in his boiler suit reading *Walden*. If he wanted a little light activity he could mend a few broken chair legs.

We could have a sign inside the front door saying "Next Christmas: December-" and then give the year. That way, adult children visiting the house during the year would be able to discreetly note it in their diaries, and no-one would suffer embarrassment or hurt feelings when the subject of Christmas was raised in those difficult parent-offspring telephone conversations that often occur in September. Outside the house, my husband could erect a sign directing carol singers and other assorted revellers towards the appropriate location.

So, that's decided, then. We'll buy a Christmas Shed and get started. The only problem now is to decide whether we start the new regime with an ON Christmas or an OFF Christmas. He says we've had Christmas for thirty years, so this year should be OFF. I say I did without the tree last year, so Christmas should be ON.

I hope you have the kind of Christmas you like – whether it is ON or OFF or non-existent.

This year our Christmas is ON.

December 31st 2010

New Year quote

"We must try to contribute joy to the world. That is true no matter what our problems, our health, our circumstances. We must try. I didn't always know this, and am happy I lived long enough to find it out."

Roger Ebert

2011

JANUARY

January 2nd 2011

There are some things you can't turn off

I've been lying in bed fretting about my mother's house, which we sold in August. It's been empty since then. My brother in Wensleydale rang last night to wish me happy new year, and he told me that one of my mother's neighbours had heard rushing water and another had a key, and they went in to turn the water off, and found burst pipes in the bathroom, and extensive damage. I put down the phone and felt sad.

You might think it has nothing to do with me any more, but that's not how these things work. An elderly friend of ours died in September and his brother has been worrying about the empty house (now sold) and fretting about whether the new owners had turned off the water and drained the system.

These properties are not in our care now, but we can't turn off our concern for them. My 80-year-old friend was brought up in what became his brother's house. And my mother's house was the centre of family happiness for 45 years. Yes, yes, I know. Houses are houses. They don't love. They don't care. They don't suffer. But when they have been such a stable part of your life for so many years, *you can't turn off your concern for them as easily as exchanging contracts.* You want people to treasure them, the way you have.

January 3rd 2011

Growing more brains

Yesterday my daughter rang while I was practising my sax, and in the course of our chat I said, "Hey, Zoë, I read in the *Guardian* on Saturday that if you learn a musical instrument when you are an adult, you grow more neurones and expand your brain. Isn't that great? I don't have to worry about Alzheimer's any more."

Zoë: "You told me the same thing yesterday."

January 4th 2011

My family and the earthquake

The news of an earthquake with the epicentre in Yorkshire reminded me of the earth tremor we had here some years ago. I had a piece about it in *The Times*. It's my favourite ever piece, because it has all my family in it. Here it is -

There we were, quaking in our boots

Derbyshire. Monday morning 12.54 a.m. We wake to a sound like a bowling ball rolling across the wooden floorboards of our bedroom. My husband switches on the light and sits up, "What the hell was that?"

"Don't know," I say. "Weird. Let's go back to sleep."

But he is sitting up, fretting. Is it settlement? Subsidence? Last year we built an extension and now we are sleeping in it. "What the hell was that noise?" says DIY man again.

I want to sleep, but I need a pee. My adult daughter – who is staying with us – hears me out of bed and calls out, petrified: "What's happening? The walls were shaking. The roof was rumbling. The wardrobe doors came open and now they won't shut."

She had been lying in bed unable to sleep, so was writing a to-do list for the following day. I give her a hug, thinking *Silly billy, fussing again: she lives her life on the margins of hysteria.* Then I remember her ringing me on September 11th last year telling me to turn on the telly, and my refusing because I had to post a birthday card.

I return to our bedroom to find DIY man getting up. He has heard daughter speak of the shaking walls, and thinks the house is falling down. He dons a dressing gown and wellington boots (the mission is too urgent to find the beloved boiler suit) and prowls around outside for fifteen minutes with a torch, looking for cracks, subsidence, disaster.

He finds nothing. He comes back inside and engages in anxious discussions with daughter while I retreat under the duvet and long for sleep. The front door opens: it's our younger son. He has been sitting on the village recreation ground under the full moon, having a philosophical discussion with his friend.

Only on arrival at our garden gate did he become unnerved – not by unusual shakes or rumbles, having felt nothing and heard nothing - but by the freakishness of all the house lights being on after half past ten. A rarer sight is DIY man still up and about. Younger son is phlegmatic, but he is also an *X files* fan, and suggests to DIY man and sister that the noise was supernatural.

DIY man comes back to bed and props himself up in worry mode, arms tense, head twitching. His next theory is that something has happened to our older son, who was flying to Denver and arriving there in the middle of our night. You hear stories, he says, of people dying and doors opening in family houses miles away. He gets up and leaves a message on our son's mobile phone: "Are you safe?"

More effectively, younger son (in the UK) logs onto the internet, gets instant messaging and immediately contacts older son (in the US.)

[01:40] son in UK: isaac. say something

[01:40] son in US: hello. wozzup?

[01:40] son in UK: thank god for that

[01:40] son in US: :S

[01:40] son in UK: theres some weird shit goin down here

[01:40] son in US: o no... what?

[01:40] son in UK: hang on, let me tell peeps youre ok. brb

Younger son tells aged parents that older son is safe, then returns to the computer.

[01:43] son in US: what gives?

[01:44] son in UK: i got back at 130 to find everyone up and wandering around the house looking worried

[01:45] son in US: there's been an earthquake

[01:45] son in UK: where?

[01:45] son in US:
uk. http://news.bbc.co.uk/1/hi/uk/2275158.stm

[01:45] son in UK: haha coool

The lights are off and I am just dropping off – oh bliss - when younger son brings us the printout from BBC news online: an earth tremor shakes the Midlands – 4.8 on the Richter scale.

"Great. Can we go to sleep now?" I say.

"Are we insured for earthquake damage?" says DIY man.

Morning breaks and I go downstairs to find him outside checking the drains. He has heard of damaged drains and wants no truck with them.

If something needs fixing he will fix it. If the earth moves, he will steady it. Failing that there's always the BBC. (But yes. The drains are fine.)

FEBRUARY

February 17th 2011

The planets

Don't tell me that astrology doesn't work. Yesterday I had Mars (energy/conflict) opposition (in difficult aspect to) Mercury (communication).

I woke up from a nightmare in which someone was saying nasty things to me

I spilled a full mug of tea all over the bed and the floor

I crashed my laptop

I went to the local library in Bakewell with my 5-page permission request to fax to David E Kelley Productions in Los Angeles, and when I got there realised I had forgotten the fax number

so I Googled it at the library and sent the fax

then got home and checked the fax number and found I had used the wrong one so had to go back to the library to fax again

came home and had a spat with the family member who declines to be named.

Fortunately, after that, things improved. I got to see Zoë and my grandsons. The six-year-old showed me the book he had written about the planets (astronomy is his latest craze) which has a contents page and what he calls a "blurb" on the back. How does he know what he knows? He is a marvel.

February 27th 2011

Verbal tics

I like to make the dialogue in my books distinctive and interesting, so I'm a keen listener to what people say AND the way that I say it. I try to capture peoples' verbal tics and give them to my characters.

Dave has a lot of verbal tics. They change over time. At present his favourite is to add "and stuff" to the ends of his sentences. Someone else in the family uses the word "obviously" a lot – often when it's *not* obvious. One of my good friends frequently says "to be honest."

I've been asking Dave for ages to spot my verbal tics, and he hasn't been able to come up with any.

This morning he said "*That's* a verbal tic of yours!"

"What is?"

"*How very odd,*" he said. "You say *How very odd,* usually in situations when you've just been proved wrong about something."

Me proved *wrong*? How very odd.

MARCH

March 1st 2011

PR

I am sitting here in bed with my laptop, reading through my "manuscript" one last time before it goes to press. You have no idea how tedious it is when it gets to this stage. How many times have I read this thing?

Oops! Bad PR!

What I should be saying is

Gosh, it doesn't matter how many times I read this book it still seems fresh - such riveting prose, such wonderful characters, such sparkling dialogue! It makes me laugh, it makes me cry! I love it! and what did that agent say about it? "...the novel is lovely - clever, funny, subtle, wry, sad and uplifting all at once." And who wrote the novel? Oh yes – me!

March 10th 2011

Writer? Grandmother? Writer?

I've been waiting excitedly for the hard copy of my book cover to arrive from Isaac in San Francisco. I've seen it on screen, but I was dying to see it for real. Today it arrived. Fedex banged on the door and I rushed to answer. As I tore open the packet I saw there was something else in there - some A4-size photographs of Lux. I forgot the book cover, pounced on the photos and oohed and aahed. "Isn't she lovely? Look at this one! Look at *this* one! Oh, look at *this* one!"

Then I looked at the book cover and drooled over that.

Perhaps I'm a grandmother before I'm a writer. Who would have thought it? Certainly not the me of 7 years ago.

March 18th 2011

Still waiting

I'm still getting over the virus I had, and can only manage half a day on normal activities before I get tired. That's OK. I have a safe warm house, and nothing pressing that I must do. Yesterday I was lying on the sofa by the fire looking out at the bare branches of the mock orange against the cold sky, and missing my mother. I'd spoken to one sister on the phone in the morning, had an email from the other, and I'd emailed both my brothers. We keep in touch. I love them all. I'm very lucky. Sometimes, though, I feel as though we're chatting amongst ourselves and keeping each other company while we wait for Ma to come back.

APRIL

April 1st 2011

Perfection

Thinking about perfection and imperfection with regards to the proof copy of my book that came the other day, I remembered this piece I had in *The Times* some years ago:

The idea of perfection

Reading the Orange Prize winner *The Idea of Perfection* has made me consider the thorniness of liking things *just so*. I loved the book, but in my Picador edition there were no quotation marks used to enclose the direct speech. And I hated that.

Popular culture abounds with characters with fine discrimination, or obsessive pickiness, depending on your point of view. Remember Meg Ryan as Sally in *When Harry Met Sally*? "I'd like apple pie a la mode. But I'd like the pie heated and I don't want the ice cream on top I want it on the side. And I'd like strawberry instead of vanilla if you have it. If not, then no ice cream, just whipped cream, but only if it's real. If it's out of a can, then nothing." You could say she was picky.

But if there were a team event for pickiness in the Olympics, my family would get the Gold medal, every time. At fifteen my brother was ironing his own shirts, because my mother didn't do it well enough. Now if you wash up for him he will tell you to turn the teaspoons upside down on the draining board so that they drain efficiently. I am picky about everything. So picky that last time I had breakfast in bed, my husband - who can never remember precisely what I like, but who wanted me to enjoy the treat - brought me three different mugs for my tea, three spreads, and three different types of jam. My father, a Grand Master of pickiness, will spurn every kipper that isn't from Craster. But if you send him one from that blessed haven you give him exquisite pleasure, and he will be sweet for days.

At least you can be sure of giving great pleasure to high maintenance types if you make the effort and get it right. Those people who say "I'm easy," or "I don't mind," can be impossible to please. How can you possibly know how to delight those colourless children who come round to tea, and who "don't mind" whether they have fish fingers or pizza or baked beans on toast?

Pickiness becomes truly unbearable, though, when it extends to a delusion that other people want to know your opinion about everything on every occasion even when you haven't been asked. This week I am dreading my father coming to stay, and casting his critical eye over my treasured garden, because I know he will make derogatory comments about how I have pruned the blackcurrants or let blackspot infest my roses. When someone picks at an expression of your creativity, that's when it hurts the most.

72

So if someone actually *asks* your opinion about something which they care deeply, and in which you can see an imperfection, what do you tell them? If they have just spent three months stitching a tapestry and they ask you if you think that it matters that they ran out of blue and had to use another dye lot and can you see the difference, and does it matter? If you can, and it does, what do you say?

When planting our new garden my husband asked exactly where I wanted him to place the silver birch tree, so I marked the spot in the ground with a stick. "We work to fine tolerances here," he said. When I viewed the tree later from the kitchen, I thought it was nine inches too far to the right, but I bit my tongue and said nothing. I was rewarded for this uncharacteristic forbearance when in the evening he looked through the window and decided that the tree needed moving, about nine inches to the left. Such miracles are rare.

I know I'm difficult. But being the pick*er* can be just as uncomfortable as being the pick*ee*. It is not easy when someone you love has just sanded and varnished a wooden floor for you, and every time you sit down on the sofa you notice a white paint stain (he missed) under the varnish.

I do find it helps to remind myself that in some cultures craftsmen deliberately include a mistake in their work, because only God can create things perfect. It also helps to read the motto my husband gave me "Perfection is our aim. We must learn to tolerate excellence."

April 4th 2011

Busy, busy, busy

I'm really busy working on the PR campaign for my book and although I keep getting ideas for the blog – e.g. Would Catullus have used Twitter? – I haven't got time to write these posts. I'm sorry. Please will you make do for now with this old *Times* piece which I showed (new parent) Isaac at the weekend, and which he enjoyed?

What the Green Paper left out

The Green Paper on parental leave misses the point. Parents don't need maternity leave or paternity leave. Tired, stressed, burnt-out parents don't need leave to **see** their children, they need leave *from* their children. If only the government would issue parental respite vouchers along with Child Benefit, parents could take short sabbaticals from parenting at those flashpoints when the going gets too tough.

Think of the early infant years when you stumble zombie-like through a chain of frazzled days and sleepless nights, measuring out your life with feeds and nappy changes. Wouldn't three nights of parental respite put your body and mind back together, remind you who you were, and also why you wanted a baby in the first place?

Later, when there are two under-fives in the house, and you've just vicariously suffered two consecutive bouts of chicken pox, closely followed by 48 hour sickness and diarrhoea, you could cash in one of your vouchers. A stimulating city break or a weekend away in unfettered fresh air would give you the strength to carry on.

Once sick children are past the easy stage of being feverish, weak and pathetic, and have reached the downstairs-in-the-sitting-room-playing-with-Lego-phase, it's wearing. They are well enough to be crabby, but not well enough to have a friend to play. Being cooped up together with no dilution in each other's company for seven hours every day can make you both feel pretty murderous, no matter how much you love each other. After several weeks of my son's tonsillitis and quinsy I remember stamping down the cellar steps to fetch coal, saying "I hate him, I hate him, I hate him" and on returning with a full bucket found him behind the door whispering "I hate her, I hate her, I hate her." If someone had offered me parental respite of just two days we would have both leaped for joy.

Different people have different strengths: a parent may sail through one childhood phase, only to be floored by the next. I find new born babies irresistible, but when they get to four-months-old I find them boring, and dream of putting them in a time capsule, to get them out again when they are old enough to talk.

There are some parents who do not feel up to making costumes for the nativity play at junior school, or fiddling with all those Blue Peter models. They shrink from the thought of a dozen pairs of greasy hands when it's their turn on the class cooking rota, and they would rather sign up for a course in lion taming than help on a school trip.

Other parents are a dab hand with all that primary stuff but find it too cold and tedious standing on the touch-line for pubescent hockey and football matches, and too nerve racking watching their sons risk paraplegia by playing in the school rugby team. They also get worn down by a house awash with swirling hormones, a fridge that needs restocking daily, conversations conducted at ten decibels, providing a 24 hour taxi service, and fielding phone calls from teachers pursuing missing coursework.

My personal current blackspot is cooking for a teenage vegetarian who doesn't like vegetables. I love cooking, but as far as making healthy, balanced meals for someone who only wants junk food is concerned, I'm burnt out. I'm battle weary from arguing with someone who at ten paces can recognise and reject anything containing a shred of fibre or an infinitesimal trace of a vitamin. Fights over meeting GCSE coursework deadlines are bad enough - who needs extra grief?

I've shot through my diligent, dutiful catering phase, and serve up instant junk vegetarian every other day, boosted by synthetic vitamins and minerals. If only my innovative parental respite system had been in operation, I might have been able to sustain the provision of healthy food until he left for University, and worried about his own baked beans.

Look, the system needs fine tuning but it doesn't have to be too complicated. Each parent would have a set number of vouchers for each year of the child's life, up to the age of eighteen. These vouchers could then be cashed in with pensioners who became registered providers of parental respite, and they in turn would be reimbursed by the Benefits Agency. The system would thus be doubly beneficial. It would boost pensioners' incomes as well as relieving pressure on families.

No doubt the Benefits Agency would want to evaluate how parents used their vouchers. Parents new to the job would probably practise spend-as-they-grow, whereas more experienced parents might save their vouchers and have one long decadent splurge during the most arduous phase of adolescence. During a lengthy happy-families phase an insouciant parent might altruistically donate a few vouchers to the PTA fund raising auction. A desperate parent might organise after dinner poker with vouchers as the stakes.

Those especially blessed people born with huge reserves of patience and deep wellsprings of parental instinct may find that their children leave home before all the vouchers are spent. You can just imagine the classified ad: "For sale: cot, box of assorted Lego, inline skates size 5, Nintendo, and fifty parental respite vouchers. Will separate."

April 11th 2011

Panacea

Yesterday morning…

Sue (lying in bed): I feel sick.

Dave: Why don't you go downstairs and look at your box of pre-release books? That'll make you feel better.

Sue: I don't need to. I've got one here on my bedside table I can fondle.

MAY

May 1st 2011

May Day

Dave and I should have been up on Longstone Edge this morning at dawn, singing "To welcome in the summer, to welcome in the May-o!" as we usually do, but we didn't wake up till a quarter past five: too late. We had a bit of sleep to catch up on. I don't know if you've ever slept on a boat, but when I come back home I always feel as if the bed is bobbing about on water.

We've been round the Avon ring, made up of the Worcester and Birmingham canal, the Stratford canal, the river Avon and the river Severn, and in case you're interested, we went through 132 locks, all but two operated manually by us and our two friends on the boat. May is my favourite month, and combining it with boating in a week of sustained sunshine was pretty awesome.

The holiday was great because it gave me respite from *my exploding brain*, and being home is great, too. I am sitting in bed as I write this, and sunshine is streaming in through the mucky windows onto the patchwork quilt. Outside, the wind is rustling the new green leaves on the row of lime trees opposite, and the copper beeches in the garden. Through the side window I can see may blossom and cotoneaster blossom. This is a beautiful place to come home to after a holiday. It never feels like a let down.

May 9th 2011

The couple who need to be connected

So there I was, gaily telling everyone that the narrowboat we're currently sailing on had wifi and I could keep in touch with printers, wholesalers, the ISBN agency, journalists, BBC Radio producers, Waterstone's, my family and friends (note how they come last in the list these days) and yet, and yet, the wifi has been non-existent, and I've been freaking out.

Dave, too, has concerns he needed to keep in touch with.

Now we are moored in a spot that works. Yay! I have dealt with my gazillion emails, and paid the printer. Now he can print my book. Phew.

The boat we're on has a different kind of toilet facility from the hire boats. Hire boats have a ceramic loo and a sewage tank on board and you have to pay to have it pumped out once a fortnight. This boat has a plastic loo with a toilet box

79

underneath which fills up every two days, and you have to find a sanitary facility where you can empty it. That's fine for me: Dave is happy to do the honours. But when we arrived in Banbury yesterday and got a speedy internet connection and a place to get some food – Morrisons – it was a treat to use the flushing loo there.

"I think everyone on the boat should have their own toilet box," said Dave this morning, when we were chatting in the bedroom.

Me: "Why on earth do you say that? That's the kind of thing a character in one of my novels would say."

Dave: "No doubt they will."

Sue: "That's very funny. I'll have to put it on the blog."

He drew the curtains.

Sue: "Hang on, is there anyone on the towpath?"

Dave: "No. But people don't look in, anyway."

Sue: "I do."

Dave: "Well, thankfully the towpath isn't teeming with writers searching for copy."

Sue: "That's very bloggable."

Dave: "See. It's not even 6 a.m. and I've contributed two things to the blog already."

May 15th 2011

I'm not fitted for this life

Today I was standing in the teensy-weensy bath on the barge, having a shower. When you have a shower you're supposed to turn on the water pump to empty the water into the canal. I forgot until half way through the shower, so I was standing up to my ankles in shower water. Then I knocked the plug into the bath and didn't notice that it had found it's own way into the plughole. So then when I finished the shower I was still standing up to my ankles in shower water, the pump was still going, and the plug had been sucked so tightly into the hole that I couldn't pull it out.

I am a stranger in the world of even simple mechanics. I just *look* at the mop for swabbing the deck and the head falls off.

Dave fixes everything. He's my man.

May 27th 2011

The Monsal Trail

I'm rushing around like a mad thing every day, sorting out book-related stuff, and then after tea I collapse and slump in front of junk TV.

But – but – I did find time one early morning to cycle up the Monsal Trail, a local disused railway line.

Dave and I have lived within half a mile of the Monsal Trail for 16 years. We've walked on it three times a week, and it's always been my preferred cycle route into Bakewell. Now the Peak Park has opened it up in the other direction for another eight miles, and one or both of us will cycle up the new track almost every day.

It goes through five tunnels, and across a couple of high viaducts, and the scenery is fabulous. The views are spectacular, and the silence is lovely. For several miles it is completely silent on the Trail, apart from birdsong, because the limestone hills shield the Trail from traffic noise. I have a favourite spot between the Cressbrook and Litton tunnels. I stop and lean on the railings and look down into the deep river gorge and listen to the birds. It's a perfect way to start my day.

Dave and I feel as though we've discovered a pot of hidden treasure in our back garden. It's such a great thing to be organised by the powers that be, that we're half expecting an announcement that it's all a mistake, and the thing is now closed.

JUNE

June 9th 2011

Launch day!

It's book launch day and I'm sitting here in bed with my laptop and first mug of Yorkshire tea, trying <u>not</u> to make lists in my head of things to do this morning. First I need to wake up.

Dave just said "Well this time tomorrow it'll all be over."

There was a look of relief in his eyes.

June 15th 2011

Clueless

Life is hectic this week. But yesterday afternoon was a rare interlude of R & R and I managed to get to my saxophone lesson. I have told my teacher, Mel, I want to learn to improvise. And to do that, I need to know some music theory. At present I don't know any. None at all. Zilch. Yes, I can play, yes I can sight read, but that is the limit to my musical knowledge. So yesterday Mel spent fifty minutes on Major chords. Isn't it complicated? Isn't it challenging? Isn't it dull?

Oh my God.

But this year I have learned how to publish a book. Maybe I can also learn the intricacies of music theory. Wish me luck:

it's my latest challenge. Even if I don't succeed, the attempt should keep my brain alive.

June 20th 2011

Not J K Rowling

Book promotion is exhausting.

I just had three events in the space of four days, and after yesterday's signing at Hassop Station on the Monsal Trail (which actually means approaching people and handing over your book for perusal, because punters are far too shy to actually come up to your table and say "Hello") I came home and went to bed at six o'clock and lay there in a stupor unable to switch off and go to sleep, but too tired even to listen to the radio. After two hours of lying there, I sat up and watched two episodes of *Neighbours* (so shoot me), had some cocoa, and slept for nine hours.

Now I feel human. Thankfully I have five days before the next event.

June 29th 2011

Jam today

Yesterday was the day I did my tax return.

Today it's jam!

Sue: "Don't forget, Dave. We can only get 6lbs of fruit in a jam pan."

Dave: "I wonder what's the minimum amount of jam it's possible to make."

Sue: "With a pound of fruit I should think."

Dave: "No, theoretically speaking. Would it be possible, for example, to make jam with only two blackcurrants…in a test tube?"

JULY

July 13th 2011

In praise of 7 year olds

It was my elder grandson's birthday this week and when I rang him in the morning *and* when I saw him in the afternoon, he told me joyfully that he'd been given some wine gums and a ten pound note. He loved his other presents – one of which was a pocket digital camera – but oh the joy he got from the wine gums and the ten pound note!

He is a beautiful sunny boy, thoughtful and sensitive, enthusiastic and affectionate, and I told him there was no-one else like him in the world.

"But there might be," he said.

"No, love. There's no-one like you."

"There might be someone like me." He paused for thought. "But they probably wouldn't have a ten pound note."

July 22nd 2011

Treasure

I asked my grandson if he'd broken into his precious ten pound note, and he said, "Yes! I've spent £3.50, and bought a bag of Fool's Gold."

AUGUST

August 4th 2011

It's the little things

You want to send flowers to a friend in hospital in Manhattan.

First you ring the hospital to check you're allowed to send flowers.

Then you ring up a florist in Manhattan to order flowers. You discuss the flowers you want. They say it's a bad idea to send fragrant flowers to someone in hospital, and no they don't know what sea holly is, or eryngium, and they say you must send a vase as well if they're going to a US hospital, and you tell them the flowers you don't want (carnations, chrysanthemums.)

And then they take your name. 'What? Egworth? Epworse?'

You spell it out.

Then you tell them your message – *Get better soon, lots of love, Sue and Dave.*

And a few hours later you get an email saying –

Just got beautiful flowers along with the lovely wish to

'Get Well Soom'

August 22nd 2011

You can't be a minimalist if you're sentimental

I had a perfect holiday, doing nothing with my sister Jen.

The first day it rained and we spent the afternoon clearing out the top drawer of Ma's sewing chest. It's much easier to do that kind of job with someone else, especially if they are sentimental as well as practical. There are times when in order to be able to throw things away, you need permission from someone who is also emotionally engaged with the material. We only had one tiny temporary tiff, relating to a pair of damaged, rusty scissors in a scabbard made from the finger of a leather glove. I wanted to keep it as an example of Ma's recycling (the finger of the glove) but Jen wanted to chuck it because the scissors were rubbish, and the scabbard was not made with care. "Come on – two staples! Not Ma's best effort!"

She was right.

Meanwhile, I have at home a pewter ash tray made by Pa at school in the 1930s. No-one wants it, but no-one wants to chuck it out. Jen and I can remember Pa lying on the carpet in front of the fire, reading aloud his latest article for *Farm and Country* so Ma could make editorial comments. He would be smoking, and using this ash tray. I've had it in my kitchen for three years (since Ma died) and Jen has agreed to have it now. When she's fed up with it, I'll take it back.

SEPTEMBER

September 4th 2011

This and that

People often ask me how much of my books are taken from my own life.

We-e-el-l-lll, one bit in the latest book is certainly true – I did meet a woman at a peace demo in San Francisco on the first day of one of my visits, and she did show me round the city and we did become friends. And TODAY she and her husband are coming to stay for a couple of days – Woo-hoo!

I have seen her home, but she has never been here and seen how beautiful the Peak District is, and we are both outdoorsy types, and I want to take her cycling on the Monsal Trail, and on our favourite walks round here, and rain is forecast forever and ever amen so please can you all keep your fingers crossed that we'll have at least one dry day? I'm not even asking for sunshine though that would be nice - just one dry day.

The other news at Hepworth Towers is that we are now officially a no television household. Our area went digital and we have no way of watching the big old box in the corner and Dave doesn't want to have a telly, anyway, so while I consider what I want, I have not renewed our licence. I am willing to give it a go and do without a telly for now.

The fact is that my head is so full of Karen and John coming, and then in less than two weeks my trip to the sunshine to see Isaac and Wendy and Lux in San Francisco, that tellies (is that how you spell the plural?) are the last thing on my mind. I told Karen this and she said "Oh but I wanted to watch *Neighbours* with you and see why you liked it" – so I told her she would have the full Hepworth *Neighbours* experience – huddled round my laptop with a glass of wine and a packet of crisps, because we have never been able to receive Channel 5 in our village anyway – digital switchover or no digital switchover.

I am going to get up and get weaving, but before that I might just watch Monday's episode as I haven't seen it yet.

September 18th 2011

Carpe Diem

Here's a quote from my *Quaker Faith and Practice*:

"Are you able to contemplate your death and the death of those closest to you? Accepting the fact of death, we are freed to live more fully."

And here are some quotes from Martial:

'If someone knows how to live, why would they delay?'

'Trust me: a wise man doesn't say "Life starts tomorrow". Living tomorrow is too late. Live today.'

I went to a friend's 60th birthday party the other night and caught up with a lot of people I haven't seen for ages. It was fascinating to find out what they're all doing, but even more interesting to see how they're approaching retirement.

Some are embracing it and exploring their creative side, taking up activities they've hitherto not had the time for. Others have felt they're on the brink of a scary chasm and have panicked and taken on armfuls of voluntary jobs. One person, a retired senior civil servant, had decided he wanted to see if he was able to earn some money in the big bad world.

It was a big shock to me when I turned 60, but now I've adjusted, I am carpe diem-ing as if there's no tomorrow. I want to cram in everything I can before I'm too old or ill to enjoy the activities I love. There was a fab little trio at the party with a tenor sax playing the kind of music I love – *The Nearness of You, How insensitive, Desafinado*, you know the kind of thing – and for the first time since I took up the sax (when I was 60), I thought it would be fun to play in a band. So this may be my next big aim. Watch this space.

What's on my mind this morning, though, is that I'll be seeing Lux in 2 days. D.V.

September 22nd 2011

Fog City

This is my fifth visit to San Francisco, and I've always denied seeing fog. But that was then - when Isaac and family lived in The Mission, a district that doesn't see fog. Now they live on Bernal Hill, I am always at their sitting room window gazing out at the long wide view, saying "Look at the fog, creeping in from the coast. Look at it - it's sinister!" and they laugh at me, poor wee innocent that I am. It can be a baking hot day and then at 4 o clock, I see it swirl in from the Golden Gate and cover areas of the city not protected by the contours of the landscape, like the Mission is. So OK. I have seen the fog. And now I learn it has its very own Twitter account - @KarlTheFog. This week it tweeted: "Back early from vacation. I'm as happy about this as you are."

Karen, the aging hippie, and I had a fabulous day in North Beach yesterday, walking and talking and soaking up the sunshine. We took in the Coit Tower, and Stella's pastry shop and a couple of cafes (there was a lot of talking to do) and we ended up at the City Lights Bookstore.

Why are they always so snooty in there? There is always someone behind the counter dressed in black who is young and male and sporting some outré constellation of facial hair and they always look at me with an expression that says "You're old and grey and female, what can you possibly want in here? Why aren't you at home, knitting? We only welcome OLD people if they are male. And even then they have to be of vast intelligence and with impeccable literary and political connections. Only old people like that are allowed past our portal."

When Karen asked if they had a copy of *How to retire, happy wild and free* the guy said "Oh, we don't carry books like that," as if we were in a Christian Bookshop and asking for porn.

I really think they should lighten up in there. If they can carry babies' onesies emblazoned with the word HOWL, they have no right to be so high and mighty about their stock. Or about anything else. And besides, Karen has exquisite credentials. She is a bona fide aging hippie who lived in Haight when it was all happening, and you can bet she's read more books than Mr Snootismo has had hot dinners.

September 26th 2011

I love you, Margarita

If you're lucky enough to be staying in San Francisco, and your luck is so extravagantly awesome that you also have a warm, understanding, zany and hilarious daughter-in-law, who can turn any evening into a party, then get yourself down to the Velvet Cantina on 23rd and Bartlett. Start the evening with their perfect margaritas and something to eat with the second margarita. Do you expect me to give you details of the scrummy food? I can't remember what I had to eat! Come on, I'm upright and my head is clear - isn't that enough for you?

September 27th 2011

Road trip

Today I am going with my friend Karen (aka the Aging Hippie) to see the Grand Canyon. Yippeee!

We are flying to Las Vegas on a cheapo-cheapo airline and then renting a car and driving for five hours to get to the Canyon. Karen has kindly arranged and booked it all - bless her - and she will be doing the driving. I said to her that driving through the desert with her would be just like *Thelma and Louise* (never having seen the film.) So she said that first of all, I HAD to see the film before we set off, and secondly (or "second of all" as they say over here) I mustn't be taking a gun.

OK, Karen.

September 30th 2011

A new obsession

It seemed like a good idea to drive from Las Vegas to the South Rim of the Grand Canyon (280 miles and 5 hours) with an ageing hippie for whom a USA coast-to-coast drive is the equivalent of a Saturday morning trip to Sainsbury's, but it might have been better if we hadn't been using her map from 1971.

Moving swiftly along (which we didn't) - the Grand Canyon is more awesome than I ever imagined. We gazed down into it, we watched the changing shadows and colours, we walked along the rim, and we hiked down into it on the Bright Angel Trail.

The information leaflet said it was one and a half hour's walk to get to the first restroom (an earth closet and a water tap) 1,000 feet down. The path was narrow and stony, slippery in some places because of the surface dust, and at the side there was often a vertiginous drop. We got there in an hour and a quarter, but then I discovered we had only gone one and a half miles down! Pathetic! It is seven miles to the river at the bottom. It took us an hour and a half to get back up, and the air is thin at 7,000 feet, so I got a bit puffed.

But now I am totally hooked! I want to fly over it, sail through it on a boat, and walk right down the trail to the bottom, a feat which takes a day. The problem - apart from the arthritic knee and the advanced age - is that I couldn't carry all the stuff I would need to sleep at the bottom for two nights, before I tried to climb back up again.

So I am on the lookout for a fit young man who will do the honours, by which I mean - carry my backpack. He has to be thoughtful and sensitive and patient, and not a macho type. I want someone who has a good relationship with his mother. I don't care about perfect abs. (For the record, Brad Pitt in *Thelma and Louise* did not turn me on.)

So if you know such a person, point him in my direction.

OCTOBER

October 12th 2011

Here and there

I've finally stopped dreaming I'm in America, and waking in the night wondering where the hell I am. My sleep cycles are set to England, and specifically Hepworth Towers, and my brain works from 7 a.m. onwards everyday. But I just got an email from Wendy, giving me domestic and family news, and I'm back in their living room in Bernal Heights, watching laughing Lux chase up and down.

How on earth did people manage with emigrating families before air travel and phone and email? I guess when you kissed them goodbye at Southampton or Liverpool, it really was goodbye. I'm so glad that's not how it is for me.

And now it's made me think of a piece I had in *The Times*, some years ago…

The continuing story of the empty nest: optimum distance

An empty nest is a place that is heartening to look forward to, in the way that the suffering, in olden times, looked forward to heaven. And now I have achieved nirvana I relish it.

But I still love to spend time with my children. Nor is my caring role redundant.

That ridiculous term "life long parenting" - to describe the phenomenon of adult children returning to live with their parents - must have been coined by a non-parent. Haven't children always been for life, and not just for Christmas? Whatever their offspring's pain - whether it be a trapped finger or a mangled heart - a mother always wishes she could bear it for them. Soppy? It's true.

The very week the 18-year-old moved out and left us in peace, the 29-year-old rang to inform us *he* had just spent the night hooked up to monitors after an emergency admission to hospital. The medics insisted his condition only required rest and an early check up, and sent him home, but I was unconvinced, and hopped on a train to go and make my own early check up. Mothers do that.

But even if there is an unbreakable bond, once children grow up there is an optimum distance at which parents and offspring should live: near enough to allow travel of either party for an emergency dash, or for a weekend stay, but far enough away to make it unfeasible for anyone to drop in unexpectedly.

Parents, just like children, have their own lives to lead, and their own need of privacy. If a couple of old fogeys are agile enough to want to make love on the kitchen table, they won't welcome someone with a front door key waltzing in unannounced.

The other advantage of having children easily accessible but at a distance is that a weekend visit provides a chance to get away from middle aged cosiness. For several years my eldest two children have lived in London, thus providing me with comfortable bolt-holes from which they could take me out to sample the delights of young urban chic entertainment.

How else would I - a country bumpkin who has led a sheltered life - have the chance to sample tequila slammers in an ex-engineering-workshop bar in Hoxton, with décor so uncompromisingly industrial I expected the ladies loos to consist of a row of galvanised buckets? My last exciting foray into their lives led to cocktails in a private bar with a secret Soho location, which, when I entered the blacked-out frontage, made me feel as if I was time travelling back to the prohibition.

But now one of these children has moved to live within half an hour of here (Derbyshire) closing one of my bolt-holes; and the second child is threatening not just to leave London, but to flee the country. Last week he told us of his plans to stop teleworking for his American employer and to move out to Denver to work on site.

I wanted to scream "Don't do it - I'll miss you too much!" but I didn't. I was well behaved and breezy. I couldn't quite squeeze out "What a great idea," as the old man did (with no apparent effort, incidentally), but I did manage some intelligent questions about living in lofts.

Vacating the nest is one thing: leaving the continent is another. What is the point of having children if you can't spend time with them and enjoy their company? And how can you do this if they live a ten hour flight away?

What is troubling me now is the thought that because I voiced no protest he might think I don't care about his going, and that I really shall not miss him. It's the same kind of bind you get into when young adult offspring hint, for the first time, that they might not come back for Christmas. You wish they would come home but genuinely don't want to apply any pressure; but then you worry that if you don't sound disappointed they might think you don't want to see them. And then there is the Christmas when you long for a quiet time a deux with your spouse, but don't want to offend the offspring by suggesting they stay away.

It's a tricky skill to master, this next stage of parenting.

Also, the caring role has started to hover between the generations before it finally settles on the younger one. It was my adult children who were looking after me on our nights out in London. But on one occasion when waiting for the midnight tube, I wondered how safe we were, and if my children ever got nervous, and I heard myself ask "If I weren't here, would you be scared?"

But we are getting there. On a recent protest march with my children my elder son left early, with the words (to me) "Take care. Have fun." Then, pointing to the other two, he said "Make sure you stay with them."

A woman walking alongside me overheard and laughed.

"That," she said, "must be your son."

October 17th 2011

A certain symptom

There's a story in my favourite book - Garrison Keillor's *Leaving Home* - where the whole town of Lake Wobegon gets the Swedish flu -

It's the usual flu with chills, fever, diarrhoea, vomiting, achiness and personal guilt, but it's accompanied by an overpowering urge to put things in order. Before you collapse into bed, you iron the sheets. Before you vomit, you plan your family's meals for the upcoming week.

Dave had a flu-like cold at the weekend. Usually when he's ill, he doesn't go to bed. He scorns the very mention of bed. This is his usual mantra: "I'm going out on my bike to teach this cold a lesson."

But this time he was so ill he *did* go to bed. I wanted to look after him. I like looking after poorly people (at least I do until it gets boring.) I wanted to make him drinks, fluff up his pillow, bring him treats and a nice cold flannel for his fevered brow, but he spurned all my offers.

Dave: "Do you think I'm going to die?"

Sue: "No, Dave. You've just got a nasty cold. Would you like me to make you a drink?"

Dave: "Are you being a bit impatient with me today?"

He said this three times on Saturday and three times on Sunday, and I kept answering – patiently, of course, "No. I'm not being impatient. I think you're ultra-sensitive because you're feeling so rough. I'm actually being extremely sweet to you. Don't I keep offering to do things for you?"

Could paranoia be one of his symptoms?

This morning he was his usual self again, and even though he was coughing, and his head was aching, and his chest felt as if someone was sticking a loo brush down it, he went out on his bike.

I, however, started sniffing, and then worrying that I was getting his cold, and then manically swallowing aconite every two hours as a prophylactic. And no-one was being very nice to me: Zoë sounded unfriendly on the phone, and the man in the cafe was rather off. Didn't they like me?

Now Dave is sleeping in the other room so as not to disturb me with his coughing. Or is it because *he* doesn't like me? And I am sitting here at midnight unable to sleep, two hours past my bedtime, because my nose is running and my face hurts, and now my eyes are sore.

7 a.m. the next morning. I have got it. And Dave just came in and brought me a mug of sweet tea, without my asking. He always looks after me beautifully when I'm under par.

October 19th 2011

Bulletin from the house of doom, formerly known as Hepworth Towers

I spent a feverish night but have managed to eat some porridge for breakfast.

Dave felt better from his killer bug, went outside to work on the new fence, and cracked a rib.

This morning he has flashing lights in both eyes.

October 21st 2011

Choosing the right verb

Dave: 'Well, you look a tad less corpse-like this morning. You look as if you might be climbing out of the pit of illness, not cavorting in the bottom.'

Sue: 'People don't cavort when they're ill.'

Dave: 'No. It sounds like cavorting, it's only when you look down that you see they're wrestling with death.'

NOVEMBER

November 30th 2011

On bravery

A friend emailed and said she thought I was brave to open myself up in my blog and in my books, but you know what? It doesn't feel like bravery to me.

This is brave: driving SOLO from San Francisco, out of the city, over the Bay Bridge, and up to Yosemite 200 miles away. And then doing the return trip three days later. I was driving out of the city in what felt like hundreds of lanes of hurtling traffic and gripping the wheel as tightly as I could and thinking "What's the worst that can happen? I might die. Well, I'm not afraid of dying, so that's all right."

DECEMBER

December 10th 2011

Saturday morning

I went to Bakewell to get some odds and ends, and in the Deli found myself explaining to three American women the difference between a Bakewell tart and a Bakewell pudding. They bought the pudding because I told them they could get a Bakewell tart from anywhere but you have to come to Bakewell to buy a Bakewell pudding. When I bumped into them later outside another shop, I almost, *almost* told them that if they went to the Bakewell Bookshop they could buy a signed copy of a novel set in Bakewell – namely, *But I Told You Last Year That I Loved You*. I couldn't get over the almost, though. Do you think I should have done?

December 14th 2011

Hepworth's hypothesis on short term memory loss

For the past two weeks I have been carrying my mother around in my head – or rather a yearning to see my mother. A hopeless melancholic wish to see her has been there at the end of every thought, as I finish every task, waking up in the morning, or settling down to sleep at night. Just when I thought I was not going to feel that sadness any more, it sweeps in and stays for a while.

103

But then yesterday, when the Higgs boson announcement was made, I cheered up. Not because I am into that kind of stuff, but because Ma was. I thought – *Ah, she'd be so delighted. She and Dave would be talking excitedly on the phone about it, even now.* And the weather changed in my head: weird.

Brains are odd. Mine is odd, anyway. My mother lives in there all of the time, mostly quietly and happily. I wonder if old people lose their short-term memories because their brains are so full of dead people they've lost so there isn't enough room for all the new stuff they encounter.

December 22nd 2011

My Christmas edition

You know how the newspapers use stuff they've prepared earlier (and not news) in their Christmas editions?

Well here's my version of that – a piece I had in *The Times*…

Party Time

"The best thing about being self-employed is that I don't have to think of an excuse for missing the office party," said my fellow home-worker – my husband.

I, however, am in need of some fun and games. Living up a lane in the Peak District is heavenly for three seasons of the year, but when the looming mists swirl in and blank out the fabulous views, and I can't go anywhere without wellies, and it feels as though the long dark tea-time of the soul has set in till March, I get desperate for bright lights and company.

Unfortunately the man at the computer upstairs is not a party animal: he neither goes to parties, nor understands what they are for. I remember when I decided to have one for my fortieth birthday, he asked "Why on earth would you want to celebrate getting older and moving another few steps downhill? All we're heading for now is death."

He couldn't face attending the party, but was concerned about the hordes of people I would be having in the house, and wanted to make a contribution to the preparations. He did. He calculated the tonnage of the assembled revellers, worried that the sitting room floor might collapse because dancers would refuse to keep to the edges of the rooms, and he went down to the cellar, where he used chunky four by four wooden posts to prop up the floor from underneath.

Apart from that, the only other time he's been anywhere near a party was one New Year's Eve when he found two of our oldest friends on the doorstep, unannounced, and waving a bottle of champagne. Unhappily, I was away, but he phoned me and while he wailed about the "scandalous imposition" of their expecting him to stay up until midnight and be jolly, I jumped up and down with frustration that I couldn't be there to join in.

He's not what you'd call a singing-and-dancing-kind-of-guy. Think less Gene Kelly and more Fraser, the Scottish undertaker in *Dad's Army* - "Doomed! We're all doomed!"

105

But he does have a tender heart, and, eager to cheer me up, he has suggested we have our own office party – just me and him.

We should have it in his study as it's bigger than mine, he says. I am just wondering how he will press me up against the filing cabinet for a quick snog when you can't get near it for all the wallet files spread out on the carpet for easy access, when he offers to clear the floor. He will also carry out into the hall the stacking plastic boxes stashed with papers and reports, and he'll even wheel his poncey, sorry, *precious* new bike out to the shed (to join my sturdy workhorse) where he thinks it might be all right, just for a couple of hours.

I'm not sure what he's got to offer by way of food and drink, though. He is teetotal, and he's never been able to grasp the concept of eating as an enjoyable activity: as far as he's concerned, eating is for refuelling. That's apart from yoghurt, of which he is a connoisseur. Our village shop gets in catering size cartons of Longley Farm natural, just for him. At Christmas when the shop is closed and he has to pre-buy in bulk, and yet I also need extra fridge space for family entertaining, he keeps his extra cartons of yoghurt cool by floating them in the water barrel in the garden.

It may be just me, but when I think of party food, yoghurt isn't the first thing that comes to mind.

I don't care though, because for the party he says he will wear a Santa hat and download a festive screensaver onto his computer.

He really knows how to show a girl a good time.

I do appreciate the offer of an office party, I say, but I wonder whether it's possible to have a party with only two people. Couldn't we invite someone else? Unfortunately, the only other people we see during our working days are the postman, a sweetie who likes to tell us how many buzzards he's seen on his round, and our neighbouring farmer, who calls when he is moving his heifers, to ask us to stand in our gateway to stop them from coming in and cavorting on the lawn.

But we do have a continuous stream of telephone callers. Perhaps during the party we could have the phone on loudspeaker, I suggest, and at least have some conference calls, maybe with a Christmas quiz, so it doesn't feel so lonely? He says we can't do that, because he's just recorded a seasonal message on the answering machine saying "Sod off, it's Christmas."

He says he's willing, but his Christmas spirit is weak. And even after detailed explanations, his grasp of partying is non-existent. So I may flip out: cabin fever does strange things to people. If you see a news report of a desperate woman in sparkly reindeer antlers streaking through a Derbyshire village shrieking "Does anyone want to party?" you'll know who it is.

December 31st 2011

Publicity!

What a fabulous way to end the old year.

My book - *But I Told You Last Year That I Loved You* - is in the *Guardian* today, in Readers' Books of the Year. Yay!

JANUARY

January 24th 2012

Got the toys, the books, the cot and the trike

I dreamed Dave had let someone in the village use my beloved saxophone without asking me (and neither of them had screwed the neckpiece on properly, either.) Dave is without remorse. He says he is not responsible for his behaviour in my dreams. I don't altogether agree.

If you don't hear any more from me this week, it's because I'm busy with my American family who are flying in today from San Francisco.

January 27th 2012

The good, the bad and the downright exhausted

Jet-lag and toddlers don't mix.

Jet-lag and toddlers who are teething don't mix.

Jet-lag and irrepressible, never-sit-still toddlers don't mix – at least not for the parents.

The west coast Hepworths staying at Hepworth Towers are merely grazing on sleep, but…Lux is doing just fine.

January 30th 2012

Back to real life

She's gone. They've gone. As I write this, they are flying Virgin Atlantic back to San Francisco.

The last week was very special, even though Lux couldn't settle into our UK time zone and was awake and playing for several hours in the middle of every night. We stumbled around in various states of sleeplessness and tiredness and (for my part) bliss, and even though she already has her own Twitter account - @thebeean – Isaac felt she needed another one for her alter ego - @jetlagtoddler – so she tweeted under that name, these last few days...

@jetlagtoddler

i am on my very own timezone, people.

@jetlagtoddler

I will sleep ONLY WHEN YOU LEAST EXPECT IT

@jetlagtoddler

running round the house giggling at 2.24am is the best therapy.

and this is me...

@suehepworth

current status: have captured @jetlagtoddler and she's asleep in my bed. Greenwich Mean Time: 06.05. Jetlagtoddler Standard Time: who knows?

Now it's back to real life: writing fiction.

FEBRUARY

February 6th 2012

He still won't admit he's wrong

Did you know that I put a lot of what Dave says into the mouths of my fictional characters?

There is an exchange in *But I Told You Last Year That I Loved You* that comes straight from our sitting room:

They carried on watching Jessie Levine, and Jessie's flatmate said to Jessie, "You make me a margarita, and I'll make you a Sea Breeze."

"What's a Sea Breeze?" said Sol.

"A cocktail, of course."

"Really? I thought it was a rissole."

Well, last week when I was cruising the drinks aisles in Sainsbury's I noticed a bottle labelled Sea Breeze, so as soon as I got home I told Dave - "You see! I'm right! A Sea Breeze *is* a cocktail!"

"I refuse to be cowed. It is just as likely to be a product made by Captain Bird's Eye."

111

I can tell you here – because Dave rarely reads my blog – that as well as being downright infuriating, there is something rather appealing about someone who sticks to their guns and won't admit they're wrong about something really, really trivial. But I am probably a bit weird (as well).

MARCH

March 8th 2012

Small talk

I hate going to new hairdressers because they always try to make trivial conversation and ask you inane questions like "Are you off out tonight?" and I don't like small talk. I can't do small talk. Fortunately, my current hairdresser has known me for years and talks to me either about real things like family or haircuts or future life plans, or she doesn't talk at all.

Today I went to a new dentist because my usual one has retired. The new one is pleasant (except that he didn't polish my teeth) and he has a smiley dental nurse who I liked right up until she said, "Are you doing something nice this afternoon? Are you going out?" I was in fact doing something taxing and private this afternoon and I said "I don't want to talk about it." I suppose it was due to my feeling rather tense, that I blurted out this reply.

Do you consider me churlish? Or do you sympathise that the kind of nicety she was trading in was unnecessary and irritating?

As far as I'm concerned, the weather was invented so that unfamiliar hairdressers and smiley dental assistants have something to talk about so they don't have to say to you, "Are you off out tonight?" We just need to inform them all of this.

APRIL

April 1st 2012

What the Americans can teach us

I've just come back home from brunch in a cafe. I love brunch. And I love it in the USA. You can order a bottomless mimosa, and a main of almond French toast (which comes with vanilla bean cream cheese, fresh citrus compote, and Vermont syrup) along with a side order of bacon, and no-one bats an eyelid.

You can order anything you want with anything else you want at any time of day or night and the waiting staff will say "Of course" or "You're welcome." They won't say "We don't serve sandwiches in the evening," or "We stop serving lunch at 3" or some other piffling British non-service crap. Let's hear it for the Yanks!

April 3rd 2012

Hip, or what?

How hip am I? I'm sitting with Isaac's super slim laptop and a café latte in a café on the edge of the Mission district. Yesterday morning I stayed home and wrote. Today I thought I'd try it in the big hip world. It's good. I have a huge bench table to myself, and there's music playing and a view of Precita Park. But how do I go over and get a refill without worrying about the laptop? I'm thinking it's probably not cool to take it with you to the counter. Hmmm...this is when my newly acquired San Franciscan hipness fails. I'll have to check what the form is when I see Isaac tonight.

April 7th 2012

West Coast trivia

I've been away. I've been away from away. I went to Redwood City to stay with the Aging Hippie, and I've come back to the city to have a rest. She has so much energy, that woman - she ran me ragged.

I had a great time, and saw something of life in what she calls the "suburbs." To me it looked like the American Dream - wide leafy streets, immaculate front gardens, non-stop sunshine. I did lots of things I've heard about and never done, things that make up everyday life for a lot of people, things that Anne Tyler mentions in her books, and the Aging Hippie drops into her emails, and until now have not been *exactly* sure what they mean.

1/ I went to **a thrift store** and bought a beautiful cashmere jumper for only $5. The thrift store was a huge charity shop the size of a small supermarket.

2/ I went to **a garage sale** and ogled a 1930s handmade quilt, but didn't buy it because it was $65. (It was an upmarket sale - actually, an 'estate sale' and the prices were upmarket too.) There was a sofa I liked but I couldn't persuade the Aging Hippie to buy it.

3/ I went to **a line dancing class,** which I loved. Once you know the steps of a particular dance, it's a bit like a meditation.

4/ I went out for margaritas. (Oops, no change there. I do that in San Francisco. But it was a relief to get them in as they were the first I've had this trip, and my crime writer friend back home, Chrissie Poulson, wanted me to have one for her.)

5/ I heard a **screen door slam**. You know that line in Joni Mitchell's *Big Yellow taxi - Late last night, I heard the screen door slam?*

6/ I had **an American scone,** which was very cakey and very buttery and very rich, and not at all like an English scone, which probably explains why the Aging Hippie wasn't much taken with our scones when she came to visit last year.

I did other things too, such as go on two long walks, and visit a photography exhibition at the Stanford University Art Gallery. All of this was packed into two days, so you can see

115

what I mean about the AH being energetic. There *was* some down time for slugs like me, involving sitting, talking and sunshine. It was a wonderful 48 hours - thank you, AH.

April 20th 2012

The old me

Since getting back from San Francisco I've been catching up with all my friends, such as Mary, who told me how worried she gets about forgetting the most basic of facts – e.g. the names of friends' partners, and I told her not to worry, that it happens to everyone, that I once forgot the name of my brother-in-law. So she said "Oh well, if *you* do it, that's OK, because I think of you as being on-the-ball."

Later I saw Ruth and Annie, and we were all saying how we can't remember the plots of books we have read, and sometimes ones we've read in the last month. I left Ruth's house and walked down the dark rainy street under my umbrella, and found the car and had a struggle to get in, with my umbrella and basket and big bag of books. When I put the key in the ignition it wouldn't turn. I switched on the light to see why not, and saw that the car seats were grey, and not black, like mine. I was in the wrong Polo!

This is me, signing off, the woman who is on-the-ball.

April 30ᵗʰ 2012

Blessings

Sisters are one of God's better inventions.

You can get the train to Bingley together and see the Five Rise Locks for the second time this spring (but this time in sunshine) and then walk the 3 miles down the towpath to Saltaire and eat your lunch in the sun in your shirtsleeves, overlooking the River Aire and the park and the wooded hill beyond. You can hold a young mother's baby while she eats her lunch, and think that while it is a very nice baby, it is not as nice as any of your own (of either generation).

You can wander round the Mill and check out the titles of novels in the spacious bookshop, looking for inspiration for your own. My favourites today were *Care of Wooden Floors*, *Cheating at Canasta*, and *The Particular Sadness of Lemon Cake*.

You can curse together that the Hockney exhibition is closed on Mondays, but read about the history of Saltaire and its massive Mill, and watch the documentary about *Titus Salt*, and relish the narrator's soft Yorkshire accent.

You can have a coffee in Salts Diner, forget to pay and only remember when you have walked down four flights of stone steps and down the road, and you're leaning on the bridge over the canal, and have to go up the road again and the four flights of stone steps to make an honest woman of yourself.

You can sit together in companionable silence waiting in the sunshine for your train, while you munch on apples and idly watch the two pigeons in front of you picking at a squashed Ferrerro Rocher on the platform.

And as an end to a perfect sunny day in the midst of a fortnight of rain, you can hug and part, and lose yourself in *The Secret Garden* on the train home and almost miss your stop.

MAY

May 8th 2012

Sally Howe/Sue Hepworth crossover

Sometimes people ask me if Sally Howe (in *Plotting for Beginners*) is me. The answer is "no" but nevertheless, some of the things that happen to Sally have happened to me. And *some* of her opinions are the same as mine. Some of them.

And I have a feeling that in the sequel to *Plotting* (which is on the verge of having a title) Sally is going to mock the sleeveless trench that appears in her latest copy of the *Pure* catalogue.

A sleeveless trench? Give me strength. The catalogue says - "it is a real statement piece…" Too right. It states: "If you're wearing this, you're a bozo." Don't they realise that rain falls on your arms as well as your body?

May 29th 2012

The Monsal Trail

We are so, so lucky to live so near to the Monsal Trail which runs through beautiful limestone country. Because it's so high, there are fabulous views, and on a warm, clear day it's a real treat to cycle up it at eight in the morning, before it gets busy, or at teatime, when all the tourists have gone. I usually stop between Cressbrook Tunnel and Litton Tunnel, where there is no view of houses, or civilisation, and no sound but birdsong. I sit on the cliff edge and look at the river below, and listen to the birds, and think about the day – to come, or just past – and about all my family, and all my other concerns. Then I cycle home feeling better.

The last two times I've been, someone has left litter and I've brought it back to chuck in the bin. I'm always puzzled as to how someone who has the sensibility to choose to walk or cycle miles up a trail in the countryside, can also think it OK to leave their litter there. Last time it was a plastic carton for an Asda Spicy Chicken Pot. Oh my God.

June 12th 2012

Where the week went – ordinary life at Hepworth Towers

My life is a quiet life, and sometimes when it comes round to bin day (like today) I think *Oh, another week has flown past*, and I wonder what I have to show for it. These are a few of the things I've done in the last week – so it's not so bad -

finished writing the first draft of Chapter 3 of *Plotting for Grown-ups*;

read and critiqued Chrissie Poulson's new novel – first draft – and had a meeting with her about it;

felt miffed that of 32 dwarf climbing bean seeds I planted, only four have came up, and one of these was eaten by slugs;

refused the kind offer of some replacement runner beans (which I don't much like) from someone at Quaker Meeting – who said that everyone has too many beans this year because of the weather;

finished reading Penelope Lively's latest book – *How It All Began*, which I loved. Enjoyable and thought-provoking;

been really chuffed that the Christmas tree in a pot which I bought last year has begun to sprout, which means I won't have to get another one this year. The garden centre man told me when I bought it that it would take till June to know if it was alive or dead – AND – he would give me my money back if the latter;

got my patchwork project out of the drawer because it was so wet outside. I am still unsure about the arrangement, and also whether or not it is too loud and too busy to go on our bed, so Zoë is coming to advise me tomorrow;

made good progress with learning to improvise variations on my sax to *Lady be Good*, *Honeysuckle Rose* and *Tea for Two* (the book describes the latter as a hoary old standard, with which I agree, but Mel, my teacher, likes it for some odd reason);

been for three rides up the Monsal Trail on my bike;

visited some inspiring craft and art exhibitions in Open Arts Derbyshire;

successfully cooked shoulder of lamb for the first time for a group of friends (There are so many vegetarians in my family I rarely see meat);

assisted at my younger grandson's birthday tea;

finished making a tiny cardigan for Isaac and Wendy's new baby – who has decided *while I have been writing this post*, that today is his/her birthday - whoopee! - sister or brother to Lux.

How one earth am I going to concentrate on making the alterations to Chapter 3 – suggested by Jane – while I am following Isaac's tweets about Wendy in labour?????

June 13th 2012

Baby bulletin

She's arrived! My lovely new American grand-daughter. 7lbs 8ozs and healthy. Wendy is fine, too. After Lux's lengthy and difficult birth we are all very thankful that everything went well. Well done, Wendy! Tomorrow there will be a name.

June 14th 2012

Frankenstein's monster

I've just been chatting with Isaac, 5,000 miles away, and he told me the name of the new baby, and I asked if it was bloggable, and he said they had not announced it yet. "And," he said, "you broke the news of the baby's sex yesterday." I did. It's true –here on my blog, and also in a tweet.

I apologised profusely. I didn't know it wasn't in the public arena. So with the name, I have been instructed not to blog or tweet about it, yet. I am genuinely sorry I broke his embargo (unwittingly) but at the same time it is rather amusing that the grey-haired mother of a Twitter employee has gone live in the cybersphere with information before said Twitter employee. Think of all that time he wanted me to go on email, then get broadband, then get a blog, then start tweeting, and now he is having to rein me in.

But I can show a photo, as it is on his Flickr account and so are up for grabs.

June 16th 2012

The baby's name is...

...*Cecilia*: the patron saint of music.

I think it's a lovely name.

And I know I can announce it now, because I just read Isaac's tweet.

JULY

July 19th 2012

Jam today

Why do Dave and I make jam? He never eats it, and I might eat a jar in two months. And yet every year I pick the blackcurrants, wash them, weigh them, collect and prepare the secondhand jars, and buy the sugar, and we stand around in the kitchen on rainy summer days, making jam.

By the middle of August we'll have probably 80 jars of jam, and I will spend the rest of the year giving them away.

Why do we do it? Why do we like it? Don't know why, don't care why. Maybe it's the homeliness of the activity, maybe it's the conversations we have. Dave usually cracks me up with something he says on a jam-making session.

One year the blackcurrants will be ripe and one of us won't be here. I think things like that these days. That's why I want jam today.

July 20th 2012

Jam today (continued)

The jam did not set.

And it is my fault.

I do all the measuring and I always reduce the sugar a bit and then forget to reduce the water as well. Then, being the one who tests it and says when it is ready, and being impatient, and getting fed up of standing around (despite the fascinating conversation) tell Dave the jam is ready when it isn't. So my name is mud, and we'll be tossing the jam back into the pan for another attempt.

Meanwhile, it rains and it rains and it rains, and I am thinking of bringing my SAD light down from the attic.

AUGUST

August 1st 2012

Tea and Siblings

My sister Jen rang last night to ask exactly what time my train is arriving, and to suggest I take some Yorkshire tea, as I hate her tea. (i.e what she calls "tea." I think it's Tetley's or PG Tips – don't go there.) I love my family. I love it that we can be honest with each other.

I know I have a thing about tea and I make no apology for it. I often mention it on my blog. I wrote a piece about it in Belgium when I was staying with my brother. He doesn't understand tea, either.

Enough about tea. Here is a piece I had in the *Times* some years ago. I've put it on my blog before, but I'm not apologising. (I'm in a very non-apologetic mood this morning – bullish, I am – it's probably because I'm excited about going to stay with Jen.) Anyway, I'm posting the piece again, because I love my sibs and they should get full credit for being fab.

The Comfort of Siblings

I am a late developer, and so it is no great wonder that it has taken me fifty years, and my father's death, to appreciate fully the worth of my brothers and sisters.

I don't deny that siblings can be some of the most annoying of God's creations, especially when young. Sisters are apt to borrow your opal ring, wear it to clean the hen-house, and then come and tell you they've lost it. Brothers are apt to lean from their bedroom window and give a running commentary while you kiss your boyfriend goodnight, or write in the cream on your wedding reception trifle "Wot, no shotgun?"

Siblings may also out-perform you at school, or in my case, something worse: be seen as having more common sense, so that when in the middle of my degree course I told my mother I was pregnant, she said "Oh Sue, I always said it would be *you.*"

I know that in some families the death of a parent brings out the worst in those left behind, with scrabbling over legacies, and recriminations about how little this one or that one has contributed. Or there are arguments over the gravestone or where to scatter the ashes.

In my family it has been the opposite. During my father's last illness we combined efforts to support my mother in her caring role. Then when my father was in hospital we shared the visiting.

When I left my father at the hospital, I would drive disconsolately back up the dale to my mother's house. Wanting to share my distress at my father's deteriorating condition before I saw my mother, I'd ring my younger brother (a gardener) and he would tell me which village and in which garden he was working. I'd meet him at the gate for a hug and a chat, so I was sufficiently restored not to burden my mother with my tears.

In my father's last week we took turns to sit by his bed - sometimes alone, sometimes in twos or threes. And between his death and his burial we stayed at my parents' house. All through the days we spent together with my mother we lurched between tears and laughter in a way that was both comforting and liberating. We all knew that each was upset, and we didn't have to be proper, or to make any kind of pretence. The closeness, the intimacy, the warmth and the comfort from being all there together, with no hangers on in the shape of spouses or children, felt special. We had not been assembled like that, with no-one else, since we were children. In the worst of times I found the best of times.

When other family members appeared on the scene for the burial at the end of the week this cocoon of ease-amid-grief evaporated.

Siblings, more than others, can understand why one is grieving for someone who in his latter years was grumpy and often less than loveable, because they too remember him as a fine and handsome hero.

Having so many siblings, I have one for every season of grief. There's one to be practical and effective, one to be sensitive, one to listen, one who, while missing the missing father, remains cheerful and good humoured and insists on looking to the future.

I can share family in-jokes and memories of my father with all of them. I can see my father's eyes in my brother's and my father's character traits in the others. And the fact that not all

127

these characteristics are attractive helps me to be realistic about the father I have lost.

Last month I went on holiday with my elder brother and sister, something we haven't done before. It was as easy as being with close friends, but better.

At dinner we toasted my father. And during the meal my brother winked at me for no reason other than affection - just as my father used to do. After dinner he offered me some chocolate, giving me instructions on how to open the packet and tear the wrapper - just as my father would tell me how to cut the stilton.

August 15th 2012

My co-writer

One of the reasons I like co-writing books with Jane is because, like me, she thinks of our characters as real.

Sometimes this can get tricky, however. She told me in the spring that one of the characters in the new book buys his steak pies from a butcher in Hackney (a place near Bakewell), so some months later, when I had a visitor staying who I thought might like a steak pie, I emailed Jane to ask her where the butcher's shop at Hackney was, and got this reply - "What butcher's shop at Hackney? There isn't one."

In the meantime, my new granddaughter Cecilia is definitely real – and I am going to see her in three weeks time. Yay!

August 20th 2012

Little things I like

driving down our lane and arriving home – whether it's from Bakewell, London or San Francisco

days when it's warm enough to cook in bare feet

evenings when it's warm enough to sit outside

watching *Neighbours* with my friend Ella, with a glass of wine in one hand and a bag of crisps in the other

playing hockey in the garden with little children

sitting in Quaker meeting in bare feet, on a warm Sunday morning with the windows wide open

chatting to my children on the phone

reading Allan Ahlberg books to children who are enjoying them as much as me

sitting here in perfect peace, because everyone else is asleep or out

picking sweet peas in the back garden

seeing a new photo of one of my grandchildren

"For in the dew of little things, the heart finds its morning and is refreshed."

SEPTEMBER

September 7th 2012

Fashion tips

Yay!

I am here in San Francisco. The flight was good: quiet, uneventful, on time. *Good job,* British Airways - see, I have the local lingo already - it slips off the tongue (or keypad) as if I've never been away.

And Wendy took me for my traditional pedicure this morning, which is a big SF treat. As well as having pretty feet at the end of a peaceful hour of self-indulgence, it's a rare chance to catch up with women's magazines, which I never buy. Today I read *Elle, Bazaar* and *Vogue,* and found a host of helpful titbits. I discovered that there's such a thing as "tight pants syndrome," which you get from wearing too-tight jeans, and which can lead to a long list of unpleasant health problems. Also, there's a blog called *Man Repeller,* which tells you what not to wear if you care about attracting men. My favourite quote, though, was this: "Dresses have become too trendy. I am convinced by trousers."

Ooh, ooh, almost forgot... the day in a life of Michael Kors, a fashion designer, who said "I'm definitely a man who loves his tote collection....I have an L.L.Bean leather tote from the 40s...that I was fortunate to find while vintage shopping here in New York. As soon as I saw it I was like, Oh my God."

It's that last sentence that creases me up.

September 26th 2012

Home is where the heart is

A friend had a holiday in Wensleydale in August and I told her how much I miss the place. She said, "Ah, your heart is there," and I said, "Well, yes. But it's also here. I love my home."

When Dave retired, we had a three week holiday in Northumberland together, and Isaac said, "That's the longest time you've ever been away from home," and without thinking, I said, "No, I wasn't away from home. Dave was there."

DECEMBER

December 6th 2012

Thursday and frantic

It is 7.35 a.m. and I have already bought a Lego fishing boat from Argos for my younger grandson for Christmas – delivery free – oh, I love internet shopping from the comfort of my own cosy bed.

Now I must jump out and get ready for more arduous Christmas shopping in Sheffield. Wish me luck. I would far rather be here, tweaking *Plotting for Grown-ups.*

Meanwhile, there is a voice from the bathroom calling out: "Don't you worry about all the fiscal incontinence around at Christmas?"

Bah! Humbug! I don't call £12.59 (delivery free) fiscal incontinence.

December 7th 2012

Customer service

Yep, I'm a grumpy old woman.

I had a full on day yesterday (starting at 5.45 a.m) which included work on the book, a visit to the homeopath, a welcome cuppa with the family member who declines to be named, and long hours of Christmas shopping, in which I went in Waterstones looking for Julia Donaldson books. Neither of the young assistants in there knew who Julia Donaldson was, or what she writes (she is the Children's Laureate! the prolific genius who wrote *The Gruffalo* and *Stickman*, and *Tiddler* and so many more!) and then when we had finally tracked them down, I asked for the *Deadly Sixty Annual* and it took a <u>customer</u> to find it for me. If they are going to have extra assistants in there for Christmas, why don't they have ones who know their onions?

Then I went in John Lewis, oh shop of shops, not just my favourite shop, but Sally Howe's too. (Sally Howe is the heroine of *Plotting for Beginners*.) There, it was a different story:

two young Christmas women on separate floors were helpful and efficient, listened to my needs and solved my problems.

The last stop before home was Chatsworth Farm Shop (another of Sally Howe's favourite shops, but no longer mine) to buy something for tea, where at the checkout, the young man – who I have never met before - said "Hello, how are you?" and I bridled. Why is it the current custom for people in one stroke interactions to ask you how you are? Aaargghh! One does not expect this in Chatsworth Farm Shop: he must have missed his induction day.

I mumbled "OK," without looking at him (not wanting to encourage his dastardly behaviour) and then he said "Do you have any plans for the evening?" and I wanted to say "Yes, but they are none of your business. It is 4.15, I have had a hectic, tiring day, and all I want is my sausages and my rare breed pork chop. I do not want to answer personal questions or engage in meaningless banter with someone I have never met before. If I wanted that I would go to a new hairdresser." He needed to be told that God invented the weather so it could be a topic for small talk but I didn't say owt. I am writing this blog post instead. This is Grumpy Old Woman signing off.

p.s. I have just ordered some books online from The Book Depository, and there was a link to click, if I wanted to "watch people shop." Are they crazy? Don't they know that shopping is bad enough without watching other people do it as well?

December 27th 2012

Nora Ephron was right (as usual)

It's mid-October, after your narrowboat holiday, and you're gloating because you've lost half a stone through all the opening and closing of heavy lock gates and traipsing up and down the tow path, and your tight jeans finally fit you with *moving* room, and you are ecstatic.

And you sail through November feeling great. But as the days pass, and it rains and rains, you cycle less and less, and you also start thinking things like, "I am sick of Ryvita, wouldn't just one real sandwich be nice?" And you're still in that land where your jeans fit and your partner actually comments favourably on your size. You read something by your heroine Nora Ephron where she says - "At the age of 55 you will get a saggy roll just above your waist even if you are painfully thin," and you want to ring her up and say "Hey, Nora! Not me!" but you can't, because sadly, she recently died.

And then December comes and you eat just four mince pies in the whole of the month, and when you go to Sainsbury's for the Christmas shop, you treat yourself to one of those clingy T shirts in a colour that suits you, and you like it so much you wear it with your jeans on Christmas Day with your silver necklace and silver earrings and you feel very glam.

And the family member who declines to be named arrives and sits in the kitchen to chat to you while you're cooking, and he says, "Those jeans are very tight" and you think to yourself *Yes, well, they were clean on today and they haven't*

134

stretched yet, and you carry on shoving more and more food items into the cooker, unperturbed about said jeans, but bamboozled as to how you are going to find room in the cooker for every damn thing…

At lunchtime, the OFF Christmas Elf decides (uncharacteristically) to take some unposed photos of the assembled hordes enjoying their Christmas lunch, and he takes several standing behind you.

Then in the evening, when the family have departed and you collapse on the sofa and look at said photos, you realise with horror that Nora was right, and you go back to her original quote and find her next paragraph - "This saggy roll just above your waist will be especially visible from the back and will force you to re-evaluate half the clothes in your closet, especially the white shirts," and you want to ring her up and say, "It's not a roll, it's a wodge!" and you know that the game is up, and it's back on the treadmill of NO BREAD, NO CAKES, NO PUDDINGS, forever and ever, Amen.

And if you think I am going to show you one of the aforementioned photos, you're nuts.

December 31st 2012

Pollyanna

I've got my sinus problem back, and I'm sick to death of the dark grey wet Derbyshire winter, so I'm trying to be cheerful, and to think of all the things I'm thankful for. So here are the first blessings that come to mind…

my warm bed

my morning shower

the log burning stove

Dave's oatcakes

Dave

the lemon curd I made yesterday

my grandchildren

my children

the fact that the two married ones have lovely partners

my techie guy Adrian for diagnosing a knackered fan on my laptop and fixing a new one, which means, I hope, that I don't have to buy a replacement yet. (The decisions required are as bad as the money.)

the fact we don't live on a flood plain

the chest of drawers my mother left me. It's right beside me now as I write, and is a huge comfort, reminding me as it does of her. It even has a strip from an old pair of tights still tied round one of the handles. She used to cut up old tights and use them for tying up parcels and raspberry canes and anything else you can think of. If you cut them into loops, they are great for bundling up small packets. My mother was so well known in the family for her tights fetish, that at her funeral someone said we should have let her coffin down into the grave with ropes woven from old tights. Ma would have loved the joke.

my parents and sibs

You can see why 'Pollyanna' could be a term of derision – it's so easy to get mushy when you count up your blessings.

JANUARY

January 22nd 2013

Cabin fever

I am trying to stay cheerful.

Dave is trying to stay cheerful.

We are trying to stay cheerful.

The truth is – we have cabin fever. He wants to go out on his bike and he can't. I want to drive to my sax lesson and can't. I have a day trip train ticket to London for tomorrow and no idea if I'll be able to get to the station, let alone London, get home again, etc, etc, etc.

The days are filled with long, long tramps through the snow so our bodies don't atrophy at home. Yesterday even Hassop Station Cafe on the Monsal Trail was closed on account of the snowy roads, so we walked in the other direction.

I am also playing my sax a lot. Since I heard a flashmob on the net singing and playing *Here Comes the Sun* so beautifully, I've been trying to nail it myself.

My Fair Isle hoodie is almost finished. I had to design the hood myself, having no pattern, and the first attempt was a failure, but this second try is working well and I should be sewing the whole thing up this afternoon. Yay!

Meanwhile, Dave has been keeping himself occupied with baking batch after batch of oatcakes, blogging, and yesterday he went down the Monsal Trail to Bakewell in search of fresh fruit, on his scooter, or *kick bike*, as the aficionados term it. He is totally nuts. But also rather wonderful.

When the sun comes out, the landscape looks pretty. But we still wish the snow would melt.

January 29th 2013

Finding your writer's voice

When I started writing creatively about 15 years ago, I read a lot of stuff about "the importance of finding your voice." I worried about this. What was my writer's voice? Would I know when I had found it? I didn't really understand what these people meant. I did what you're supposed to do and wrote as much as I could – screeds of stuff in my journal, poetry, short pieces, a novel (all right, an attempt at a novel – I shudder to think about it now) – and I thought "Have I found my voice yet? When will I know?"

When I first started trying to get pieces in *The Times*, I showed them to Dave for his comments, and he would say things like "You need to make it more vivid. How about saying *this*, and putting it like *this*, and…"

I listened to him because he's so clever, and has a huge vocabulary and is an entertaining raconteur. But then when I read the pieces again after his insertions and alterations, I felt uncomfortable. It was then that I had my first inklings about what is meant by a writer's voice. His suggestions and his writing were sharp and clever and expressive, but they weren't how I express myself. I am understated, dry (when I'm writing well) and minimalist. He is the opposite. *He has a wonderful voice*, but it's not my voice. Here is my voice from ten years ago in *The Times*...

Home is where the clutter is

Next time you open that kitchen drawer full of jumble and groan, don't even think of calling a clutter consultant or a Feng Shui space clearer. Just be thankful instead. When I lost all my things in a fire, there were times when I yearned for my very own tangle of fossilised rubber bands, ancient postcards, last year's advent candle, furry balls of Blu-tak, crushed paper flowers from playgroup, tatty plant labels, tacky plastic novelties from Christmas crackers and old matchbox cars with scratched paintwork. The relics in that drawer are symbols of your family history, and in their own way are as precious as the antique oak bureau in the dining room or the original oil painting over the mantelpiece. Only when your belongings are snatched away do you learn which ones are irreplaceable.

When we sold our house and temporarily moved into furnished, rented accommodation I didn't think twice about putting our things into storage with the removal company. But my 10-year -old son refused to store a single item, and took every last Lego brick, four years worth of Beanos, and his complete rock and fossil collection.

We were still renting 18 months later, when we received a letter from the removal firm informing us that a fire had completely destroyed all our things. For me, it took a week for the reality to sink in, but my husband – ever practical, resourceful and proactive - came round sooner. He went to the warehouse with a garden fork and spade to sift through the ashes in search of any traces of our former existence, anything to soften our bereavement. When he arrived, he found a blackened shell of a building knee deep in filthy sludge, with burnt out washing machines and fridges poking out above the surface.

We had a brief summary inventory of what had been stored in our six containers and my husband set about locating the detritus from them by looking for a large non-flammable object from each, such as our tandem, my daughter's bicycle, a stone garden trough. He managed to position all but one of the containers and retrieved just a few things from the disgusting, sodden ashes.

Most of these objects were pathetic items, but to us they were treasures. Amazingly, the plastic twin dolls I had dressed and played with as a child were there, twisted and deformed, but still dressed in the clothes I had made for them and to me, still loveable. He found his father's old spring balance and the disfigured brass face of one of our grandfather clocks. He discovered a handful of blue and green marbles from the collection I had kept in a carafe on the windowsill for the sun to shine through. They were blackened but reclaimable, and although they were not unique or valuable, to me they were priceless. At that time, with no tangible past, and no concrete future in the shape of a new home, the marbles gave me a link with our previous existence, and in a strange way, a feeling of security.

He managed to find something significant belonging to each member of our family, except for my daughter. She was living abroad when we moved and I had spent hours packing up her many books, unusual art posters, distinctive art deco furniture, and all her photographs. We searched painstakingly for something of Zoë's, but found nothing. The most heart-wrenching loss was the three storey Victorian dolls house my husband had made for her, and which she as a girl had decorated and furnished and cherished.

When it came to the insurance claim, having to list every lost item was a torture in its own right. Falling asleep at night I would remember something else, and think "oh no...." Trying to list our hundreds of books became a black parlour game. Lying back in the bath I would remember yet another book, and rush naked onto the landing, shouting a title down to my husband before I forgot it. We did get up to 637 books, but since then have missed dozens more.

Four years on it is still too painful to recall all the irreplaceable items that we lost. It is not the money, although we did lose out financially to some extent. What is painful is the loss of all the trivial and substantial accretions of 25 years of family life, our books, and some inherited antique furniture, all with family connections and sentimental meaning. The plain, modest grandfather clock we had bought for my father-in-law when he first became a grandfather, and which we gave him a week before he unexpectedly died. The small chair my adored grandmother had been given as a child, and which my sister and I would race to sit in when visiting her house as children.

As an only child, and with no living family, my husband feels as though he has let his parents down by losing their things. He feels brutally cut off from his childhood and his roots, with nothing tangible remaining to connect him to his past. Gone is the oak swivel chair which his father sat in when he was resting from serving in his shop. Gone is the barometer that his father used to tap first thing every day. Gone are his family photographs.

But the most bitter loss of all is that of the albums containing all the photographs of our adult children when they were young. I can still close my eyes and see many of these photographs, but I will not be able to turn the pages and share them with our children and their children in later life. Friends and family have kindly raided their albums and old packets of photos for replacements for us, and this has been a great help. But so many favourite family photographs are of unposed moments, of funny games in the bath, dressing up in the back garden, or a child fallen asleep in a high chair, with a face sunk into soggy Marmite fingers. Photos from others are posed family groups. They don't appeal like the tasty memories committed quickly to posterity by a quick snap with that cheap camera you keep in the kitchen cupboard.

I am sad we have no things with family associations to pass on to our children. I had hoarded for any future grandchildren all the favourite pre-school books, and the best wooden bricks and toddler toys. I thought I was being frugal, and that in the future they would remind me of my children's babyhood. I had packed away the Moses basket I had lined for my youngest child, and writing this I am in tears again.

It's common on suffering traumatic events to look for lessons and meanings in the hardship. The practical lessons for us are easy: don't trust anyone else to look after things that are irreplaceable, and be properly insured for what you do put in store. I have also learned what is precious and what is not: I can throw things away more easily, but what I keep I treasure. Any other lessons are more difficult to work out. Two months after the fire, I was diagnosed as having breast cancer and had a mastectomy. Compared with the fire, that felt like a piece of cake. Does this mean I am an unredeemed materialist? We didn't lose any of our family, so why are we grieving?

But I have learned another lesson. As an irrepressible optimist I subscribed to Adrian Henri's sentiment "Don't worry, baby, everything's going to be all right." Now I can admit the possibility that pessimists might sometimes be right. I am more sensitive to others' anxieties, more moved by others' hardships, more empathetic to others' losses.

Our new house is now fully furnished, and I'm pleased with the effect. And although it will be a long time before it truly feels like home, my cluttered kitchen drawer is coming on a treat.

FEBRUARY

February 3rd 2013

Random

I was sitting on the sofa in front of the fire with a glass of wine at teatime the other day, when Dave told me a quote he'd found (and liked) on the internet -

"Courage does not always roar. Sometimes courage is the quiet voice at the end of the day saying, 'I will try again tomorrow.'" Radmacher

I liked the quote, too. And suddenly from nowhere I was missing my mother, and in tears.

Where do these waves of sadness come from? Was it because I'd been looking at a photo of the latest addition to the family tree – my newborn great niece – whom my mother will never see? Or was it because when I consider the word *encouragement*, I immediately think of my mother?

Maybe it was neither. Grief follows no pattern: It can ambush you years after you thought you'd left it behind.

February 7th 2013

Meanwhile...and then

I woke up feeling dreary, lay here for ages feeling worse, sat up and wrote a long email to a dear friend, a litany of problems and complaints, ending with, "Meanwhile it is February."

Then I had a second mug of Yorkshire tea, two home-made oatcakes with home-made lemon curd, the sun came up, and Dave and I had a chat about the tricky art of translating poetry.

Things felt better.

February 20th 2013

Interlude

I may have two granddaughters who live too far away for comfort, but I do have two grandsons very close by. Zoë brought them over yesterday as it was half term. I admired their latest Lego acquisition: a derelict house on fire with flames that disappear when the fire engine arrives with foam and water. Then we got out the Lego boxes that live upstairs and messed around on the sitting room floor. But the boys

146

were full of beans, and it was a bright cold sunny spring day, so we walked down the Monsal Trail to Hassop Station. These two guys are such good friends with each other, it warms my heart. Yesterday they were just like those idealised kids you get on adverts. They aren't always like that.

On the way home they played Romans and Celts. When I was little, it was cowboys and Indians. (I know it's no longer acceptable to say "Indians," and I don't, usually.) Whatever the factions – it's blood and death. I'm a pacifist, and my parents were pacifists, and yet my Gran made me a Davy Crockett hat, and all five of us had pistols and holsters and contests to see who was the quickest on the draw. Those were happy days. Yesterday I had another to add to my collection.

February 28th 2013

"In the midst of total uncertainty, we can love."
- Terrance Keenan

MARCH

March 4th 2013

Death is part of life, and all that crap

I'm not talking about my death here: I am not afraid of dying, I'd just rather not do it quite yet. I want to see if my younger grandson becomes the comedian he wants to be, and if my elder grandson becomes – based on his current proclivities - a palaeontologist, an astronomer or (please God not) a banker. And if Lux becomes the first Californian nudist pianist, as she so loves running around naked, and has such amazingly long fingers. And what becomes of smiling Cecilia.

And I would also like to see some more of America, to play my sax in a flashmob, to turn down an offer from a publisher, and to see if Microsoft ever get their act together so I don't regret not replacing my PC for an Apple (oh how I detest Windows Picture Viewer).

No. The title of this post relates to the death of a loved one and the things people say in a misguided attempt to cheer you up when you're bereaved.

There IS no comfort, or as one of my characters in *Plotting for Grown-Ups* says about something else:

Thank God for Richard. He sees hardship for what it is. He understands the darker side of life. He does not try to pretend that horrible things that happen are anything other than horrible things that happen. He does not buff them up into shining opportunities, he doesn't frame them as transforming planetary transits which are for the ultimate good of the inner self, like Wendy does (God help her). Richard sees crap for what it is.

Death may be "part of life" but that doesn't make the death of someone you love a happy, pleasurable or even an acceptable experience. Clearing up vomit, dealing with exploding nappies, and the pains of childbirth are part of being a mother, but does that make them nice? At least there's a baby involved. With bereavement, all you get is a vast black hole (even if there is the relief of not having to put up with someone who uses Zoflora in the kitchen so your dish cloth stinks and the work surfaces taint every bit of food you absentmindedly put on them – a fairly trivial blessing, I think I can live without.)

When I was grieving for my father, the most comforting piece of writing I found on the subject was not that "I am just in the next room" rubbish (to which I always wanted to retort – "Well why don't you walk in here where I can see you, then?") but Edna St Vincent Millay's poem, *Dirge Without Music*, which begins: *I am not resigned to the shutting away of loving hearts in the hard ground.*

March 8th 2013

Inside Sol's head

Some people who read *But I Told You Last Year That I Loved You* said they would have liked me to have included Sol's point of view in the novel – i.e. to see the world through his Asperger eyes.

If you'd like to see the world through an Aspie's eyes, you can read this from Dave – my husband of 42 years.

As Large as Alone

It's a mistake to think I have Aspergers. Closer to the truth: Aspergers has me. On a good day I like to think I call the shots in my life, but the reality is different. In one way or another Aspergers runs the game. It always did.

We don't see things as they are, we see things as we are.

Things always look slightly odd to me, and Anais Nin was probably on the money.

There are some things I am pretty good at. Not many, but some, at least. Mostly they are useless things, like crosswords, having a terrible memory that can't forget anything, being able to hear more than most people think possible, Latin, music, some amusing maths. Being able to figure out how things work.

How things work. I never could figure out how people work.

Or rather, I don't have a sense of how people work, think, feel. Their motivations are inexplicable to me, so I tend to project onto them my own motivations, and I am not always sure even what they are. A lot of effort goes into trying to figure out what is going on. I can often get there in the end, but it is an exhausting mental effort to analyse even the most trivial situations to reach some kind of understanding.

Larkin, considering the experience of being dead, talks of "nothing to love or link with". For many with Aspergers, that is the experience of being alive. It is a lonely condition, and one is conscious of being always essentially alone, even in a crowd of people.

Aspergers people tend not to have circles of friends, but rather the dot of a friend. (Singular).

We seem to have difficulty with linking, I mean really linking. We might KNOW that we are loved, but we tend not to be able to FEEL it. When I was a kid, a constant question in the house was "Are you friends?" No-one was sure. It's a question I still ask at 62, and will keep on asking, just to feel temporarily surer. It is peculiar question, and insane to anyone with normal circuitry. But checking that out has been as compulsive as hitching up my trousers to check that I haven't gained a stone since breakfast.

As for loving and linking, well, for Aspergers people, those are hard to feel. The intellectual constructs seem to make sense, but feeling them is different. Aspergers gives you a burning need to come home, but you always find yourself locked out. It is hard to describe this exactly, but it is somehow being quite unable to feel what people express towards you. You know something is there, but it as if you are trying to feel a texture without any nerve endings in your fingers. You know it is rough, silky, warm, but simply do not have the apparatus to feel that. Love is as large as alone.

And, of course, without the resilience that comes from feeling loved, self-esteem is at best brittle and uncertain, and small setbacks and large can be devastating, undermining. There is a strong chance that this seems unfathomable to you, reading this. Aspergers separates us with a chasm of mutual emotional incomprehension. (And there is an uncomfortable joke there, too, in the interminable tense symbiosis of thought and feeling.)

Someone said to me recently that Aspergers was like seeing life from behind a glass screen. It made me think a lot. To me it feels more like trying to watch a movie through a keyhole while wearing slightly inefficient earplugs. You know that something is happening beyond the keyhole, but no end of scrabbling about is going to get you through that door. When you understand a few frames of plot you are flushed with a sense of triumph.

Kurt Vonnegut created an alien from the imaginary planet of Tralfamadore. He had an important message to deliver to earth, but his only means of communication was though a combination of tap-dancing and farting. His message was lost in translation (actually before translation) and he was clubbed to death. There is something of Aspergers tucked up in that image.

Yes, Anais Nin was right.

152

If you want to know how Aspergers feels, look closely at the next heron you see. They look how we feel.

March 11, 2013

Yes, we have snow. Again.

But not much. And it brightens up the Monsal Trail, and our village church. And the sun is out, shining on the ancient stiles and pathways round the village. And my Pollyanna approach to the bitter east wind is possible because I am flying off to California on Thursday, where there may be rain (as it's spring) but there sure as hell won't be snow. Forgive my smugness: I really need a break.

update: the snow was horizontal this afternoon. I hate the stuff.

March 23rd 2013

Iffy and squiffy

It is warm and wonderful where I am. Warm enough to be outside in shirtsleeves but not too warm to comfortably walk up the 1 in 4 hill to Isaac's house, pushing Cece in the stroller.

Last night was a girls' night out. Wendy took me to a bar called Blondies which she said was a bit iffy (not her word) but it didn't seem as iffy as the bar they took me to last year which was a dark and dingy gay bar just over the hill from here.

Whatever - we had margaritas. Two margaritas - that was enough to get me squiffy. I'd be a really cheap date if I was in the market for dates. Thankfully, all that is behind me, unlike Sally Howe, heroine of the upcoming *Plotting for Grown-ups*. I digress. After the two margaritas, Wendy helped me outside and into a cab where a tiny TV screen was showing a man getting his legs waxed. A wild night out or what?

Next stop was Wendy's favourite burger place - Umami Burger. Yum.

She took me home while the night was still young, because I am not.

This morning, Cece was up and shouting from 5 a.m. She is a happy baby, but very shouty. Lux woke up at 6 a.m. I did stagger upstairs to the living room to offer my babysitting services to the parent in charge, but thankfully was told they had it covered. I staggered back down to bed, and lurked there till I smelled coffee and saw the sun peeping through the blinds.

I had a fab, fun time with Wendy and the margaritas, but the pace of life at Hepworth Towers in Derbyshire (even under three feet of snow) is probably more suited to me on a long-term basis. The problem is that I did not discover margaritas until a few years ago, and I have a lot of lost time to make up. I will have to drink them a lot in my next life - the one where I am a rock chick and have my hair in an urchin cut, and it's bleached.

154

March 30th 2013

Henry Miller did not marry Marilyn Monroe. That was Arthur Miller.

As Karen (aka the Aging Hippie) and I were driving along Highway 1 in Big Sur, the road wove away from the ocean and into the redwoods and something caught our eye: The Henry Miller Memorial Library. It was intriguing and enticing and we parked and went in.

It was a shack next to the forest, with a large deck outside and a table with free tea and coffee. They had a variety of tea-bags, but I'd taken my own Yorkshire teabags (naturally.) There was also free wi-fi. Inside was a funky yet serious bookshop, and a young man (I can say that as he was probably a third of my age - OMG, I am ancient) who was charming and helpful and who treated us, not as if we were two grey haired women, but as if we were valued guests. He said "The place was made for people like you, people who just want to hang out." He could teach the staff of the City Lights bookstore in SF a thing or two. They are so horribly snooty in City Lights, and look down their noses at you, even when you're buying something they probably approve of such as a Tom Waits CD or a Bukowski anthology. Yep, I think the guy in the Henry Miller Memorial Library should run training courses for the staff of City Lights.

We hung out in the sunshine for a couple of hours, emailing, reading, drinking tea, and stroking the resident cat. It was hard to drag ourselves away.

And in case you'd forgotten, Henry Miller was a prolific writer, but is probably best known as the author of *Tropic of Cancer* and *Tropic of Capricorn*.

APRIL

April 3rd 2013

Home

I am back in Derbyshire. There are huge piles of snow everywhere. It's the middle of the night. I have jet lag. I have Cece's cold. My nose is dripping on the keyboard.

It's so great to see Dave. It's so good to be home.

April 8th 2013

On the nature of blogs

We have several substantial problems at Hepworth Towers and there's not a one I can tell you about.

Some people have said that when they read my blog they feel as though they are intruding, as if they are voyeurs. But you don't need to feel like that. I share what I want to share. Often I share my own problems. But naturally, there are some I wouldn't share, and nor do I want to share problems of other family members.

There is a woman in New Zealand who writes a daily blog about her everyday family life. I am gripped by it. She doesn't say much, and a lot of it is minutiae. The blog posts are very short. She used to have a sentence at the side of the blog saying she was devoted to the beauty of the quotidian. I am too. But it is her style which makes a gem out of matters which in others hands would be nothing but the dullest dross. Also, she always has an eye on the sublime, the numinous, the meaning of life, the way to live. She often has interesting quotes on there.

At the moment I am reading her blog everyday. Sometimes I only read it occasionally - in the middle of the night when I can't sleep. Whatever she is feeling – depressed, sad, defeated, happy, joyous, amused - it is a delight to tune in. I realised recently why this is. She opens her heart, and in doing so, touches other people. I have never met her, I don't know her. But the common thread of our humanity and the human condition – particularly the condition of women who are at home, and whose lives centre around their families, and the desire to make her life count - that is what links me to her. Her blog is called *The Scent of Water*.

April 18th 2013

I have no idea what this post is about

Yesterday, a dear friend and I were talking about how we felt the minute we woke up in the morning: was our habitual frame of mind positive or negative? Cheerful or gloomy? And

I said that I usually wake up cheerful. Lately, this hasn't been the case. You might have noticed that I've been veering wildly between gloomy and sunny-side-up. Just one of the less significant reasons has been my continuing sinus troubles, which make me feel as though my head is full of jelly, so thinking clearly is a challenge. It also saps my energy.

I had a good day yesterday – my head was slightly clearer, and I knocked several admin tasks off my to-do list. I didn't play my sax, but I did get a short bike ride in along the Monsal Trail.

But then last night I couldn't sleep because of the 65 mph gales, and because I was thinking about the death of a woman in our village. She died on Tuesday in a car crash. It is a huge shock to everyone. She was much respected, and a key figure in our community. We can't believe it has happened. The circumstances of her life make her death appear like one last definitive kick in the teeth from fate.

But what's in my head is the tenuousness of life, and the way that we have to pretend it isn't tenuous, that our life is sure, that the lives of those we love are sure, certain, safe. If we didn't have this notion fixed in our heads, how could we go on? We'd be paralysed by anxiety.

As for me, I think I am coming up for air. I am bobbing up and down, but I hope that soon I will be my usual optimistic, positive, Pollyanna self, floating evenly and calmly, balanced in the blue.

April 29th 2013

The trouble with blogging

Sometimes I can't write my blog because I can't share what's in my heart. There are some things that aren't up for sharing.

After my mother died you, dear readers, could see the course of my grief. It ran beneath the surface of my days, but every now and then it would emerge on the blog. I felt justified in writing about her death and my bereavement here, because my mother wasn't around to upset or offend, and because her troubles were over.

Right now there are three people I am close to, people I love, who have potentially life threatening health problems. It is they who have the problems. I am someone on the sidelines, someone anxious and concerned for them, eager to support them, and at the same time anxious for me because I don't want to lose them. But I can't write about any of that on here.

Meanwhile, there is an ebook of *Plotting for Beginners* to be prepared for publication, and a paperback and ebook of *Plotting for Grown-Ups* which need to be sent to press. The paperback will be delayed because of lack of time and emotional energy to attend to everything entailed in its launch, but the ebook will be out before too long.

Life is hectic (next week the Californian family are coming to stay – yay!) ……and life is also full of stresses, so if you don't hear from me for days at a time, I know you'll understand. I'll be back.

159

MAY

May 1st 2013

May Day

Dave and I have just been up Longstone Edge to welcome in the May.

We drove past the village shop where Nick was sorting out the papers for delivery. At noon today, the village will be crammed into the church for his sister Christine's funeral, who died two weeks ago.

We always aim to be at the top of Longstone Edge before dawn, but it was 5.30, and light, and the birds were singing, though the sun was still below the horizon.

We stood on the edge of the hill and listened to the birds for several minutes, then we sang a traditional May Day song – Hal an Tow, with the chorus–

Hal an tow, jolly rumbalo

We were up long before the day o

To welcome in the summer

To welcome in the may o

For summer is a comin in

And winter's gone away o

I broke down in the first chorus and Dave continued alone. I joined in with the next verse and managed to sing to the end.

Dave asked me why I cried, and I said "Because we don't know what the summer will bring."

And he said, "We never know what the summer will bring."

May 2nd 2013

At this age

I woke up with the sun straining to get in past the blinds, and it was delicious.

Then I checked my Inbox and found a stream of lovely messages from friends and family, and some WONDERFUL pictures of two little sisters having an absolute ball, racing in the countryside, and messing about in their bedroom with a giant tutu. I felt really blessed and loved and then I drew the blinds and saw my view of the Derbyshire countryside waking up to spring sunshine. The hawthorn leaves are at last beginning to unfurl, and the conker tree leaves are saying a tentative hello. It was joyous. It IS joyous.

And then I thought a about a friend and I agreeing that life gets harder the older you get. I think that at this age my moods are more extreme that they have ever been – there is so much more joy around, delight in simple things (probably because I have more attention to give to them) but there is also so much more anxiety and more dark pits of despair to avoid.

161

OK. That's my thought for the day. Take it or leave it.

May 3rd 2013

Not even standing room

Our small village church was packed for Christine's funeral. The pews were full, the aisles were full, and there were people outside who couldn't squeeze in, listening to the service on the loudspeaker that Frank had fixed up. 300 people whose lives had been touched by Christine. 300 people is almost half the village, but there are many more who were away and couldn't be there.

Christine ran our village shop with her brother. It's like a shop from my childhood, stocking everything from Stilton to starch, party balloons to the New Statesman, toothpaste to Sauvignon Blanc. What they don't stock they will order.

They were delivering shopping years before home delivery was even on Tesco's business plan. But I'd rather go in and have a chat. They have a chair for weary customers – I remember one village lady who used to sit in the shop most weekday mornings, being served coffee when the family were brewing for themselves.

After school on Fridays, the children queue up with their pocket money to buy lurid sweets from plastic boxes stacked on the counter. It doesn't matter how long they dither between liquorice sticks and rainbow drops, they are treated with patience, respect and kindness. Adults have to wait their turn, which is just as it should be.

It is my kind of shop.

Christine's life was cut short. She is missed. She will always be missed.

May 8th 2013

They can smile

Lux and Cece can smile because they are on Californian time. I can smile because they are here with us for nearly a week, and it's been wall to wall sunshine. It's harder for their poor tired parents to smile, dealing with two energetic children who are awake from who knows when to who knows when, and who settle down for the night at maybe 3 a.m.? I am rather hazy this morning about hours, as I decamped from sharing a room with Lux.

Dave was already sleeping on his study floor, and last night I slept on mine, on the grounds that two bedrooms, three beds and a cot might make the night easier for Isaac and Wendy to negotiate. I did help when I could on the two previous nights. Last night I slept well, but now feel guilty that I did nothing to ease the tribulations of the others, who have travelled 5,000 miles to see us. Oh well. I came across this saying recently – *There is no way to be a perfect mother, and a million ways to be a good one* – and this probably holds for grandmothers, too.

163

Last evening's treat as I got into my makeshift bed was having Lux climb under the duvet with me to watch *Blue's Clues* on Isaac's iPad - both modern wonders of the world. (iPad and *Blue's Clues* - the US version with my heart-throb, Steve Burns.)

The West Coast Hepworths have been with us for a week now, and Lux still shows no signs of moving to the UK time zone, although she's not on a Californian one either.

This was yesterday's sleeping/waking schedule:

Midnight – 1 a.m. EVERYONE ASLEEP

1 a.m. LUX wakes up ready to play, so WENDY gets up to look after her.

1 a.m. – 5 a.m. LUX AND WENDY play

5 a.m. DAVE wakes up. LUX, WENDY and DAVE hang out.

6 a.m. SUE wakes up. WENDY goes to bed to sleep.

6 a.m. - 8 a.m. SUE and LUX play.

8 a.m. LUX goes to bed. ISAAC and CECE wake up.

8 a.m. – 11 a.m. an ADULT plays with CECE.

11 a.m. CECE goes to bed or falls asleep.

11 a.m. – Noon. Free time for all adults who are not asleep.

Noon.　CECE wakes up. SOMEONE plays with her.

12.30 p.m. WENDY wakes up.

1 p.m. ISAAC takes a nap.

1 p.m. – 3 p.m. WENDY, SUE, DAVE and CECE hang out/play. ISAAC may or may not wake up and join in.

3.30 p.m.(ish) LUX wakes up. EVERYONE IS AWAKE! Yesterday we walked down the Monsal Trail to Hassop Station Cafe.

3.30 p.m. - 8 p.m. EVERYONE awake in various moods – somnolent, energetic/too tired to walk and needing to be carried, crabby, hungry, happy, desperate, loving, snippy, tipsy, etc. etc.

8 p.m. CECE goes to bed.

9 p.m. LUX and DAVE go to bed.

10 p.m. ISAAC, WENDY AND SUE go to bed.

10 p.m. – Midnight. EVERYONE IS ASLEEP, though CECE sometimes bucks the trend.

Eating is another matter and will not be dealt with here.

May 15th 2013

Too tired to blog

The chundies have returned to San Francisco, the house is quiet and tidy, the toys are stacked away, and I am too tired to blog. 5,000 miles away, the girls have slotted back seamlessly into a sleep routine appropriate to their location, and their parents are recovering from the 20 hour door-to-door journey, after a week of sleep deprivation and jet-lag.

Bless them for coming.

May 18th 2013

The wisdom of 2-year-olds

What Lux said to her mother this week:

"You open the book page and then you go on an adventure."

May 26th 2013

A small pleasure is...

...going out for a short bike ride on a rare sunny teatime when most of the tourists have gone home from the Monsal Trail, and saying hello to my lovely neighbours on the way back, and being urged to join them for a Pimms in the sunshine. So we sat on their terrace in the sunshine and chatted and laughed and looked at their garden and the fields beyond, and I realised that the last time I was in a similar situation - garden, sunshine, fields, Pimms, laughing - was with my mother, and the realisation enhanced a moment which was already beyond delight.

May 30th 2013

mish-mash

a bundle of unrelated thoughts and all in lower case a la e e cummings with scanty punctuation because it suits the mish-mash effect and is less effort and also in homage to giovanna, a character in plotting for beginners who took to writing her emails in lower case with no punctuation:

two dear people start chemotherapy this week. i think about them all the time

i have had a good week working my way through a list of tasks and was about to upload the first ebook to amazon when i hit a problem and now i have to wait to speak to isaac before i can sort it out, and he is in san francisco and asleep till this afternoon

the trees are fully out here but the may blossom has not appeared and it will be june in two days. will that make it june blossom?

dave persuaded me he needed another narrowboat holiday so although i have a million things to do at home which include three weeks gardening and various publishing matters we got a cut-price-for-late-booking one on the leeds-liverpool canal for next week

this is my tweet of the week (cut and pasted from twitter so not in lower case)

Sue Hepworth: *My husband learned today that a shower cap is for keeping your hair dry in the shower. He'd hitherto thought it a fashion item.*

JUNE

June 1st 2013

The odd men who visit my house

While I was out doing last minute shopping for our trip to Gargrave and beyond, Dave was in the front garden, basking, and there he was prey to a man who comes house to house (in his car) selling tasteless calendars and the wrong sized baking tins, synthetic tea-towels and gadgets you really, really don't want. I thought we'd seen the back of this guy: he hasn't called for a year or two. I thought I'd managed to categorise myself as "an unrewarding customer." Dave always berated me for being so mean. I have nothing against pedlars (actually, I think the concept is romantic) if they are selling useful stuff I want, but this guy never was. Eventually Dave and I came to an agreement that whoever answered the door to the guy could decide whether or not to raid the family budget and there would be no recriminations afterwards, either way.

When I got home with the coffee and bananas, Dave flourished a new 'feather' duster, on which there were no feathers.

Dave is the one who notices cobwebs, and he's been wanting a new 'feather duster' for some time.

"It's tat!" I said.

"It's 100% lambswool!" he said.

I smelled it. It was. "I thought I'd seen the guy off," I said.

"He said I was so nice, you'd be wanting to hang on to me."

"Hmmph!"

"Oh, and he said – *Give my regards to your wife*."

June 9th 2013

Other people's time zones

When Dave and I go away on a narrowboat with the usual suspects, we set sail around 9 a.m. after breakfast and as many showers as the hot water supply will allow. This means that Dave, who gets up at 5 a.m. (OMG) has been pacing the towpath for several hours, muttering the mantra "We need to get going. This is no way to beat the queues."

When Dave and I go away on our own, we set off early. This last trip I indulged him and agreed to wake up at 6 and we'd set off half an hour later, after my two mugs of Yorkshire tea. This, dear readers, is a huge concession. I am *useless* first thing in the morning and I feel *appalling*.

On some canals I can stay in bed while we travel. Not so last week. The trouble with the lower reaches of the Leeds Liverpool canal is the plethora of swing bridges. Whereas an experienced lone boater can manage most locks solo if they have to (although it's a faff), and swing bridges are not *impossible*, the latter really need two people: one to open the

169

bridge, and the other to steer the boat through the gap. This is because the bridge always swings *away* from the towpath and you need to be on the other side to open and close it.

One afternoon we moored up early above a set of six locks and sat in the sunshine reading. We decided we'd go down the locks the following morning. Bad mistake. A long stream of boats came down the locks and with every one that passed us, Dave's twitchiness increased: "Have we misjudged the journey? Should we be going down them now? What do they know that we don't? Shall we change our plan and go tonight?" For someone who doesn't give a damn about the norm, or the motley crowd, or the grunts of the inferior, he was surprisingly fretful. I insisted we should go down in the morning when it was quiet, at half past six.

The following morning at 5.20, an intermittent banging on the side of the boat woke me up. Ah, I thought. Dave must be filling the top lock, so when it's time to go, the lock is ready. I turned over and snoozed. At 5.30 I opened my eyes and saw through the gap in the curtains that the trees were moving past the window, though the boat was silent. What? I stumbled into the kitchen and looked out to see that the boat was already in the lock. Dave had *towed* it down the canal for 100 yards.

He clambered on board and said "Are you surprised? Can I turn the engine on now? Do you want to steer the boat while I do the paddles and the gates?"

"NO!"

By 5.55 a.m. I was on the lock side, the bottom paddles were open, and Dave was on the boat in the emptying lock. I was barely awake, but the air was chill. That helped. Everything was quiet apart from the sheep, the birds, the throbbing engine and the clunk of the catches on the gate paddles (now silent.) Oh, and the gushing water.

By 8 a.m. we had gone down six locks, emptied the rubbish, had a chat with another boater, and taken photographs.

June 12th 2013

The given

When Dave and I are on a canal trip à deux, there are two givens. One is that I will fall over against the steel hull at least once, and come away with several large bruises, and the other is that on the very first morning we will have a spat. There are limitless possibilities for marital wrangling, as you will know. Last year the spat was about which one of us had locked us out of the barge on a chilly morning at 7.30 a.m. with me still in my pyjamas. I blamed Dave. He blamed me. He was stressed. I was relaxed (if shivering) as there has never been a practical mess we've been in that Dave hasn't been able to get us out of. And my faith was justified: he got us out of that one, accompanied by much muttering.

Last week our first morning squabble began with my asking how to steer the boat in reverse. Dave – being an ex-teacher – likes to explain things from first principles. The problem with this is that first, I don't have a practical mind like his, and second, I want speedy answers, not something along the lines of.. "OK, forget the reversing for a minute…think of the boat in this way…….blah….blah…"

However kindly it's meant, I don't want a half hour lecture. I want specifics. e.g. "Look, all I want to know is…if I am this far from the bank with the stern pointing to the middle of the canal, and I want to get there. Do I point the tiller this way or that way?"

The way to resolve these disputes is not to talk things through, but to back off and go and get some breakfast. There wouldn't be any fighting if a girl was allowed to wake up slowly and quietly and to have her two mugs of Yorkshire tea and her muesli before she was expected to be compos mentis. And I speak as someone who has just spilled her mug of tea on the bedroom floor because she put it on a sloping pile of books on the bedside table…

It doesn't matter: after that little tiff on our first morning, it's always plain sailing.

June 19th 2013

You never stop worrying about them

I was thinking about *Isaac's being 40 this week*, and lines from Evangeline Paterson's poem *A Wish for my Children* were hovering in my head -

May you not
skin your knees. May you
not catch your fingers
in car doors. May
your hearts not break.

….and I thought – oh well, at least I don't have to worry about minor injuries, these days. And then Isaac rang up from San Francisco (when he should have been asleep) to say he didn't want me to see his tweets and to wonder what was happening and to worry, so he was ringing up to tell me he had broken his thumb.

I hate his being so far away anyway, but when he has hurt himself I hate it even more. He may be 40, he may have an important job at Twitter, he may be a father of two, I still want to give him a hug when he's hurt himself. Not that Wendy can't do it just as sweetly, but I am his mother, and (as I said in a piece once) "Whatever their offspring's pain - whether it be a trapped finger or a mangled heart - a mother always wishes she could bear it for them."

June 23rd 2013

A newly opened door closes again

When I was last staying with my sister I found a clothes shop in a small town in Hampshire that had clothes that apparently had been designed with me in mind, and my sister was with me, sitting next to the mirror, egging me on to buy them.

And when I got home I found another branch of the same shop in Bakewell (my local town) that I had hitherto ignored as not being relevant to me and my taste?

Well, one of the linen blouses I bought in Hampshire hung on a clothes hanger in the bedroom for a week or so and every time I looked at it, I wondered why I didn't want to wear it when the colour and fabric were perfect. Then one day I realised I didn't like the collar and neckline. So I took it back to the shop in Bakewell (they have an exemplary returns policy) and got my money back and then asked if they had in stock the dark navy linen jacket my sister had failed to persuade me to buy. No, they said, but they would order it.

It came, I tried it on, it was too small. They ordered the next size up, I tried it on, dithered, tried on the smaller one, dithered, bought the larger one and that then hung in the bedroom for several days. Yesterday, I took it back. It was a different assistant and I found myself uttering a long stream of reasons why this jacket was not for me – the sleeves were too long, it didn't fit quite right, the colour was too dark, it was more formal than the things I usually wear, I went shopping with my sister and her taste is not the same as mine....my excuses went on and on in an embarrassing stream until eventually the assistant said, "If it's not right, it's not right."

She gave me back my money and I slunk out of the shop more mortified than I have been since I was 14.

I still ADORE the first linen blouse I bought – the boxy cut, the asymmetric neckline, the fact that if I wear it with indigo jeans I look smart (I live in jeans).

But I feel as if I can't go back to the shop again. Ever. Or if I do dare cross the portal, I shall have to buy something and <u>not</u> take it back, whatever their policy on returns. Oh dear. Now I remember why I like shopping by post.

June 29th 2013

Too mean to lend a book

Yesterday I felt ashamed.

A good friend came for the day – to walk on the Monsal Trail and to take me out to lunch. When she comes to visit she always brings an armful of books as presents for me and for Dave.

We had a wonderful walk, despite the showers (I wish you could see the banks of ox-eye daisies on the Trail) and we talked for nigh on five hours. I told her, amongst other things, about one of my favourite books, *A Tree Grows in Brooklyn*, and urged her to read it.

When we got back to Hepworth Towers, I fetched it from the shelf so she could write down the details, and she said "Are you sure you want to lend it me?" and without thinking, I said "No, I can't let it out of the house. I was just showing it to you." And then immediately I felt mean and selfish, and overcome with remorse and after a bit of to-ing and fro-ing, I said "Yes, do borrow it."

Being a lovely person who understands the importance of books, she immediately said "Are you sure?"

I hesitated. I knew perfectly well she would look after it. And I knew perfectly well I would get it back soon. It is just that there are some books I cannot bear to leave the house. I think it stems from when we lost 95% of our possessions in a fire, including thousands of books.

I explained this to her later, on the phone, after she'd left (and I had let her take the book.)

And being a lovely person, she said "I expect that if I'd wanted almost any other book in the house, you wouldn't have worried."

This is true.

But then I thought about what other books I always want close at hand, just in case, and these are they:

Leaving Home by Garrison Keillor

Homestead by Rosina Lippi

Writing Down the Bones by Natalie Goldberg

Heartburn by Nora Ephron

The Diary of a Provincial Lady by E.M. Delafield

and lastly and oddly – because I don't like any other Mary Wesley book – *Part of the Furniture*

When I was little, I thought real life was like *The Waltons*. That's probably why all but one of these books are comfort reading.

AUGUST

August 3rd 2013

Real life? Fiction? There's so often a confusion

From *Plotting for Grown-ups*, written last year…

I asked Richard again what the woman looks like. "What colour hair does she have?"

"Medium."

"Is she fat or thin?"

"Medium."

"Does she have a weird nose?"

"Maybe."

Absolutely hopeless. It's a good job the woman isn't a criminal with Richard expected to give an eyewitness account to the police.

From real life at Hepworth Towers last week…

Sue: What does he look like?

Dave: I have no idea.

Sue: You spent four hours with him! What does he look like?

Dave: Really – I haven't a clue.

Sue: What colour is his hair – is he dark or blond? Is he tall or small? Does he have a fat face? A flat face? You must remember *something*.

Dave: He has a blue anorak.

August 29th 2013

Sue Hepworth is a ratbag - again

Sources close to Hepworth Towers say I've been grumpy and snappish, lately. This may be true. It's sometimes hard to judge from the inside whether it's you that is being irritable or whether other people are being particularly annoying and exasperating.

Whatever, I have been feeling stressed. At the height of tussles with Amazon and worries about the book, I saw an advert for a pot-washer in a local café, and it looked like an attractive option. I know, I know – I have no experience of being a PAID pot washer - but what I thought was – *Oh, how restful, how undemanding - a job with no decisions or anxieties. I'd be able to drift off into a quiet reflective reverie.*

What was I thinking?

OCTOBER

October 20th 2013

Here's the thing

You may read a lot of books. You may read them really fast, you may get through them like I consume films on a transatlantic flight.

But the author of the latest book you read took months (or more likely) years to write said book. They sweated over the plot. They rewrote the first chapter seven times. What's more, the characters are their friends. The characters are so real to them that they see them walking down the lane, or maybe the writer even *buys groceries for them.* I did that once.

Sometimes authors pine for their characters after the writing is finished and the book is published. Sometimes authors keep imagining their characters in real-life situations.

So, all that being true, next time you meet an author who knows that you recently bought their new book, please, please, say something about the book to them. It may not be at the forefront of *your* mind, but it sure as hell is what they are thinking about, when they see you walking towards them on the street.

If you hated the book, say "I read your book. I liked" – and then pick one thing you *did* like about it, even if it was only the cover. And then if they start to ask you more, have a carefully prepared sentence such as "Hmm, well, you did such and such well, but I really preferred ….[your last one]"

Of course, you may have loved the book, and if that is the case, please put the author out of their misery **now!**

October 25th 2013

News from the slow lane

I LOVE waking up without a list in my head.

I love not caring if Dave interrupts what I'm doing to tell me something 'interesting' he has just heard on the radio. I love being able to sit in an easy chair with a cup of tea and look out of the window at the sky and the autumn leaves and not think I should be doing something more productive.

I am still in that post publication-frenzy hiatus which (as my friend Chrissie said) is like the time when all your exams are finished and you feel free to stay up late or stay in bed late, or not get up at all.

I am getting up. I am doing stuff like taking down the sweet pea canes, mending holes that have worn in three favourite jumpers, having my hair cut.

And I have joined a small, newly-formed jazz band, much to *my* delight and that of my sax teacher Mel. She seems to think that a single practice session has already improved my timing.

And when it rains I clear the drain down the lane. Every year it gets clogged up with leaves and other wayside debris and a torrent of water runs down the hill. There is something very satisfying about clearing drains. It reminds me of damming streams when I was little. It's about changing the course of water. It's messing about. I am becoming Compo in *Last of the Summer Wine.*

NOVEMBER

November 6th 2013

It is possible to have too many tables

When we moved into this house with not very much (our furniture and belongings from 25 years of family life having been lost in a warehouse fire) I wanted a kitchen drawer like the one in our old house.

I wanted a drawer full of the detritus of everyday family life – a domestic archaeology to ground me – fossilised rubber bands, ancient postcards, last year's advent candle, crushed paper flowers from playgroup, buttons and safety pins, plant labels, tacky plastic novelties from Christmas crackers, old matchbox cars with scratched paintwork.

Since then I have been developing such a drawer as this, and it was only this September that I felt it was time to transform it. Now it is a treasure trove of interesting bits and bobs that the grandchildren like to ransack when they visit. It is time – after seventeen years - to clear some clutter. Unfortunately I am fighting a rising tide from the other person who lives here. And the real trouble is that his clutter is large and beautiful.

He likes making tables out of recycled wood. In the sitting room alone we have one coffee table made from an exceptionally chunky old oak gatepost, two made from old teak science lab benches and one glass one with beech legs.

Two years ago, a good friend gave him her old office parquet floor. It has been stacked in the shed since then, but now its time has come. Dave is making tables from it. He has installed the new table top on his desk in his study (phew).

But Dave is always so delighted with his successes that he goes on to repeat them again and again.

I don't know where he intends to put the latest one. He won't want to sell it, because he will love it so much.

Yesterday, he told his adopted sister (a happy recipient of three coffee tables made from reclaimed mahogany) that he was making another parquet table.

She was silent for several seconds, and then she said "Oh dear."

Quite.

November 12th 2013

"Have nothing in your house that you do not know to be useful, or believe to be beautiful."

Yesterday I did some more clutter clearing. I was working on the back porch, which is too small to fit any kind of table in, whether or not it is lovely and made from reclaimed wood. Even so, the place is a key battleground at Hepworth Towers in the fight between order and minimalism and the ever-threatening tsunami of grubby items of mysterious usefulness (never mind beauty.)

If I went away for a year, I would not be able to get into the porch for stuff that should live in the shed.

In my view, the presence of the following items is acceptable:

the cat tray

a tidy rack of hiking boots, working boots and wellies

a hook with spare coats

the central heating boiler

an airing rack suspended from the ceiling

a compost bucket

a hat and glove basket

the cat's bed on top of the boiler, which she has currently disdained in favour of the basket chair in the kitchen

the vegetable box

183

The following will be tolerated (with gritted teeth):

one bike which is apparently too important to live in the shed with mine, even though this bike leans up against the shoe rack obstructing access.

What I do not want to tolerate is a list of DIY stuff, the list being so long I am not going to bore you with it.

However, yesterday I found this item nestled on the windowsill between a spare inner tube and a bicycle pump: my Gran's toaster. This toaster is imbued with intensely happy memories of holidays at her house in Morecambe. After she died, my mother adopted it, which means that the grandchildren remember it on *their* Gran's breakfast table.

Unfortunately, as well as a good clean up, the toaster needs a new element, which I don't think is available. You can buy very similar toasters on eBay, but they would not be Gran's.

Yesterday I sent out a family email asking if any of my four siblings or their children or associates would like the toaster, saying if I didn't hear by Friday, I would throw it away. I held my breath, desperately hoping someone would want it, because I didn't think I could *actually* throw it away when Friday came.

A trickle of emails arrived throughout the day, renouncing the toaster. (Oh ye of hard hearts – I have your number now.) Then late on, Isaac (my son who lives in San Francisco) said he would give it a home. Last thing at night, my younger brother said he would have it if no-one else stepped up.

I now have a new measure of family sentimentality (and I love you guys for it.) Also, there is a bit more space in the porch.

November 15th 2013

Eat your heart out Stieg Larsson, Jodi Picoult and all the rest...

Last night I learned that my novel *But I Told You Last Year That I Loved You* has been named by the National Autistic Society as one of their six favourite novels about autism, alongside the bestselling *The Curious Incident of the Dog in the Night time.*

The other four novels are: *A rock and a hard place, Al Capone does my shirts, Of Mice and Aliens,* and *Einstein's Dream.*

November 23rd 2013

Cataract city

The doctor was ace, my op went well, and my distance vision in my new (left) eye is better than that in my right eye when it's wearing a contact lens. Roll on the op on the right eye.

Have a nice weekend.

November 26th 2013

What really happened

I wanted to tell you the lurid details of my cataract op but I am from a family of robust, no-nonsense women, who already think I'm a wimp.

Also, when so many people have worse problems to deal with, it felt self-indulgent to whimper. I mean – I was lucky to have a top eye surgeon on the NHS and for everything to go smoothly and to suffer no pain.

Then on Sunday a good friend told me that she hated having ops on her eyes, and after they were done, she always wanted to hide in a hole. She pointed out to me that all our instincts are to protect our eyes, so we are fighting those instincts in lying on a table awake, and letting a stranger poke medical implements into them. She said I wasn't a wimp to hate it. This made me feel better.

So I'm telling you now, that after the op I was cold for five hours. I had to go to bed with all my clothes on, under a duvet, quilt and blanket, and even then switch on the electric blanket.

Bed is the only place I wanted to be, curled up watching crap TV on the iPad, and then catching up with *The Archers*.

The woman next to me in the hospital waiting room said she would have to have a general anaesthetic if someone wanted to operate on her feet. She couldn't stand it otherwise.

I talked to Dave about this.

Me: "Would you be nervous about having surgery on a particular part of your body?"

Dave: "I think I'd feel unnerved if they removed my head."

November 27th 2013

…on second thoughts…

I have been puzzling about my reaction to the cataract op when I have had three major operations under general anaesthetic and I didn't want to crawl into a hole afterwards (although, having said that, I was in bed anyway). Therefore, it must be the fact that I was awake throughout the proceedings, as much as the fact that they were meddling with my eye.

Case closed.

Tomorrow I shall write about something completely different, you'll be pleased to hear.

DECEMBER

December 8th 2013

Temporary Remedy

If your Christmas tree in the garden is almost bald, and you've had enough of the short days and the long nights and your SAD light doesn't seem to make much difference and you've tried playing Pollyanna's Glad Game for a week while you avoid the news and you've still got the winter blues, I recommend watching back-to-back episodes of *Frasier* while you begin to knit your daughter a pair of Fair Isle arm warmers for Christmas. It cheered me up, even if just for a couple of hours.

December 10th 2013

Cheering words

I played the Glad Game last week. The effect was patchy. Sometimes I felt cheery, and sometimes I felt bad.

This week I'm trying another tack. I'm going to share some things Dave has said to me over the years when he's been trying to cheer me up.

Yesterday, it was this:

"At least you're not at risk of cannibalism. If you were a depressed Neanderthal, you'd be an easy straggler for the neighbours to pick off."

December 11th 2013

Wednesday's child is full of woe

I've been feeling really low. Last night I cried my way through most of *Billy Elliot*. I haven't felt this bad for such a sustained period since the year after my mother died, though the present malaise is different from how I felt then.

This week I'm trying to lighten up by remembering things Dave has said to me in an attempt to cheer me up.

Today:

Me: "I'm really fed up, Dave. Actually, I think I might be depressed."

Dave: "Don't worry – it'll pass. Either that, or you'll die."

December 12th 2013

Comfort and Joy

I had a good day yesterday. I worked all morning on my own in the garden. That's what I like to do at the moment. I don't want to talk to anyone. And it was sunny.

We watched *Billy Eliot* again – this time for screenplay-examining purposes (and I only cried twice.)

And loving people sent me messages. Barbara sent *me* a short animation, which I liked a lot.

I read Megan's post again on her *Scent of Water* blog *about* making good art, and hope.

But as it's *Quotes from Dave* week, here is another gem – so good that I used it in *But I Told You Last Year That I Loved You.*

I was worrying about being old…

Me: "I've just noticed I've got those old people's freckles on the backs of my hands!"

Dave: "I've had those for some time. I keep telling you how ancient we are. Stranded in the grey, dank land of old age, and everywhere the stench of death. I'll make our coffins this winter."

December 13th 2013

Pub quiz as mini-break

Who would have thought that an evening in a local pub the size of our sitting room, doing a pub quiz with a bunch of friendly women I didn't know would be such a treat? And such a holiday from the stuff inside my head? Well it was. I feel a bit better today. Maybe I should go out every night and then I wouldn't have to worry about how the world is falling apart.

Here is the last of the week's cheering quotes from Dave:

Me: "We're really old."

Him: "Fortunately, nature has its own way of sorting that problem out."

December 16th 2013

The Marie Celeste Christmas tree

My half-dressed tree has nothing to do with our ON-OFF Christmas and everything to do with me rushing off to hospital in the middle of decorating it.

A word of advice….

Don't keep your post-operative eye drops on the same shelf as your contact lens cleaner. Otherwise you might go upstairs to put your eye drop in and grab the cleaning solution by mistake and squirt that in your eye.

This will necessitate a trip to the local emergency eye clinic so that the sweet young doctor (oh how ancient I am) can clip your eye open so you look like an anatomical dummy (thanks, Dave) and hose down your eye with two litres of saline solution, and THEN do unspeakable things to your eye with a cotton bud. That last manoeuvre alone is enough to teach me a lesson.

The good news is that we only live half an hour away from the wonderful Royal Hallamshire Hospital and the other good news is that the sweet young doctor said it wouldn't have harmed my new lens. It was my cornea that needed attention. But the Ph was back to normal when I left and they don't want to see me again, and I don't blame them.

They do want me to keep my bottles on separate shelves.

December 18th 2013

The story of the Christmas shed

Our ON-OFF Christmas (aka Christmas in the Shed) – which is now part of the biennial domestic landscape at Hepworth Towers - has an interesting history, as well as being immortalised in the novel *Plotting for Beginners*.

1. It began as a jokey idea of Dave's.

2. I wrote a piece about it for the *Times,* thinking everyone would know it was a joke.

3. The following year I sent a clipping of the piece to a glossy women's magazine.

4.They rang me up, and this is what happened next – and I quote from the fictional version in *Plotting for Beginners*. But the bulk of this is TRUE.

"The features editor of Hearth and Home [fictional title] rang. She said that everyone in the office had been rolling around laughing at Gus's zany idea on how to spend Christmas, and they would like to give us a double page spread in the November issue (which is in fact the Christmas issue — what?)

Gus and I are going to be in a feel-good feature about people who have unusual Christmases.

The entire piece was a spoof. It was bloody obvious it was a joke.

Not so to Mrs Features Editor.

She asked me if this was an OFF year or an ON year.

"Why?" I asked.

"We'd like to have a picture of you in your Christmas Shed."

"Oh, we don't have a shed just for Christmas," I said.

"So you decorate your normal shed?"

"Well, actually," I said, "it's an ON year this year, which means I'll be decorating the house." This is true. With Gus away, I am going to have a Christmas celebration such as Goose Lane has never seen. "So unfortunately," I went on, "it wouldn't make a very interesting picture—it would look like everyone else's Christmas."

"That needn't be a problem," she said. "Would you be willing to pretend—for the sake of a good story for our readers—that this Christmas is an OFF one, and that you'll be decorating the shed? It would only be like time shifting it a year, just as the photoshoot is made to look as if it's in December but actually takes place in September."

"I suppose that would be all right," I said. I know it was stupid to agree, but at the time it sounded so reasonable: she had caught me up in the idea of providing a good story for her readers.

"So I can send a photographer to shoot you sitting in your deckchair in your decorated shed, then?"

"Yes."

"Would tomorrow, or next week suit?"

"It'll have to be tomorrow. I'm going away on Saturday."

"Fine. Tomorrow. And don't fret about a tree," she said. "Our consumer department has a batch of artificial ones we're reviewing. And I'll get the art department to sort out some decorations."

"Could you send some extra lights?" I asked.

I can't believe what I have agreed to. One minute I'm telling her we don't have a Christmas Shed, and the next minute I'm arranging for them to come and photograph me in it. I should have told her to make sure that when the photographer comes to shoot me he brings some ammunition."

Only several years later did we decide to put the joke into practice.

December 19th 2013

What happens now

We've hit on a happy compromise for the OFF Christmas: Christmas is confined to my study, where I have a small tree but elsewhere there are no decorations, lights or cards. This year Dave said that if it would cheer me up I could do whatever I liked, but that didn't seem fair (and anyway, the depression is nothing to do with Christmas, ON or OFF.)

But I have allowed myself a few cards on the dresser, and a lovely decoration on the dining room table involving ceramic stars.

The ceramic stars were handmade by Zoë, who came over on Tuesday to take me out to lunch (as loving daughters do.) It was a beautiful clear sunny day, so we walked up the Trail and over the fields to the pub not much bigger than our sitting room. It's been a ladies-who-lunch week. On Monday I had a wonderful Christmas dinner at Hassop Station with a friend, and yesterday I met my big sister half way between her house and mine – an hour's drive. We saw a fab exhibition of Quentin Blake drawings.

It was so good to see Kath. Sometimes, there is no substitute for a hug from a sibling.

December 23rd 2013

Some of us have a reputation for not being able to control what we say when we have had a drink

It comes to a pretty pass when you are single-handedly in the process of assembling a festive family meal comprising:

roast free range chicken, sausage, bacon, nut roast, veggie sausages, parsnips, sprouts, peas, potatoes, stuffing, force meat balls, gravy, mushroom gravy (V) and caramelised onion gravy (V),

(which – incidentally – was all ready at the predicted time of 5.30 p.m.)

and two of your children tell you that because an unexpected guest is now coming, you may not have anything to drink during the festivities lest you embarrass said visitor, said children, yourself or the cat, and this includes the champagne that is already cooling in the fridge door, and your one ally in this situation (your daughter-in-law who is at that moment on the phone) is 5,000 miles away, so cannot shout them down.

I acquiesced, and then because I acquitted myself with grace amongst the assembled hordes, the children relented.

You know what they say? A good time was had by all.

But I was the one who had the best time…

…there is nothing so sweet has having your family assembled around the same table, happily pulling crackers, and having a grandson say after EVERY cracker joke "Why is that funny?"

And my only sadness was that the West Coast Hepworths couldn't be there. But you can't have everything.

And now, it really is an OFF Christmas.

December 24ᵗʰ 2013

Lazy day of wind and rain

I got up late yesterday, so was late at Bakewell market and then even later because I bumped into an old friend who bundled me into the nearest cafe for a catch-up. Then when I did get to my favourite greengrocery stall at 10.30, they were selling their stuff off cheap, so I snagged some bargains.

Dave and I had an old peoples' afternoon and evening. We lit the fire, and I knitted, and Dave did the Christmas crossword and then entertained me by reading out unwittingly comic small ads from the *Peak Advertiser*. I flicked through the SALE catalogue from Celtic and idly considered buying the Darley Pocket Dress in 100% Geelong lambswool, now half price…not because I have the figure to wear a knitted dress, but because the thing is obviously warm and a real bargain and I always think that a knitted dress would be just the thing to wear over my pyjamas on cold mornings when I'm writing.

So there we were at teatime, each lying on a sofa in a quiet house, on an OFF Christmas, curtains drawn, fire blazing, with no shopping to do and no guests expected for four whole days, and he said with utter sincerity:

"As we're approaching the corona of Christmas, how do we avoid burn-up?"

December 31st 2013

Courage and hope

2013 has been a trying year.

Three people I love were diagnosed with, and/or treated for life-threatening conditions. Then there was Isaac breaking his thumb and Wendy coming off the motor scooter, and there were other upsetting things that I can't tell you about.

And outside of my domestic sphere, the world became nastier, and that was deeply upsetting, but I am not talking politics on here.

A dear friend asked me the other day if I was feeling better. She understood that my depression was not about feeling sorry for myself; it was about losing courage and hope.

I am feeling better, but I'm still wondering where to find that courage and hope.

Here's that thought again from Mary Ann Radmacher: *'Courage doesn't always roar. Sometimes courage is the little voice at the end of the day that says 'I will try again tomorrow.'*

I wish all of you courage and hope for 2014.

2014

JANUARY

January 7ᵗʰ 2014

What's important

In the heat of battling with life, bad news from every direction, trying to get fit on the bike again after the bad-weather break so every trip up the Monsal Trail doesn't feel like forced labour, it's easy to forget what I achieved last year…so I've been thinking back to encourage myself and reassure myself that it's OK to be distracted from writing by the drive to clear out clutter (oh this Protestant Work Ethic is a hard thing to shake – actually – it's not that, it's my much loved mother always saying when she rang up "And what are you making/working on/writing?") ….so back to what I achieved last year…two ebooks published, one paperback published, that fantastic launch, beating down internet pirates, having *But I Told You Last Year That I Loved You* named as one of the National Autistic Society's favourite novels about autism, finally finishing the Fair Isle hoodie.

But the thing is, two of my grandchildren came to play yesterday and I had a brilliant time playing with castle Lego, and when Zoë said they had been very excited about coming over, <u>that</u> felt like a bigger achievement than any of the other more worldly ones above. Just like when Lux ran across the concourse in San Francisco Airport last March, shouting "Sue! Sue!" and I knew I'd hit the big time.

January 10th 2014

Three

Yesterday was a trying day but three small sweet things happened, even so.

I had my first sax lesson of the year and Mel had found me a book of Jazz Solos for the tenor sax that has backing tracks and some lines of blank stave for me to improvise. This is all part of the Sue-learns-to-improvise-on-her-sax-plan. I am so excited! Watch out *Corcovado*, *All the Things you Are* and *In a Sentimental Mood*. I dismissed *The Way You Look Tonight* because they had pepped it up. Some musicians are weird. The song is slow and romantic – no two ways about it. What were these bozos thinking?

The second nice thing was an unexpected letter from an unexpected person.

The third was my arriving at 7.45 at the Bakewell chippie after an exhausting afternoon and evening in Sheffield, and being told by the woman cleaning the counter that they only had one fishcake plus chips left, and they were getting ready to close. But then the sweet young man (well, young to me) who was mopping the floor, took pity on me and cooked me a fish. And his wife (?) said as I left, "You look very tired. Go home and have your supper and a rest."

So I did, and Dave had lit the stove. (Fourth nice thing.)

January 12th 2014

Airport security for cats

The trouble with having someone else clean your house – unless you have been married to them for 43 years - is that if they are incompetent, you end up doing the job anyway and if they *are* good at their job, you feel you have to clean before they come so they don't despise you for being a dirty Dora.

I have only once paid someone to clean my house, not because of any principle – after all, some people like cleaning, and why not earn a living doing it? – but because the woman cried off the following week with some excuse, and never came back, and I am sure it was because she was overwhelmed by the hopelessness of the task.

But why am I wittering on about cleaning?

Partly because the windows are filthy, and partly because that thing about having to tidy up before the cleaner comes, is like the situation I am in with the doctor.

Let me explain. In September, during the hectic run up to my book launch, I got a letter from the GP offering me an over 60 check up, and not having any spare time, I tossed it to the back of my desk. After the book launch, I went to California, then I had my cataract removed, and then it was Christmas. Now I have run out of excuses.

But.... it is after Christmas and of course I have put on weight. I know how strict the nurse is at our surgery – a friend went down for her over 60 check-up – a fit friend, a friend I would not have thought was more than half a stone overweight - and was told she was almost three stone overweight and apple-shaped. I was furious on her behalf, but that's not the point. The point is – I DON'T WANT TO BE TOLD I AM OVERWEIGHT WHEN I KNOW I AM, AND I CERTAINLY DON'T WANT TO BE TOLD I AM APPLE SHAPED WHEN I AM CERTAINLY NOT.

So now I have to lose my Christmas weight before I go for my check-up. You see, if I get back to my normal weight, I can say to the nurse, "I have been this weight for years and years and have never had anything seriously wrong with me," and so stub her out.

And what has airport security for cats got to do with any of this?

We don't have a cat-flap because we don't want the cat to bring in presents for us in the form of livestock. That rabbit was bad enough. This means that there are dirty paw marks on all of our windows from when she signals to us that she wants to come in, and the low winter sun shows them up. We need a cat-flap that doesn't allow the cat to bring anything inside the house, not even paw-luggage.

And I need to ask Dave to clean the windows.

January 15th 2014

Think global, act local

I was thinking about how depressed I was in December, and how the root of it was the loss of courage and hope. Yesterday I realised that a feeling of defeat was in there, too…a feeling that there was nothing I could do to make the world a better place.

I went to Greenham, marched against Britain entering a war with Iraq, demonstrated here there and everywhere, signed petitions, hawked petitions round door-to-door, volunteered at CAB, boycotted Israeli goods, knitted blankets, filled up *Aquaboxes*, donated money, etc, etc.

Everywhere there is injustice, suffering, poverty and war. Politicians can't or won't solve the problems. Is there any hope?

Yesterday I had a messaging chat with the Aging Hippie who has just been accepted for the Peace Corps, the US equivalent of Voluntary Service Overseas.

AH, whom I am proud to know, said: "I just watched a TV programme called 1964. My time! We wanted to change the world!"

Me: "I am defeated with that one but you are still going strong. Kudos to you!"

Her: "I still want to, but actually don't think I can any more."

Me: "But you are! What else is VSO about?"

Her: "It's about friendship, sharing, witnessing, helping."

Yes.

January 21st 2014

Winter struggles

It was foggy yesterday, and frosty, and the sun didn't cut through till the afternoon. I wrapped up warm and went out on my bike on the Monsal Trail.

It was cold and I felt as if I was working inordinately hard, but I pushed on and got to my favourite turning spot, stopped, and had a think for ten minutes while I looked at the limestone cliffs opposite, and the river below, and saw a heron fly downstream.

Then I struggled to cycle home, even though it's downhill for most of the way: I felt limp and weak and hot, as if I'd been suddenly struck down with flu, and all I could think about as I battled on was a slice of white bread spread with butter and golden syrup.

I am going to get a new bike. This one is like Sally's in *Plotting for Grown-Ups* – old and cronky with broken mudguards held on by plastic ties. Which pretty much describes how I felt when I got home and flopped on the sofa, and Dave said, "You look as if you might die."

I am rereading *The Secret Garden*. It's a good book to read in the winter. It's full of hope, renewal and The Spring. This morning it moved me to tears.

January 27th 2014

Standing in the gutter and looking at the stars

I like to live it up a little and yesterday's living it up involved waking up late (8 a.m.) so I had time only to blog before I rushed out to Quaker meeting, and then after lunch I was just trying to decide between writing and playing my sax when the rain stopped and the sun came out and gave me other options.

Dave didn't want to go for a walk. He was ensconced in what we euphemistically call his "study" but which is really an indoor shed, and he was already getting some cold January air - the window was wide open and the heating was turned off. He was wearing an apron and a beret, and cutting a stained glass piece while listening to a recording of T S Eliot reading the *Four Quartets*. He was sorted.

So I went out alone, on my bike up the Trail. The lanes were awash with rain draining off the fields, and the drains on the lane were blocked again. So on the way home I spent a glorious ten minutes unblocking the main one. You know how I love unblocking drains on the lane.

At dusk we drove up over Longstone Edge in search of starling murmurations. And we found one.

January 28th 2014

Planning the future

Yesterday morning early I was lying in bed looking at the latest catalogue from *Wrap* that had dropped unbidden through my letterbox. I was turning down the corners of pages to mark the items I liked.

Later in the morning I inadvertently saw a side view of my face, and my spirits plummeted far lower than my sagging neck. There is no getting away from it: I look my age. The trouble is that inside my head I am still 41. Oh *Wrap*, you turn my head with your skinny boyfriend jeans and your biker jackets.

Do you have plans for your next life? I do. I was embellishing them yesterday as I sat freezing on a country station platform waiting for a train to take me to Sheffield to see *Inside Llewyn Davis*. (I dropped that bit in to impress people who think that all I do is watch Rom-Coms, and not critically acclaimed Coen Brothers films.)

So these are my current plans for my next life…

I shall have a body like Audrey Hepburn's, and I'll bleach my hair and have it in an urchin cut. My style will be rock chick.

I will take up the saxophone at 20 instead of 60, becoming expert at trad jazz improvisation. I will travel during my twenties, and most importantly, I'll hike to the bottom of the Grand Canyon and camp there before hiking back.

At 30, I shall begin to write, and also have my children. By the time they are all at school I shall be a published novelist.

In my forties I will be a hard-hitting and influential columnist, writing about social injustice, and the oppression of the Palestinian people.

In my fifties I'll have a wild time.

In my sixties I will join the slow lane and spend a lot of time with my grandchildren.

In my seventies, I will take up photography.

After all that, I think I'll be satisfied.

January 30th 2014

It's addictive

You'd think a broken-down old writer would be pleased when it's a grey rainy January day because there are no lures competing with the desk and the emerging work-in-progress (despite the fact that writing a screenplay is turning out to be soooo much harder than writing a novel, especially when it's an adaptation of your own novel – I mean – how can a woman slice out whole sections of prose which she thought were important enough to include in the first place?)

deep breath – Even so, be that as it may, and notwithstanding, (just using too many words there as a form of rebellion against screenwriting) by yesterday afternoon I was feeling twitchy and desperate for exercise. This was despite the fact that I have

207

Fair Isle arm warmers to knit for Zoë, and a patchwork quilt of my own that requires weeks of work.

It's all due to the new diet and fitness regime designed to shed those Christmas pounds, so I could go to the GP for the over-60s health check. I can now sit comfortably on the sofa after tea (dinner or supper to you lot down south) without undoing the waistband of my jeans. I can now get to the third tunnel on the Trail and back again without needing mouth-to-mouth.

The upshot of getting fit is that you can't bear to get no exercise for more than two days at a time. So I braved the rain and went out. But the mud! The mud!

I have booked my check-up appointment for next Wednesday. I am fit, and almost my normal weight again. Let the nurse call me apple-shaped. I'll give her what for.

FEBRUARY

February 4th 2014

You don't have to be perfect to be lovable

It's so liberating to wake up this morning having had a good night's sleep.

I feel ready for anything.

Yesterday morning I felt dire, and when my friend rang up to ask if we could cancel lunch and eat at her house instead and would a poached egg be OK, I said "I hate poached eggs. I'll bring my own lunch." I knew this wouldn't offend her, and it didn't. That's the kind of friend she is. Later, she commented on my being grumpy – but not as a complaint, merely as a statement. She loves me, even when I'm grumpy.

Also, I can tell her anything. I am so lucky to have her as a friend.

February 8th 2014

One pass, one fail

These are testing times.

I had the dreaded over 40s (apparently – not over 60s) health check this week. My cholesterol level was good, but my waist was 1 and a half inches too big. It wasn't in the RED DANGER ZONE, but in the yellow zone, which means the nurse doesn't thrust diet pamphlets at you, and look appalled, but points at the tape measure and says mildly, "It would be good if you could get it down to *this*."

She asked me all about my diet, and also, how much I drank. I said, truthfully, one glass of wine a day.

"And do you have an alcohol-free day?" she said.

"Only when the bottle runs out."

She was not amused.

My 18-year-old car has definitely run out of bottle. Yesterday, it failed its *MOT*. Dave has almost convinced me it should go for scrap. I am *so* fed up. I like my car. I think the lichen on the window seals adds character. Who cares about the broken central locking? And I have learned to live with the damp problem. There is no sign of rust, because I bought it from my sister in the sunny south. I am *so* fed up. I have liked having a car that no-one wants to steal.

Now I have to decide if we can manage living in the country with just one car, when that car was not my choice, and is really a van masquerading as a car, and actually feels like a truck, and in order to reverse, you have to use the wing mirrors, rather than turning round and looking through the back window, and what is more it's BEIGE.

February 10th 2014

Deleted Scene

My big sister, who lives 50 miles east of here, says the weather's been kind and she's been gardening. Here we've had relentless rain and wind for days and days, the rivers are broad and swirling, and the fields are flooded.

There was a winter walk by just such a swollen river in the first draft of *But I Told You Last Year That I Loved You*, but in later drafts it was cut.

Here it is – my very own deleted scene….

210

They walked along the Monsal Trail, a disused railway track reclaimed by the Peak District National Park as a bridleway. They got as far as Monsal Dale, where the sky loomed over them, a charcoal grey. Her feet were wet and cold and she was ready to turn round and make for home, but Sol wanted to carry on, and they had a bad-tempered spat. He was usually very considerate, but since he'd found the letter, he'd not been quite the same.

As they crossed the bridge over the mill race at Water-cum-Jolly, she looked at the fierce, noisy torrent and shuddered. How easy it would be to lose someone by throwing them in.

"You won't ever chuck me in here, will you?" she said as a joke, trying to smooth things over.

"You don't need to worry about that," he said. "The barrier's too high and you'd struggle too much."

They climbed up onto the ridge and trudged along the sheep track through the bare trees, whipped by the January wind, and down again to cross the swollen river on another bridge.

"Look how the river's flooded - look at the way it's swirling around those trees," she said.

"The current's much slower," said Sol. "Do you think someone could be swept away just here?"

"You're not really thinking of throwing me in, are you?"

"Don't be daft. You'd make too much noise."

February 15th 2014

Old and new

The scrap man came on Wednesday and took my car and I was sad.

And I was surprised at being sad. Dave kept saying "It's only a car," and I kept replying, "I know. But I am sad. Please just try to *pretend* you understand."

The car was 18 years old. The central locking had gone; the window seals leaked, so the boot smelled as if twenty tom cats had been trapped in there for a fortnight, and worse, the whole car steamed up horribly on cold days; the aerial was broken so I couldn't listen to the radio; my big sister said it was too scruffy for me – an author trying to publicise her latest book – to drive; the repairs on it have cost a fortune; but I liked the car. I still don't understand why I was so sad, though. Was it because:

1/ I bought it from my sister

2/ I bought it with some money my mother left me

3/ It was my private space (like my study) where I could listen to my sax music and no-one would complain

4/ I could listen to Fun playing *We are young* REALLY REALLY LOUD, and pretend I was Sally in *Plotting for Grown-ups*, driving along with Kit

5/ I could run away whenever I wanted, even if Dave was out with his/the family car

212

6/ Although it needed money spending on it to fix it, it wasn't rusty. It seemed like a huge waste to scrap it.

But there we are. It is gone. And for the moment (and maybe forever) I shall be sharing the *beige* car with Dave. Ugh.

February 19th 2014

Front garden floorshow

Did you have a lovely warm spring day yesterday, as we did here?

So there we were in the back garden at 4.15, oiling my (old) bike chain (which means that I was watching Dave do it) and a loud unfamiliar noise started somewhere on the lane.

Dave said: "What's that rushing water? It sounds like a burst water main."

I said: "No it doesn't, it sounds like some kind of farm machinery."

We finished oiling the chain and then Dave disappeared round the side of the house in search of the noise. Two minutes later he was back.

"It's starlings in the field across the road!"

We stood on the lane in front of our house and saw and heard a HUGE flock of starlings sitting on one of the trees. The noise was weird and wonderful. They took off and flew around for a couple of minutes and then alighted back on the tree. Then after another 3 or 4 minutes, they took off and flew over the hill to join the main roost.

One day, I'll have the camera with the zoom lens all lined up and ready. I wish you'd seen them with us. It was breathtaking.

February 21st 2014

grey (bike) and beige (car)

I've chosen a new bike! I'm slightly disappointed because they only do it in charcoal grey, and driving around in Dave's beige car is bad enough. Tell me – why would anyone even *dream* of making a car that's beige?

But hey – I'm having a new bike!

The other problem yet to be solved is what width of seat to have. You may as well know that when I was first pregnant with Isaac (42 years ago) the doctor examined me and said "Plenty of room in there for a nice ten pounder" so when Jim in the bike shop said "We have a device for measuring what size seat you should have," my mind reeled. Not wanting him anywhere near my bum with a tape measure, I said "Oh, I'll just try a couple of seats, shall I?"

I tried a couple and still hadn't found a comfy one so I asked him exactly how they measured customers in order to find the right seat. I needn't have worried. It's a broad strip of gel that you sit on and your ischial tuberosities dent it more than the rest of your bum, and they measure between the two points and look on a chart and hey presto – this is the size of seat you need. But they hadn't got my size in stock (which I must tell you was not the widest) and nor could they order it, and I ran out of time. I had to pick up my grandsons from school. But the bike is ordered, and when it gets here, I'll sort out the seat.

JULY

July 16th 2014

Nostalgia

You know I had a cataract removed last November? Well, in June I had the other eye sorted, and Monday saw my follow-up appointment with the optician. Our optician is fantastic. She is the opposite of flash: she has a tiny office and writes her notes on index cards. She gives you as much time as you need, and will explain everything. She also comes to the rescue with free, emergency disposable contact lenses when you are flying to America the next day and have lost your permanent contact lens on the bathroom floor. Dave and I think she is tops.

Anyway, she said that the reason my eye was sore was because I had scratched my cornea. We discussed how that might have happened, and the only thing I could think of was dust from the Monsal Trail. (It has been so dry lately that my bike is covered with a film of dust.)

"Perhaps you had better stay off the Trail for a bit," she said.

"I can't do that!" I said instantly without thinking.

I walk or cycle (or both) on the Trail every day. We agreed I should always wear sunglasses when cycling, until my eye is better.

When I cycle up the Trail at teatime to my thinking spot between the Cressbrook and Litton tunnels, and then cycle home again, the sun behind me, I love the warmth, the atmosphere, the wildflowers, the views, the quiet – I love them all so much – that I have this feeling that in the future, when I am ancient and unable to cycle, and perhaps live somewhere far from here, that I will look back on these summers on the Trail with huge nostalgia.

It will be like the nostalgia I feel now for the summer afternoons I sat and talked with my parents in their Wensleydale cottage garden. There are certain weather conditions that bring on those yearnings – a warm, bright afternoon, with a breeze ruffling the leaves of our copper beech.

If I were Bob Dylan, I'd express it like this -

Perhaps it's the colour of the sun cut flat
And coverin' the crossroads I'm standing at
Or maybe it's the weather or something like that
But mama you've been on my mind.

216

July 22nd 2014

Meanwhile, at Hepworth Towers

I have a lot of siblings with a lot of opinions, and one or two of them have opinions on my blog – not that they are willing to post them in the comments section, mark you. One says I shouldn't post so many photos of my grandchildren, but he hasn't got any of his own yet, so he doesn't fully appreciate the allure of the species. The other sibling with opinions says I shouldn't mention jam. According to her, I have posted on jam too many times.

Well, this is my blog and I shall do what I want.

We've been making jam. So far this year we have made 53 jars of jam and there are more blackcurrants to pick. Jam-making is part of our summer. We have five blackcurrant bushes and they are impossibly fecund, and people who are jam connoisseurs – and don't regard that pink/red sugar solution you buy in the shops as jam – they beg for our jam. My sax teacher is one, my sibling with the opinions on the pics of the grandchildren is another, my daughter's father-in-law is another. And then there's 3-year-old Lux.

Lux (looking at jam jars): "What are these for?"

Wendy: "They had jam in them."

Lux: "Why are they empty?"

Wendy: "Because you ate it all."

Lux: "Oh yes. I did. (pause) Will Sue bring me more?"

217

Wendy: "I hope so."

Lux: "Me too, cos these are empty."

July 24th 2014

The view from here

Our house is not pretty but the light and the views are stupendous. After we'd bought it, but not completed and not moved in, we would drive up the limestone edge a mile behind it and sit on the grass verge and look at it through binoculars, and poke each other in the ribs and say - "That's our house!"

This was the year of the mastectomy and the warehouse fire that destroyed 95% of our possessions, personal and domestic. The house was our happy ending.

And when we moved in, we loved its setting so much that we felt as if we were living in a holiday cottage, despite our lack of so many basic things like dining tables and sofas. In fabulous summer weather like we have this month, that feeling returns. Last evening we were sitting on the bench looking out over our front wall and our neighbour drove up and said "You look so contented."

"We are!" we said in unison. It is rare, it is very rare, for Dave and me to say anything in unison.

AUGUST

August 18ᵗʰ 2014

Be honest – what do you think of Wuthering Heights?

I first read *Wuthering Heights* when I was 19, expecting it to be a blockbusting romantic tale of passionate love that would blow me away. It wasn't, and it didn't, and I hated it. I am reading it 40-odd years later and now I just find it tiresome, and if I wasn't reading it for homework I'd have long since given up. As it is, I am half way through, Cathy has just died, and I am having a rant about the whole affair before I carry on. Now I see the book as a study in the long-term effects of child abuse and neglect: it is precisely the kind of novel I would avoid, whoever wrote it and however many prizes it had won.

Homework? I am going on a residential screenwriting course next week and one of the tutors has asked that we read *WH*, and watch the acclaimed 2011 film version (yes, that really dark one) in preparation. By the way, I just googled the film to find a link for you and in the blurb under the search results it described it as "the greatest love story ever told." Love? Really? it's not my idea of love.

When I finished reading *Unless* last week, I looked at reviews on Amazon and as always, for some ghoulish pleasure, checked out the one star reviews. I've realised that most readers who write one star reviews of well-written novels just don't "get" the book. And I'm wondering how many stars I would give *WH* if I were reviewing it on Amazon.

This second time around I am expecting nothing in terms of enjoyment, and am trying to view the book in terms of the quality of the writing, and how I would adapt it for the screen. But I do hope I'm not the only one on the course next week who detests the novel.

I haven't forgotten the desperate situation in Gaza. On Saturday, I went on a local demo to encourage people to boycott Israeli goods. A man wearing a grey suit and an angry red face shouted at us - "You dirty scum-bags!"

Who did he think he was? A character from Wuthering Heights?

August 20ᵗʰ 2014

There is trouble and suffering all over the globe

Sometimes, the news is so universally bad that it is difficult to know what to do, never mind what to write on the blog.

August 24ᵗʰ 2014

A day off

The Aging Hippie (in the US Peace Corps in Pretoria) still has no internet, but on occasional Saturdays she makes a long trip – most of it by dirt track – to her nearest town, and there in

Wimpy's she can have half an hour of wifi. I knew she'd be there yesterday so I emailed her, and found myself saying this…

"It is 8.24, a sunny autumnal morning and I am sitting in bed with my Yorkshire tea and Dave is playing his guitar downstairs – Bob Dylan's *Ramona*. I just had breakfast in bed - two of Dave's oatcakes with my homemade lemon curd. Now Dave is playing *San Francisco Bay Blues."*

Then I realised that it is not just "autumnal". It is autumn, and I changed what I'd written.

In summer, we sit outside a lot at Hepworth Towers – to read, to talk, to daydream. Today it was too chilly: I sat in the sunshine in the bay window to knit patches for the worn-out elbows of my favourite cardigan. Hey ho.

The autumn has come so soon this year. Too soon. Most teatimes in summer we play table tennis on the back lawn. Yesterday I had to do it in a boiled wool jacket.

Dave always beats me at table tennis. He beats me at Scrabble, too, and crokinole. He doesn't see why this might be a tad annoying. I have won *just one* game of table tennis in the whole of the summer.

"It's just a bit of fun," he said yesterday. "It's just a game. It doesn't matter who wins, does it?"

"Not if you're the person who always wins," I said. "And when I try my very hardest to play the best I can, it's dispiriting never to win." He isn't a bit competitive, but I am.

"Oh," he said, "I don't try my best. I know you don't like backhand spins, so I never do them."

Bugger. I am even worse than I thought.

The other thing to tell you is that I finished reading *Wuthering Heights* and ~~enjoyed it slightly more~~ hated it less after Cathy's death (the midpoint). I have also watched half of the film, which is excellent. Today I shall watch the rest. I am watching it in two sessions because it's so dark and so violent, and I can't bear violence. When I was little I used to hide behind the sofa. Now I just shut my eyes. The book has infected me, though. There is a narration inside a narration in the book, which I have unconsciously mimicked in this post.

Tomorrow I go to stay in Ted Hughes' old house for my screenwriting course. Whoop-di-doo! There is no wifi there so I won't be posting again until I get back next weekend. No radio, no Twitter, no news. Yes.

SEPTEMBER

September 1st 2014

Recovery position

When I first arrived at the screenwriting course at Lumb Bank last Monday, I was impossibly nervous. I thought everyone else would be young and hip and that I'd be the left–out, past-it, fuddy-duddy. (Oooh, hyphen overload.) I need not have worried. Yes there were a lot of young people there, but they were friendly, and there was no hint in their hellos of "What the hell are *you* doing here?"

The place we stayed – Ted Hughes' old house - was an old and comfortable country house half way down a hill, facing south, with views of woodland and hills.

I slept badly, but there were huge compensations - lovely walks, good food, and a hilarious last-night game of charades. Oh yes, and the point of it all – excellent workshops, and time to write on our own.

I got home at lunchtime on Saturday in a zombie-like state of exhaustion, but at the same time so wound-up that all I could do was lie flat on my bed for several hours in a semi-conscious torpor, neither awake nor asleep. I didn't recover enough to talk to Dave in any meaningful way until Sunday.

Now I am enthused. I'm no longer working on a film version of *But I Told You Last Year That I Loved You*. It's going to be a television serial, and the first task is to examine the structure of the story and work out how many one hour episodes I need. It's so exciting that I'm no longer dreading the winter.

September 3rd 2014

Life is a bacon sandwich

We had such delicious salads on the course last week, that I considered – again - becoming a vegetarian, like so many of my immediate family. But then waiting for the train home on the station platform, another student and I smelled bacon, and we simultaneously sniffed and said - "Ooh, bacon!"

Bacon is definitely the deal breaker when it comes to giving up meat. I heard on the news that every bacon sandwich you eat takes an hour off your life. I didn't pause much for thought, not because I don't value every moment, but because I believe I have bacon-proof genes. My mother lived to be 91 and my father 84, and they certainly never knowingly turned down a bacon sandwich.

Bearing all this in mind I was still rather discomfited by something that happened on Monday when I was having lunch at Hassop Station with Chrissie Poulson, crime writer extraordinaire.

The lovely Lisa, who usually works in the bookshop, was working in the café that day. She's only ever sold me books, but when she brought our orders to the table – an BLT with salad, and summer vegetable soup - she said "Hi Sue, I guess this is yours," and handed me the BLT. Chrissie got the soup.

"How did you know?" I asked, aghast.

She merely laughed.

It's worrying, though. Can you tell someone loves bacon sandwiches just by looking at them?

September 12th 2014

Taking the plunge

If you are over 60 and not completely happy with the way your body looks in a bathing suit, get your fat ass over to Glenwood Hotsprings in the Rockies on a sunny weekday in term-time before 11 a.m. 80% of the bathers in the hot pool there (aka the therapy pool) are over 70 and there is every body type known to woman.

I have not been swimming for 25 years. Most of my children and grandchildren love to swim; some even find it therapeutic. In a covered pool under artificial light and in chlorinated water it holds no allure for me. I'll go further - swimming is a perverse activity. We were designed to walk around in fresh air, not to struggle to make progress in another element (water). (Oooh, I love having a blog - I can be as outrageously contentious as I like.)

However, the main claim to fame of Glenwood Springs, where I was yesterday, are the hotsprings, so of course I took a dip in my 30-year-old cossie.

I went in the hot pool and the not so hot pool and it was fab. Really fab. Doing a gentle breaststroke in warm water so rich in minerals that you more or less float without effort, and

225

surrounded by a cradle of mountains was blissful. If you're ever in Glenwood Springs, give it a go!

If you've not been in your cossie for 25 years, I recommend avoiding all mirrors, however. What you see may come as a shock.

September 13th 2014

Amtrak through the Rockies

When I come to stay out west with Isaac and family, I usually take a mid-trip trip with the Aging Hippie. But as most of you know, she's buggered off to join the Peace Corps so I went to Glenwood Springs for two nights on my own.

I travelled on Amtrak with a rotten head cold, the kind where you're wiping your nose every five minutes. I've not been on Amtrak before and was impressed by the warm-hearted staff, the spaciousness of the seats, and the relatively low cost of the fares. Unfortunately, the weather en route through the Rockies was dark, overcast, misty and rainy. I managed to take some photos through the window, but although the scenery was stunning, it reminded me - in that weather - of the worst excesses of Snowdonia on a rainy day. (I am not a fan of the looming Welsh mountains of dark slate. So bite me.)

We got as high as 9,000 feet going through the Moffatt tunnel, which goes through the continental divide. When you get to the other end of the tunnel you notice the rivers run in the opposite direction, and the weather is often vastly different. On Tuesday it wasn't.

Amtrak is wonderful. What is not wonderful is that freight trains always have priority, and Amtrak has to put up with it. We had to stop for an hour on the journey while workmen finished whatever they were doing on the track, and later we had to stop for two and a half hours while some other guys came up to move a boulder on the line (no-one's fault.) This meant that a six-hour journey became a nine and a half hour one - the same time it took me to fly from Heathrow to Denver.

My cold was getting worse and worse, as they do when you have chronic sinus trouble, so I was not a happy bunny when we arrived in Glenwood Springs. I got the cold from Lux when I first arrived in Boulder, but hey....you don't travel halfway round the world to see your grandchildren to then spurn their cuddles on account of their snotty noses.

The journey home on Thursday was sunny, and I wiped my nose only once.

September 18th 2014

Americans and tea

I don't know if you noticed on a previous post, but eight of my ten favourite books were written by Americans. There are hundreds of things to like about America and Americans, and here are a few: the stunning physical geography; the friendliness; the way waitresses say "You're welcome" and not the dreadful "No problem" adopted by their British counterparts (why would serving a customer be a problem?); the way when you walk in a cafe for breakfast they give you a coffee immediately and then come back for your order for food; the way they keep topping up your coffee without being asked; the fact that they will give you anything you want at any time if it's on the menu. (There's none of this "we don't serve sandwiches in the evening" and no raised eyebrows if you order a coffee and a vodka gimlet while you're deciding what to have on the fancy lunch menu.)

And I love the fact that Americans understand what constitutes good bacon. I just wish someone would explain to them about tea. The default offering in public places, cafes, hotels, even Amtrak, is Lipton's. OMG. It is a right strawy tea – I find it weak and tasteless.

In most American supermarkets there may be a whole shelving unit with packets and packets of so called tea - herbal, fruit, chai, spice, green, ad nauseum - but you're a lucky woman if you can find a decent breakfast tea, such as Twinings (let alone the gold standard - Yorkshire tea.) *Wholefoods* sells them both, but you may have to take out a second mortgage.

A lack of appreciation of decent tea is evident even in the UK, in the most surprising places. One evening on my screenwriting course, a fellow student of the same age said despairingly on looking in the kitchen cupboard and scanning the multitude of coloured boxes containing tea, "I just want a decent cup of ordinary tea. I wish I'd brought some Yorkshire Gold with me, but I didn't want to seem like a sad old woman." To which I piped up: "I brought some Yorkshire tea. I'll fetch it from my room."

I've stopped caring if people label me as an old English woman who must have her tea. Some things are more important than image, and tea is one of them.

September 20th 2014

Coming home

The upside of Dave's not travelling is that when I arrive back at Manchester airport after sixteen and a half hours journey, he is there to meet me - not tired, not jetlagged, and full of interesting things to say. And I know I've said it before, but I *always* love coming home to Dave and to Hepworth Towers, set up our quiet lane on the edge of the village.

These things make up for missing the family back in Boulder, and the gap that is left by Lux (4) not getting into my bed at 7 a.m. every morning for a chat on such topics as why my plum tree only had six plums on it this summer after years of overload, and why Dave thought it was a good idea to wash a duvet in the bath. Lux's comment: "Dave needs to calm down from his silly choices."

I am taken aback by the strength of my feelings for all of my grandchildren. It's not what I expected. I thought they might be entertaining in a sotto voce kind of way. I didn't expect to

229

love them as passionately and as tenderly as I do, and to miss so badly the ones who live half a world away.

OCTOBER

October 17th 2014

Comfort

Sometimes the best comfort for sad bad shocking news is an early morning bike ride on the Monsal Trail. That and a hug.

This morning at 7 a.m. I was sad. Now, after a ten mile ride when I saw only three dog walkers and two cyclists, autumn trees, hills, gorges, dales, cattle, sheep, sky and wet leaves...I feel better. Still sad, but sound.

Onward and upward.

October 19th 2014

Suffused with melancholy

Sad, odd times. Good and bad.

A friend died last week. Suddenly. She fell off her bike. All those who knew her are reeling with shock, and overwhelmed by sadness.

Also last week, it was my birthday, and I had smashing presents and nice times.

Chrissie invited me to tea, and took me to see a tiny travelling theatre company at a local hotel. We sat on the front row and lapped up their adaptation of *A Month in the Country*, by J.L.Carr. The family member who declines to be named took me for a lovely lunch. I cracked on with the screenplay. And I had some fabulous rides through autumn on the Trail.

But everything was suffused with melancholy. And in between times, banks of gloom swept in. Sadness for the loss of a life still vibrant and giving. Huge empathy for the immediate family.

But there was more than that. Have you noticed how a death close at hand, sad in itself, also has the ability to bring to the fore every other death you've experienced, past and imagined? For me, bereavement is one of life's horrors.

Then, one must think again about how to live. Here's a favourite quote of Dave's:

sera nimis vita est crastina: vive hodie

Living tomorrow is too late: live today

Martial

In our Quaker classic, *Advices and Queries*, there is the query:

Are you able to contemplate your death and the death of those closest to you? Accepting the fact of death, we are freed to live more fully. In

231

bereavement, give yourself time to grieve. When others mourn, let your love embrace them.

And the epigraph at the beginning of my novel *Zuzu's Petals* holds true -

Life is short and we have never too much time for gladdening the hearts of those who are travelling the dark journey with us. Oh be swift to love, make haste to be kind.

Henri Frederic Amiel

Lastly, after being a cycling helmet refusenik for years, I gave in and bought one (even though I am sure my friend would've been wearing one.)

NOVEMBER

November 5th 2014

This morning: 7.34 a.m.

I am sitting in bed working on the screenplay.

Dave is sitting in the bath reciting Latin poetry.

I like my life.

November 9th 2014

Red poppies, white poppies, and rain

We (at Bakewell Quaker Meeting) had our silent peace vigil planned for months, so we weren't going to be put off by a tiny spot of rain.

In the event, it wasn't a tiny spot. It poured down for the whole hour we stood there with our banner, which read:

We remember all victims of war - civilians and soldiers. *Let's all say no to war.*

We got very wet, despite umbrellas.

Some sensible Friends wore waterproof trousers. Some wore wellies. Some wore their navy nubuck Guat boots and got soaked to the ankles.

Some had fathers or grandfathers who had fought in a world war. Some had fathers or grandfathers who had been conscientious objectors. Some wore red poppies to remember British soldiers who died in war. Some wore white poppies, a symbol of peace, white poppies, which remember all people – of whatever country – harmed by war. Most of us wore both.

Some of the passing public wouldn't look at us. But we got some smiles, some thumbs up, one friendly V sign.

And none of us got trench foot.

Some of us want to do it again.

November 25th 2014

Love letter

It was so lovely to spend the day with my big sister Kath. Just to be with her, not to do anything special.

And I enjoyed the change of scene – the 50 mile drive there and back through Sherwood Forest and the arable lands of Nottinghamshire and Lincolnshire. She lives so near, but the countryside couldn't be more different. There's not a dry stone wall or a limestone edge in sight…just ploughed fields, some of them already green with winter wheat. And it's balmier there - some of the beeches and birches are still sporting leaves! You expect the oaks – which we don't have here – to be thick with rusty leaves, but not the other trees.

I came home to real post: a decorated card from Lux (4) with a message (which she dictated for Wendy to write.)

Dear Sue

I hope you have a good day and I love you. And I want to take care of you. I want you to have a star of good luck and many good things. You are my Sue and I love you,

Lux.

<u>You</u> are my star of good luck, Lux.

DECEMBER

December 6th 2014

Home on the range

Winter in the country can be a bummer - the dark, the cold, the mud, the leaching out of colour, the lack of access to what's going on elsewhere. It takes only half an hour for us to drive to town, but we have to go over a ridge of hills to get there, which means that if there's an event we want to attend during winter weather – ice, snow, fog – it requires skill, courage, determination, four wheel drive and snow tyres. I can say yes to only two of those.

On the other hand, when I arrive home from Sheffield on a clear night, the stars are bright. And I'm so much more aware of the sun and the moon out here, how their arcs change through the seasons. I like that I know exactly where they rise and set throughout the year.

When I drove home the three miles from Bakewell just after four yesterday, I was bewitched by the huge full moon hanging above the horizon in a clear sky. I parked the car and rushed in to drag Dave out to see it, and then I tried to take a photo of it and failed.

Yes, I took a photo. But could I capture the enormity of it? The awesomeness? The magic? No.

The last leaves have fallen from the copper beeches in the garden, the frost has turned the lingering nasturtiums by the front door to mush, and the Christmas tree is up on the village green. Starlings are gathering in flocks and flying up to their roosting place over the hill and soon we'll be driving up to see their *murmurations*. We're nearly at the winter solstice. The natural world is quiet. And you know what's next?

An ON Christmas.

December 8th 2014

One of those days

Did you ever have one of those days where you woke up late because you'd had four hours lying awake in the middle of the night (for no reason), and then when you wanted to go out you couldn't find your house keys and the last time you remember seeing them was the afternoon before when you were going out on a bike ride, and you hunt around for so long that you're three quarters of an hour late for Quaker meeting, which is only an hour long anyway, and then when you get home and decide that the keys *must* be in the house and you start a systematic search, you find them in a wellington boot – *why were they there? and more mysteriously, why did you even think of looking for them there?* – and then a family member visits and you ask her if the cardigan you've bought suits you or should it go back to the shop and she turns round suddenly and smears henna from a wet henna design on the back of her hand onto said cardigan so even when you've applied sellotape to it and got most of it off, a tiny spot remains so it's not enough to notice if you're wearing it, but it is enough to mean you can't take the thing back to the shop, so you don't have the option of dithering over the purchase any longer?

Well I had one of those days.

December 17th 2014

Darkness

I'm struggling with all kinds of darkness. And I just looked at last year's blog posts for the same week, and it was just the same then, so maybe I have seasonal affective disorder, despite the SAD light beaming out like an alien spaceship from the top of the chest of drawers.

Today I will bring in the tree. I love the tree: apart from being surrounded by family, it's my favourite bit of Christmas.

December 18th 2014

Desperate times

When you're a person who loves Christmas, but it takes you two days to decorate your three foot high tree and you hear yourself saying "Fuck off" to a bauble, you know you're feeling blue. The short days, the cloudy skies, the rain…they're all conspiring to make me want to hibernate. I forced myself to go out in the rain on the Trail for a ten mile ride on my bike yesterday and I came home dripping wet but feeling better.

A confession: sometimes when I'm fed up in the winter, I stay in bed late and dip into my favourite bits from one of my *Plotting* books to cheer myself up. Today it's been *Plotting for Grown-ups* and the bits where Sally tells her kids she has got a new man.

I love those bits even if it isn't the done thing to say so.

Here is an excerpt where Sally attempts to tell her lovable, errant son Sam that she's moving on.

"It's about me and Dad. You haven't been home for so long, I really can't remember if you know the full story. I mean, do you know that we've agreed it's over between us, and he's staying in his cabin in the Rockies for keeps?"

"Course I know. He's really cool, isn't he?"
Cool? Cool? That's not the word I would use.
"So we are separated, Sam."
"Well, yeah."
"I mean in the marriage sense."
"So?"
"Don't you care? What do you mean – so?"
"Well it hardly makes any difference, does it? I mean, you're both past it now. You've fulfilled your genetic imperative and you're finished."

Sometimes I could strangle that boy. Sometimes I could strangle Gus. They are so alike, those two! If we're talking genetics, it's clear

238

to me that I married beneath my gene pool. I am so much more evolved than either of them. I absolutely am not finished. I was very tempted to tell him about Kit and me and the last few days, but I couldn't face his reaction. Anyway, is there any point?

And here is the next time she broaches the subject:

"I told you that he's a friend, Sam, but he's more than that. We're a couple. An item. And, shock, horror, we sleep together."

"At your age?"

"Yes, at my age!"

"Oh, you mean for companionship. Like mates. Well, if that's what you want – cool. So long as you steer clear of the squelchy stuff."

"Listen, Sam. I know you think I've fulfilled my biological imperative and therefore I'm past it, but that's based on the premise that people only have sex in order to have children. I'm damn sure you and Xanthe don't want children." An awful thought struck me. "Do you?"

"Course not. But we're young. People your age having sex is perverted. I mean – how can you even fancy someone when they're as old as you? It's bordering on necrophilia. No offence."

"I'll have you know that the fastest growing incidence of sexually transmitted diseases is in the over-60s."

"Oh, gross. I'm out of here. I don't have to listen to this. It's as bad as listening to X reading out the technical bits from Fifty Shades of Grey."

Oh dear, oh dear, oh dear. Why on earth did I mention STDs?

Now I'm going to get up, finish the tree, put the boxes away in the attic, and clean. Yes: clean. Desperate times call for desperate measures.

December 21st 2014

Bad language

I've just had my usual lovely lengthy Sunday morning phone chat with my big brother, and he upbraided me for swearing on the blog. He said he was shocked. He said he didn't think I used language like that (a four letter word beginning with f) and he was especially shocked that I should use it in public.

I said I hadn't used it in public: I had *sworn at a bauble*.

But it was the first time I had ever used the word on the blog, but the fact that I had done so showed

a/ how desperate I was feeling, and

b/ that I realised it was funny to tell a bauble to f off.

Also, I'd just read something that said it was ridiculous to use swear words in print and to substitute asterisks for the middle letters of the word. When everyone can work out what the word is by the end letters and the number of asterisks, you may as well use the word. I found that a compelling argument.

We then had an interesting chat about swearing and when we do it and what words we use and how it is perfectly possible to swear freely and yet manage easily to refrain from cursing in front of the grandchildren. I also said that I like words beginning with f. I like the sound of them – fitful, fretful, feckless, frock.

I hope *you* weren't offended, dear readers. I shan't be making a habit of it.

This years ON Christmas tree is all done. It's small because it was grown in a pot and will be planted out after Christmas. I've forgotten which was the offending bauble.

December 23rd 2014

Who are you?

Zoë and I went to see *It's a Wonderful Life* at the weekend, a film I have seen once a year for the last OMG I don't know how many. I also have the film poster on my study wall.

The first time I saw it was with my father, who cried all the way through, which is exactly what Zoë and I did on Saturday. The person we were with had a different reaction. It surprised me, and it's prompted me (as a former psychologist) to devise a new personality questionnaire - the *SHCPS* (the *Sue Hepworth Christmas Personality Schedule*.)

1. When *It's a Wonderful Life* is on the TV, do you…

a/ watch it and cry at the end?

b/ watch it and cry liberally throughout?

c/ enjoy the film but feel there are loose ends, e.g. why is Mr Potter not indicted for stealing the £8000?

241

d/ rush out of the room as soon as the opening titles come on?

e/ wonder why they are still showing a black and white film from almost 70 years ago, especially when it's post-war American propagandist hogwash?

2. Christmas trees: do you…

a/ buy a real one, because amongst other things, you adore the smell of fresh pine?

b/ buy a real one only if it has a root, because you worry about the environment?

c/ buy an artificial one, because you worry about the environment?

d/ buy an artificial one, because you loathe and detest dropped needles on the carpet?

e/ buy an artificial one, because they're cleaner, cheaper and altogether more practical?

3. Mince pies.

a/ do you use homemade pastry and homemade mincemeat?

b/ do you use homemade pastry and bought mincemeat?

c/ you don't see the point of making them: what's wrong with ones from the shop?

d/ you think mince pies are old hat and bring the cool quotient down on your Christmas comestibles

if you ticked c/ skip the next question.

242

4. What others say about your mince pies...

a/ they're a perfect balance – in terms of the amount of mincemeat and of pastry

b/ they're mostly pastry, and mean on the mincemeat

c/ they're very pretty?

5. Are your Christmas tree decorations...

a/ all old ones that you keep and use year after year for sentimental reasons, no matter how tatty?

b/ a mixture of old and new?

c/ only the latest, most trendy ones?

d/ you don't have a Christmas tree?

That's it. If I carry on, you'll be getting the same old questions that all these Christmas quizzes have – I mean, I've come across that last one before.

And I've realised that if I devised a scoring system it would be impossibly skewed by my own sentimental, one-sided view of Christmas and all that pertains to it. But I do still think that the first question has real potential for an item in a serious personality questionnaire.

Today I'm going to make the nut roast for the veggies' Christmas dinner; go for a walk; hope the wind that has been blowing for four days finally stops so that my bike ride will be more enjoyable; and clean the bathroom.

I hope you have an enjoyable Christmas season wherever you are, whatever you're doing and whoever you're with. And if there's sadness in your house, I hope that Christmas doesn't make it worse. *Happy Christmas, dear readers!*

JANUARY

January 7ᵗʰ 2015

Who's the boss? You or your book?

The first time I sat next to Dave in the university library 46 years ago this month (are we really that ancient?) I was appalled by his behaviour. I'd peeked inside his T S Eliot *Selected Poems* that he carried around with him like a talisman, and saw marginalia on every page. Except does marginalia include stuff scribbled *between* stanzas and verses, as well as in the margins?

I was brought up not to write in books. Apart from that stricture – which I mostly observe - a book is a book, and is there for my enjoyment.

My good friend Chrissie reads five times as many books as I do and has a library to match, but I stopped borrowing books from her when I realised she is one of those people who won't bend the spine of a paperback: she has it open 90 degrees or less and peers inside it. Like my big brother.

Listen. I take care of my books. I am not a hoodlum. I like to keep their covers pristine, I don't bend down corners of pages, I try not to drop them in the bath, but I am not going to put a book's comfort before my own. I open my books. I want to be comfortable when I'm reading, and I am not comfortable if I am worrying about getting a crease in the spine.

Now I must go. I need to check on Abe Books, the second hand books site, to see if they have a copy of my favourite book in the same edition, *Leaving Home* by Garrison Keillor, paperback, publication date 1989, ISBN 0-571-15240-6, because this one has been read so often it's falling apart.

January 18th 2015

Good morning!

I am sitting in bed swathed in my worn and patched - and yet still holey - eau de nil cashmere hoodie (circa 2007) trying – after a week off – to remember how I write a post. It's 6.53 a.m. Now I am compos mentis, Dave has put on his bib and brace and is up in the loft working on his huge insulation project.

I've been awake for hours with stuff going round in my head, one of which was the job with a six figure salary (with my own driver) that I was offered last night. Yes it was a dream, but I always like to understand my dreams. I turned the job down, by the way. I wouldn't take any kind of salary to swap my current life for a corporate one.

I like living here and being free to decide how I spend my time, even if it does mean my cashmere hoodie is beyond any kind of repair that would make it wearable in polite society.

January 25th 2015

On my mind right now, and always in my heart

My closest friend, my friend for thirty years, is seriously ill in hospital with cancer, just half an hour's drive from here, and I can't go to see her because of this snotty virus. I can text and I can write, and I do. She has her loving and stalwart husband and kids around her, and that's what matters in the end. She knows I love her and am thinking about her, but I'm sad I can't visit and hold her hand for a while.

January 27th 2015

It's grim up North (a whinging post)

People often ask me if I find it hard to make myself sit down and write every day: does it take a lot of self-discipline? Well, it doesn't when I'm in the *middle* of a piece of fiction – novel or screenplay. But at the planning stage, the stage when I'm wrestling with plots and story arcs, the place where I am right now, it's hard. And it's exacerbated by a lack of hope and of courage: am I kidding myself? Can I do it? Am I wasting my time? Yesterday I couldn't concentrate and gave up, and got out my patchwork instead.

Another thing is that more heavy snow is forecast for Thursday so for the second week running, it looks as if I shan't be able to help Zoë out by driving into Sheffield and picking up the boys from school, etc. etc.

Last week I was tweeting about that inspirational book *Late Fragments* in which the author who is dying of cancer can still see the beauty of the everyday. At the same time, I was having a Twitter conversation with someone in London about snow. He was wishing he got snow as often as we do and I was telling him that, yes, yes, I can appreciate its aesthetic qualities, but I still loathe it because it cramps my life. That's how crap I am at playing the glad game.

January this year is turning out to be a sister to February: a month of practising determined cheerfulness, resolutions not to complain, stiff upper lips and gritted teeth. So...I am thankful for my warm house, my kindly and chatty companion, my loving family, good friends, good books, and technology. The latter means I can have a messaging chat with Isaac in Colorado when my cough wakes me up at 4.30 a.m. and I can also send loving texts to my dear friend M who is seriously ill, and whom I have still not been able to visit because of worries I will give her this tiresome virus.

I'm trying to be a Pollyanna, but I am obviously in the remedial class and need a personal trainer in cheerfulness.

You know what?

It isn't any of the above. It's whittling about my friend that's the problem. It colours everything.

FEBRUARY

February 2nd 2015

Interchange at Hepworth Towers

Dave: "You're in an odd mood today. You're not yourself."

Sue: "No. I'm being uncharacteristically stoical."

February 4th 2015

Crisis on the home front

All of Dave's jeans (four pairs) - which I bought in a January sale 5 years ago - have worn out at the same time. This is an emergency. He wears jeans 99.9% of the time, and owns just one pair of smart trousers (Hugo Boss, no less) that were hand-me-downs from Isaac when he moved to the USA in 2003. As a stop gap I have given him my over-sized dungarees that I bought in Colorado last autumn.

You know I hate shopping, don't you? It isn't that Dave hates shopping, it's that he doesn't know how it works. He thinks that if he sits on the sofa by the fire in the evening and says his clothing is at crisis point, and he really has to get some new jeans organised, they will materialise in the chest of drawers upstairs.

He has the same problem with his underpants. I used to shop for Dave's clothes, but it is a dispiriting sport. Where do you

249

think all the jokes about jeans and pants spring from in *Plotting for Grown-ups?*

<u>exhibit 1: the problem with jeans</u>

Richard called at lunchtime and I showed him a pair of jeans I'd bought in the Scouts jumble sale. They are just Richard's size, and they look quite hip to me.

He tried them on and said precisely what I expected: "The waist is far too low." Richard spends the entire day hitching whatever pair of trousers he is wearing up round his waist, and these wouldn't go high enough for his liking. They weren't the kind that exposes your pants, they were merely an inch lower than the M&S seconds he bought off Bakewell market five years ago. "I want something more robust," he said.

"They are robust!"

"I'm looking for something more workaday. I need something that genuflects less to fashion and more to safety and comfort."

"But you're trying to look attractive to women, aren't you?" I said.

He pulled up his sweatshirt and exposed the flesh above the waistband. "This low waistband is an outrageous ploy to dupe the consumer. Dickies don't skimp on material like this." (Richard worships Dickies work clothes because "they are commodious, they shrug off stains, and they have wonderful pocketry.")

"These jeans make you look ten years younger, Richard."

"I don't think I'll be wearing them," he said, vainly trying to hitch them up high again. "They look like a high risk trouser. Edgy."

250

<u>exhibit 2: the problem with pants</u>

He got up from his chair (we were sitting in the kitchen) and tugged at the seat of his trousers. Then he sat down again and said, "Some of my underpants are terrible. It's as if they're alive – I can feel them creeping down my thighs. I need to cull them."

"What you need to do when you get home is get them all out of your drawer, and lay them all out on the bed and go through them, one by–"

"I am going through them! That's the trouble! But where can I get some decent ones? I have had it up to here with M&S Y-fronts. They're hopeless!"

What is it about men and their underpants?

"You need to get something that isn't a standard Y-front, something a bit more 2011-ish. Especially now you're on the pull. I mean – what would Ms Fuchsia Pink think of them?"

"This is where Dickies could pounce," he said. "They ought to be calling in their top designers, even as we speak."

"So what do you think the perfect underpant needs?"

"Security, material that shrugs off stains, adequate ventilation – possibly assisted – and a reliable fastening. It's about time persons of quality gave their attention to the comfort and protection of the nation's manhood. Paxman tried a few years ago – do you remember all that kerfuffle on the Today programme? Nothing happened. Next thing you know, Prince Charles will be muscling in with the Poundbury Pant and the Prince's Truss."

There are several problems – as you can see - but the main one is that he thinks good quality jeans and woollen jumpers cost under £10. You, dear readers, may be able to source such prizes, but out in the sticks the discount stores are few. I have brought home too many items in the past that have been rejected on grounds of cost.

I'm waiting to see who will crack first – him or me.

February 7th 2015

The answer

My dearest friend and confidante is gravely ill and my concern for her is having a weird effect: it's making me sensitive to all kinds of exaggerated anxieties and sadnesses which are focussed on my family.

I'm not usually like that.

I expect it will pass.

And there's a helpful quote from Rohinton Mistry which I found in that book I recently read twice in one week, Kate Gross's *Late Fragments*. It especially speaks to my condition:

"There's only one way to defeat the sorrow and sadness of life – with laughter and rejoicing. Bring out the good dishes, put on your good clothes, no sense hoarding them."

-Rohinton Mistry from *Family Matters*

To that end, I am having pancakes for breakfast.

252

And I'm enjoying looking at photographs of the girls in Colorado.

And Dave is going out for the day which means I can get on with the rewrite of episode one of the screenplay undisturbed. Yay!

February 11th 2015

Current reading

This morning, feeling sad, I googled "Poems to read to the dying" and in a couple of links arrived at Anthony Wilson's wonderful *Lifesaving Poems Blog*. I have been sitting in bed reading the poems on his list. Now, I'm ordering the anthology which is to published in June by Bloodaxe.

In all my waking moments when I am not actually *doing something*, I am working my way through the poems on Anthony Wilson's blog. It seems like an appropriate response in the face of death.

February 14th 2015

Gone

Sometime in the last century I saw an advert in the paper: someone was making a TV programme about best friends, and they wanted volunteers to be on it. Being a bit of a show-off, I suggested to Mary that we should offer, and she, being a shy, private person was horrified.

Mary died yesterday at home, surrounded by her beloved family.

If she thought about it beforehand she might guess I was going to say something about her on here.

Mary could be infuriating, embarrassing, and – for the first twenty years of our friendship – invariably late. But outside of my large family (and yes, Dave, as you define family differently from me, I am including you in my family) Mary was the person in my life I have loved the most.

In so many ways we were opposites. I am driven. She was whatever the word is to define *minus* drive. I could be writing at 6 a.m. She would be eating her porridge at noon. It would have driven me insane to share living space with her. But our values overlapped completely, and as a friend she was unsurpassable. She was a huge emotional support through long tough times in my life. She was caring, compassionate, tactful, loyal, discreet, non-judgmental, and considerate. (Ten years ago, she stopped being late.)

Another dear friend sent me a sweet email yesterday saying she knew I'd be devastated by Mary's death. That about sums it up.

And here's a Dinah Craik quote which sums up Mary…

"But oh! the blessing it is to have a friend to whom one can speak fearlessly on any subject; with whom one's deepest as well as one's most foolish thoughts come out simply and safely.

Oh, the comfort — the inexpressible comfort of feeling safe with a person — having neither to weigh thoughts nor measure words, but pouring them all right out, just as they are, chaff and grain together; certain that a faithful hand will take and sift them, keep what is worth keeping, and then with the breath of kindness blow the rest away."

February 17th 2015

A burst of colour

Some of my family don't understand why I write personal stuff on here: but they love me anyway. The thing is - I am a writer, and writing is what writers do. And I like the Ted Hughes quote: "What's writing really about? It's about trying to take fuller possession of the reality of your life." And the Cecil Day-Lewis one: "We write not to be understood, we write to understand."

Every morning and at periods throughout the day, Dave, concerned, asks me how I am. So far it's been the same answer: "I'm sad. And I feel raw. As if I've been skinned."

255

A few weeks after my mother died, I wrote this on the blog:

EXPOSED

Being bereaved is like being a walking wound. Every part of you is tender. You can't settle to anything because nothing feels comfortable. Sometimes you forget you're a wound and you become absorbed by something outside yourself - like cutting back the autumn garden, sweeping up the leaves, watching three hundred crows wheeling over the field at the back of the house.

Sometimes you go to a familiar place and chat to a friend and forget you're a wound, and you laugh out loud at a shared joke and you think to yourself "I can do this. I can live without my mother and still be happy." And then you leave your friend and walk down the street and you're a wound again. I will know I am healed, I suppose, when all the happy interludes join up and there are no aching times in between. And it is getting better every day.

This morning, sitting in bed, I turned sideways and saw the burst of colour on my bedside table, and I loved it: the freesias and genista I bought for myself the day Mary died. Then I spent five happy minutes trying to get the best possible photo of it.

The sky is clear and bright today, and my grandsons are coming over. It's Pancake Day, so we'll have pancakes, and later, I'll tempt them to walk down the Trail with the lure of ice cream at Hassop Station.

I know that when they've gone home I'll feel like a walking wound again, but in the meantime I'm going to seize any colour the day has to offer.

February 24ᵗʰ 2015

Update

I don't have that raw skinned feeling this week. Now I am dazed and weird, wondering how I'm going to get by.

I had a lovely weekend away in Wensleydale with my sister Kath. We stayed at the B and B we always stay at. It feels like home there, but with better cooking.

We went for long, long walks mostly under cloudy skies. And we had lots of great food, including a meal at our brother Jonty's house. It was relaxing and stabilising. I love weekends away with Kath.

Now I'm into timing my "speech" for the funeral on Thursday.

I'm hoping to get back into the screenplay next week. In the meantime I'm pressing my sunset patchwork quilt, and measuring it up for backing and lining. No, I haven't been working on it all these months. I work on it when it's impossible to settle to writing, and when I can't face going out.

February 27th 2015

Things I can't tell her

I've just been writing in my journal all the things that have happened in the last 24 hours that I want to run past Mary, and can't. And only two of them are about her funeral yesterday.

You know how you go to some funerals and a vicar at the crematorium who doesn't know the deceased (who never went to church anyway and was probably an atheist) talks obliquely about the person who's died, and then you sing hymns that he/she probably didn't believe, and you go home feeling cheated and bereft?

Mary's funeral was the opposite of that. It was rich, full, honest and deeply meaningful. It was - above everything else - full of love. It was a fitting tribute to someone whom her nephew so perfectly described as graduating from life *summa cum laude*.

It was officiated by a humanist who was merely there to introduce the people taking part, and the pieces of music. Mary's wonderful children led a chain of family and friends in talking about Mary. I read out my blog post about her. The room was packed with people who had been touched by her quiet kindness and care. There were so many people present who thought of Mary as their best friend because they could talk to her in a way they could talk to no-one else. I realise now, as I have not before, what a privilege it was to be her friend.

I can share this with you…as I did with Zoë yesterday, on leaving the crematorium: "There are some occasions when you are never too old to have your mother lick her hankie and wipe the mascara off your cheeks."

MARCH

March 12th 2015

The lure of turquoise

People around here are beginning to notice that I like turquoise. There's even an 80 year old Quaker at my local Meeting who calls me "the turquoise lady," and when Lux and Cece see turquoise, they call it "Sue blue." I like turquoise. It suits me. You got a problem with that? (last sentence to be said in an American accent.)

I realised I was addicted last week, however, when I found myself on the verge of buying two expensive items I didn't need. Let me explain.

Toast have been sending me their catalogue for over a decade, and I don't think it's because they've read the *Plotting* books and know that Sally Howe loves *Toast*. A catalogue arrives every month these days and I was worrying about the waste of paper and thinking I'd post it back and tell them to stop, because the clothes are usually so muted you wouldn't be able to find them in a charcoal factory. This means I never even *want* the clothes, let alone worry about how much they cost. But when I had a quick flick through the latest catalogue, two items hit me in the eye: a turquoise and white skirt, and a patterned turquoise dressing gown.

And I swooned. If they had been any other colour, I would not have looked at them, because:

a/ I wear skirts once a heatwave – really. I like skirts, I just don't like tights, and I don't like my legs. Plus I only have one pair of shoes I could wear with a skirt and tights: everything else under the bed is a sandal or a boot.

b/ I already have an ancient but what my mother would call a "perfectly serviceable" towelling bathrobe, and a silk dressing gown my sister Jen gave me ten years ago, and anyway, I have a collection of silk blouses in the cupboard waiting to be made into a silk patchwork robe. So why would I want a new one, however pretty and however turquoise?

I love clothes, but I have this Puritan ethic that makes me feel guilty when I buy new ones, so I don't do it very often. So when I was invited to a swishing party to raise money for charity, my heart soared. And I came home with two velvet tops and a jacket. Admittedly they aren't turquoise, but they are lovely, and I'm a happy bunny.

p.s. I went into John Lewis recently for vacuum cleaner bags and came out with a raincoat, which was turquoise. I don't regret it.

March 14ᵗʰ 2015

Pathetic

Isn't it ridiculous - and frankly pathetic - how fed up a bad cold can make you feel?

I went to see the GP about my chronic sinus problems on Monday, and the next day came down with another cold…which went straight to my sinuses. Plus I've been missing Mary badly this week. Yesterday teatime I felt like this Charlie Smith quote:

"We are often far from home in a dark town, and our griefs are difficult to translate into a language understood by others."

And then I started missing my mother, who died six years ago. Pathetic.

I sent a miserable self-pitying email to the Aging Hippie and got an understanding, loving and encouraging email back from her, a woman who is literally far from home, and often lonely. And Dave brought me a mug of tea to bed and said "You look marginally better. Or maybe just a whisker less close to death," which made me smile. And he said that no matter how bad I felt I should definitely go to the talk about Conscientious Objectors in the two world wars that's been in my diary for two months.

So I've had my croissant and home-made lemon curd and I'm going to get up and get moving, no matter how crap I feel. I may be self-pitying and whinging, but I am loved. And really, isn't that everything?

March 22nd 2015

A new experience

On Saturday I had a new experience. A greetings card display made me cry.

I was in a gift shop in Boulder twirling a carousel of beautifully simple, colourful, block printed cards and you know how they have categories such as Birthday and Sympathy and Good Luck? There was one called Encouragement. I'm always in need of encouragement - you know what a wuss I am - so I checked out the cards. In any case, it's nice to have a bank of greetings cards when someone you love has a need of some kind.

The first one I picked up said "I made you a kite so you'd have to look up."

And my eyes filled with tears.

Why?

My best friend just died.

Yes.
And in my quiet times, I am currently engrossed in Vera Brittain's moving memoir of the First World War - *A Testament of Youth*.

But to cry at a greetings card in a shop? It's weird.

This morning I came across this tweet from Liz Winstead, the co-creator of the Daily Show. I think it holds the answer.

"When life gives you lemons you find out where all the tiny cuts on your hand are."

I think it's quite deep.

March 23rd 2015

Making whoopee

You need to know that I am not wasting my trip to Boulder weeping at peculiar stimuli. I am having a fabulous holiday full of treats and trips and just hanging out with my lovely family.

Lux has noticed that Isaac and Wendy often pronounce things differently from each other, he being English and she American. And sometimes Lux chooses the UK pronunciation and sometimes the U.S. one. She says tomato and vitamins the English way. She knows that what we call sledging, Wendy calls sledding.

Sometimes there are difficulties. I used the word torch and she admonished me "That's not a torch, Sue! It's a flashlight!"

I'd bought the kids a clutch of Alan Ahlberg *Red Nose Readers*, and Lux loved Mrs Jolly's Joke Shop, so I decided to buy them a practical joke. The trouble was that I didn't know what Americans call Whoopee Cushions.

Tentatively I said to the man behind the counter in the toy shop, "Do you know what a whoopee cushion is?"

"Yes!" he said. "Do you want one?"

The children love it. Cece (who is almost 3) and I played with it for half an hour solid yesterday. Every time she sits on it she shrieks with laughter. I wish you could see her. Yes, yes, I know I have a childish sense of humour. I also have a big butt. I am probably the only person in the world who has burst a whoopee cushion. Fortunately Wendy had some duct tape that fixed it, because Cece had been on the verge of heartbreak.

March 25th 2015

The Carousel of Happiness

When Isaac told me last year that they'd all been on The Carousel of Happiness, I thought it was Lux's name for the carousel, because the name was so naive and childlike. I didn't guess that that's what it's really called.

We drove up the Boulder Creek Canyon road on Saturday into the foothills of the Rockies to a small town called Nederland. That's where the Carousel of Happiness is. The carousel is housed in a small building. There are no other fairground rides. All the wooden animals that you ride on were carved by one man, and it took him 26 years to do it. Lux always rides on the dolphin.

They play songs like *Jeepers Creepers* on a Wurlitzer, and you can't help singing along. The whole experience is a joy. Anyone faced with something called a Carousel of Happiness who decides to have a ride will be smiling when they get off. It's irresistible. It really does make you happy. Anyone who pooh-poohs the idea, automatically rules themselves out.

APRIL

April 1st 2015

It's so green!

The only time I want to be rich is after a sleepless, endless night-flight, when I stumble off the plane past the first-class seats – you know – those ones where you can lie down flat. (Oh, and when I see amazing biker jackets in the finest, thinnest, softest, navy leather in a shop on Pearl Street, Boulder.)

It's always painful saying goodbye to my family out in the States. Isaac told Lux I was sad, so she gave me a huge loving hug and said, in an attempt to cheer me up: "Everyone has to die, Sue. And you're going to die fast."

Be that as it may (!) I'm startled by how green it is here in Derbyshire. It's spring in Boulder, but the grass has not recovered from the harsh winter snow. Weather...weather. We were eating outside there on Monday, and on Tuesday night when Dave collected me from Manchester airport and drove me home over the hills, it was snowing.

It's good to be home. It's good to be back at my own laptop so I'm not blogging on the edge. The technological uncertainties and inadequacies of mobile Blogger make blogging on holiday an activity to be undertaken only by the determined.

April 2nd 2015

Today >>>>>>World Autism Awareness Day

Regular readers know that my husband Dave has Asperger Syndrome. It's also known as Autism Spectrum Disorder (ASD). Now it's simply called *Autism*.

Phew. Now we're over the boring bits about terminology, I want to share something: a long excerpt from my novel about a woman married to an eccentric man who doesn't realise until late in the game that he is autistic. A few people have suggested that this storyline is not realistic. I beg to differ. I'd always thought Dave was eccentric and awkward, whilst being attractive, funny and lovable, but it was only when someone else in the family was diagnosed with ASD, that Dave and I realised that he has ASD too.

There is a lot of stereotyping about autism, especially in popular culture. This is understandable. It's a spectrum disorder, which means it can vary widely in the way it manifests, and this makes it hard for the ordinary punter to grasp, hence the simplification and stereotyping.

Good grief, this is turning into an academic paper, not a blog post. I'll stop droning on. Here is the excerpt from *But I Told You Last Year That I Loved You*, when Fran has realised that Sol has ASD:

"Fran couldn't imagine her life without Sol. Sol was central to everything. He was special and weird and she loved him for it. The crazy stuff he said made her laugh. He made her whole world bright with his nonsense – that stuff about sharing a bath with Wittgenstein! If she had challenged him on it and said "Don't talk rubbish – you wouldn't really share a bath with Wittgenstein," he would have said "Why not? The Romans went to the baths together. Martial and Catullus went to the baths with their friends. Why shouldn't I share a bath with Wittgenstein? But you do realise that Wittgenstein is dead, don't you? So there is, actually, no possibility of my doing so?"

Yes – you crazy weirdo – I know full well that Wittgenstein is dead. But the thing was, she wouldn't even have known who Wittgenstein was if it weren't for Sol. She would never have heard of Martial or Catullus. She wouldn't know what a gerund was. She wouldn't know the little she knew about black holes and quarks and supernova if it weren't for Sol. Her vocabulary would be so much poorer - she wouldn't know what meretricious and chimera and coruscating meant if it weren't for him. So much of her knowledge base came from him. He was intelligent and cultured and widely read. He was her own tame polymath. How could she live her life without him and make do with ordinary, normal, pastel-coloured people like George and Fiona and Debbie and Chrissie? .... Was his strange, material way of viewing their marriage due to Aspergers? How could she have been married to him all these years and not recognized that he had a definable condition? Was it because Asperger syndrome varied so much from person to person? Or was it that when you live with someone and adapt to them bit by bit over so many years, you lose the ability to be objective? You just think of the person as themselves – not as someone with *a condition*. And isn't that how you *should* think of someone, anyway? As themselves? Not as a condition or a syndrome or a disorder on legs? But all this Asperger stuff was irrelevant anyway. All that mattered was that she loved him."

April 9th 2015

Consequences

It's all very well living off the fat of the land and massaged kale in Boulder, but not if it means that the wedding outfit you bought last November no longer fits you for the wedding you are going to this Saturday. Oh dear.

Fortunately, there is something else in the wardrobe that will just about do, as long as it's sunny and warm. If not, I'm in for a chill. Also fortunately, the planned outfit was second-hand and can go back to be sold at the clothing exchange where I bought it.

I am going away till next Friday – a family wedding first, and then a jaunt, so if I don't blog while I'm away, you'll know it's because of the inadequacies of mobile Blogger. That or too much champagne. I live in hopes.

I am feeling more chipper today, dear friends, so….as the fat woman used to say at the end of The Morecambe and Wise Show - "Goodnight, and I love you all!"

April 27th 2015

À la recherche du temps perdu

The Lancaster canal - which we sailed down last week - is a few miles from Morecambe where my Gran lived. And a few miles further north, near Hest Bank, you get a view from the canal of Morecambe Bay and the Lake District hills beyond.

269

My Gran used to take us train-spotting at Hest Bank. She was disabled but had a hand-controlled car and she would park on a sloping lane that ran beside the west coast railway line from England to Scotland. She would sit in the car and knit, and Jen and I would climb through the fence and sit on the grass above the line, with our egg sandwiches and our proper trainspotters' notebooks containing all the engine numbers, ready to tick them off. Gran always looked up when a train came so she could be a third pair of eyes in case we missed a number. I loved those trips. She was a fabulous Gran.

Dave and I walked down from the canal to search for the place. It is 55 years since I was there but I knew we were on the same lane. Now the express trains travel at 125 mph and there is a huge metal fence to stop you getting near the track.

We missed the express, but managed to see a slower train.

We walked back up Pasture Lane in hot sunshine and got back to the barge in time for Dave's five o'clock fix of news headlines on the radio. Hundreds of refugees had drowned in the Mediterranean. I was overwhelmed by sadness.

When I went train-spotting with Gran in the summer holidays, I had no idea that the world was such a terrible place where millions of people lived impossible lives, and died in dreadful circumstances, and there would be nothing I could do to make it better. Sometimes I wish I was back in that time.

This month a photo of a Syrian girl went viral. She had her hands in the air because she thought the photographer's camera was a gun. She was four. How must she see the world?

April 30th 2015

Home truths

A friend is someone who knows the song in your heart and can sing it back to you when you have forgotten the words.

Anon

MAY

May 1st 2015

Fed up

I miss *Mary*.

May 2nd 2015

Escape

You know I like *Neighbours*, don't you? As does *Sally Howe*, the heroine of *Plotting for Beginners* and *Plotting for Grown-ups*....

You have to realise, Kit, that a writer can learn from any fiction, good or bad. It shows you what mistakes to avoid in your own writing – caricatures, poor plotting, unconvincing dialogue. Watching Neighbours is educative. You don't think I watch it for entertainment, do you?

I really haven't known him long enough to tell him the truth: that Neighbours is fab, that I love all the stupid plotlines – the amnesia, disputed paternity, blackmail, on-off love affairs, business wars, mistaken identities, manipulative ex-girlfriends, violent ex-boyfriends, people stuck down mine shafts, plane crashes that kill off half the street. And the characters – Paul Robinson, Karl Kennedy, Lucas, Jade – they're like family. One day I'll confess to him, but not just yet.

Yesterday I realised why I, Sue Hepworth, like *Neighbours*. It is fiction as defined by Miss Prism in *The Importance of Being Earnest*. "The good ended happily and the bad unhappily. That is what fiction means."

It doesn't matter how dastardly are the plots of the villains, you know they are always, always going to get their come-uppance, so you can enjoy the ride with a happy heart. It is so unlike real life where evil goes on all the time and there is nothing good people can do to stop it; where general elections are run by Westminster and the media and the people don't get a look in; where you can vote for the candidate who shares your vision but you know they cannot possibly be elected. (ooh, politics alert – this is a politics free zone.)

At present in *Neighbours* we have an internationally renowned cancer specialist telling the resident villain (Paul Robinson, my favourite character) that he has leukaemia, and personally treating him with chemotherapy. And it is all a lie. Paul Robinson is not ill. It is just a plot so that the visiting villain can get what he wants – a new cancer research centre. It is hilarious! It is totally ludicrous and wonderful and we know full well that the doughty nurse Georgia (who has been framed by the visiting villain) will somehow uncover this scam and be reinstated at the hospital. And Paul will recover and carry on being the (cosy) resident villain.

It's an escape from the real world. And I love it! So bite me.

May 19th 2015

Things that have been puzzling me

I've been thinking a lot about the migrants crammed into boats on the Mediterranean, suffering, desperate, and shunned by the UK. And then at the weekend I read that more than 700 migrants from Bangladesh and Myanmar had been rescued from a sinking boat off Indonesia's coast. They were fleeing religious persecution and poverty.

The conditions on these ships in the far east approach the squalor and brutality of slave ships 200 years ago. The reports are shocking. How can it be that here I am safe, secure, well fed, with time to spend as I like, and at this very moment, hundreds of people are crammed onto ships desperate to escape their lives, and they are left stranded, starving, in the middle of the Andaman Sea?

And what can I do about it?

And here is another thing that puzzles me. Last night we watched *Shadowlands*, about C.S.Lewis and Joy Gresham. As I see it, there are two strands to the film – the love story and the religious and philosophical theme. To put the latter into a very banal nutshell, Lewis preaches that suffering and pain are lessons given to us by God to make us perfect. Then his wife dies of cancer and he is challenged by his own ideas. In the film there is a scene where Joy and Lewis are happy on holiday and she wants to talk to him about her impending death. She says "The pain then is part of the happiness now."

I really don't know what this means. Do you?

May 20th 2015

My father

Thirteen years ago this week my father died. I was keeping a journal about him at the time, material which I later used in my novel *Zuzu's Petals*. I had tried to publish the journal, but although publishers liked it, and said it was good enough to publish, it wasn't marketable. I was not famous. I am still not famous, but I've been thinking about publishing it myself as an ebook. I thought I would post some entries here on my blog, as a start. Perhaps you'll tell me if you would be interested in reading it all.

Wensleydale   May 19th 2002

I slept in Pa's room at Kevock last night. I went to the nursing home at 8.30 to say goodbye to him, as I intended to go home for a few days, but he looked terrible. He was in a different room, and was lying in bed looking wild, and though he recognised me he couldn't say much. I sat with him and fed him a few of Kath's raspberries with my fingers.

I spoke to the matron who said I should not go home, but stay. He had been struggling in the night and she had sat with him for some time. She said she knew the signs.

I asked if I should ring everyone and she said yes. Kath drove Ma up straight away.

The doctor came late morning and examined Pa, and told Ma he wanted a word with her. Matron signalled to me and to Kath to come out too. We all trooped down the long corridor to her office. The doctor sat opposite mother and leaned forward close to her, his head ducked down, his voice calm and serious, making close eye contact all the time, and he said "He's not going to get better. And it looks as though it's going to be fast."

Ma said "It's better if it's fast."

"And you don't need to worry" said the doctor, "we'll make him comfortable. We won't let him be in any pain."

Jeny, my younger sister, drove up from Winchester in six hours and arrived in the afternoon. She brought a huge cool bag full of frozen meals for Ma that she'd prepared at home.

We sat with Pa all day - sometimes all of us, sometimes in twos or threes. I didn't want him to be alone. We got them to move his bed over to the window so that we could have chairs on both sides of his bed. Jonty and Rachel came in the afternoon and Jonty sat Pa up in the bed so that his lungs could drain. He also lit him a cigarette, and we fanned the smoke out of the window, though the matron had said she really didn't mind about his smoking.

Kath is staying with Pa tonight.

May 25ᵗʰ 2015

Aging well

I just binge-watched the whole of a new Netflix series, *Grace and Frankie,* about two seventy-year-old women, whose husbands have left them for each other – i.e. the men love each other and want to get married. The series has several flaws. As one example, there are issues raised which are only glanced at, when I would want them explored more fully. But this isn't a review.

The stars are Jane Fonda, Lily Tomlin, Sam Waterston and Martin Sheen. But the women are the main focus – how refreshing – and it's their different images which interests me.

Jane Fonda plays Grace, who is uptight and cold, formal, conservative, and is always, always beautifully made-up, coiffed and dressed. She is thin and beautiful. She looks 64, she plays 70, but in real life she is 77. Amazing. And yet finally (!)

276

I don't want to have her body. She looks fake. And uncomfortable. And you couldn't cuddle her.

Lily Tomlin, who plays Frankie, is the one I am mesmerised by. She is a warm aging hippie, with long thick hair, not beautiful like Fonda, but she has a really interesting face, and arty, way-out clothes, very stylish. It's Tomlin who intrigues me. And yes, she does look cuddlable. And fun.

I think I've just found out where this blog post is going: I've reached a new stage in the aging process. I no longer want to look like an aging rock chick. I want to be like Frankie: to look unconventionally stylish, interesting, comfortable and fun. And if any of you know where Lily Tomlin/Frankie gets her clothes, please tell me.

May 26th 2015

The view from the kitchen table

I was talking to my big brother at the weekend about whether or not to post on the blog my journal about my father's dying, and I realised something. When I'm writing my blog I feel as though you, dear readers, are sitting in my kitchen, and we're having a chat and it just happens to be my turn to speak.

Do you remember last year's sweet peas? How for the first summer in goodness knows how long, they failed? This year I have planted them somewhere else…in front of the strawberry patch, to see if the new location makes a difference. And the compost is mature this time. So fingers crossed. If they fail this year, I am giving up.

But what I really want to say, dear friends sitting round my kitchen table, is this: I really miss Mary.

JULY

July 22nd 2015

Some days it feels as though there are too many dead people in my life. Today was one of those days.

July 30th 2015

Everyday life

Life at Hepworth Towers has been hectic this week. Dave gets up very early (typically at 5 a.m.) and starts to dismantle something downstairs so he can paint and decorate. I stumble down at 6, comatose, for my first mug of tea, and have difficulty finding the kettle. This does my head in. Dave is usually listening to the news on the radio so when I have located and switched on said kettle (which sounds like Concorde taking off) it does his head in.

I am a pain in the neck when he is working on the house, and he likes me to go away. I like to go away when he is working on the house. The trouble is that when he gets the urge to do something he needs to get on with it pronto, and I am not going away until September.

I love what he has painted so far. I am SO LUCKY to live with a handyman. He makes a huge difference. We now have a lovely blue door to the cupboard under the stairs plus a nice new latch. We also have some nice 'new' hooks, salvaged from a demolished school, and we have a blue porch door.

I am trying to ignore the unsightly porch beyond, stuffed with messy etcetera and Dave's poncy bike that's too fancy to live in the shed with mine.

Dave is a domestic tornado. All I have to do is bite my lip, choose colours, fetch paint, administer appreciation, and put up with mess.

AUGUST

August 7th 2015

Blessing

The Monsal Trail has been a blessing lately. When the world feels as if it is falling apart, it's good to get on my bike and go.

And I saw something new. I was sitting on the edge of the Trail looking out at the valley and then I looked up and saw unripe hazel nuts, something I've never seen before. They were beautiful.

I've had two rainy rides on the Trail this week, and both were pleasant. Yes I came home soaked, but it was warm rain, and light.

One time I stood under the tall trees and felt so comfortable out there in nature with no-one else close by and tried to remember a snatch from a Mary Oliver poem, in which she talks about 'the wrists of idleness.' It plagued me all day, so I emailed Megan (who writes the blog *The Scent of Water*) to ask her what it was and she knew straight off…the last few lines of a poem called *Black Oaks*.

August 11th 2015

Grand Tour

You may or may not have noticed that I've been a bit down the last two weeks, and Dave, concerned, suggested I go on a six week tour of my four siblings to see if that would cheer me up. I only had a three day window, however, so I am staying with my sister Jen near Winchester till tomorrow.

Dave, meanwhile, is trying and failing to find the decorators caulk that I have tidied away at home. Sorry, Dave.

I've been having a wonderful time as I always do. And I AM cheered up. Jen is the most wonderful hostess. I've also expanded my culinary education by eating a heritage tomato (not done before) and seeing what uncooked prawns look like (disgusting and grey.) We've been walking in the water meadows by the river, eating out, catching up on family gossip, drinking too much wine (well, I did) and arguing about which of us has eyebrows that are most like Ma's. As you do when you're with your sister.

August 17th 2015

Grief attacks

I was talking to a spunky 80-year-old after Quaker meeting yesterday about grief. Her adult son died four years ago in very sad circumstances. She said that the grief doesn't go away but sometimes it feels much worse. It swoops in and takes her over: she calls this a "grief attack." It's an interesting expression.

I think it's what I've had lately. It's been like depression – waking up with a black cloud hovering over my head, a cloud that follows me around all day. I can be distracted for a few happy hours, but then it returns. It seems to have gone for now, thank goodness.

The only other news is that I have a verruca. Who ever heard of a pensioner with a verruca?

(which sounds very like one of Daise's one-line diary entries in *Plotting for Grown-ups*.)

August 27th 2015

At the limit

This week I've felt like one of those unfortunate teenagers who keep taking and failing GCSE Maths.

I never had trouble with school. I was one of those annoying girls who got prizes for English and Maths and other things besides. Now, for the first time in my life, I am at the limit of my capabilities. I keep writing a pitch for my screenplay, and my mentor keeps sending it back with another bunch of criticisms. Over and over.

Do you know that quote about writing? "It is easy to write. Just sit in front of your typewriter and bleed." That is how I felt yesterday. I kid you not. I was so frustrated, I cycled to the end of the Monsal Trail and beyond, when usually I only go half way along.

I have to write a half page pitch to accompany episode one, a story outline, brief character descriptions, and my CV, to send them off to a TV producer. It's the pitch that is driving me bananas.

It starts with what they call the logline. That is a one sentence description of what the film/TV series is about that will grab the attention of a jaded professional.

I CAN'T DO IT!

I can write a tweet, a blog, a broadsheet article, an academic paper, a novel, a screenplay, and a bereavement card, but trying to sum up *But I Told You Last Year That I Loved You* in one sentence, which shows why it is different from any other story about a marriage under threat – and that includes why it's funny as well as sad – well. It's beyond me.

Do any of you want to have a go?

In the meantime, the world turns and the season is changing. This morning I took the dying sweet peas from the vase on my desk to the compost heap and found the first conker.

August 31st 2015

Not writing but pitching

I've just been making lemon curd to take my mind off the bloody pitch that's been screwing up my brain for the past ~~week month~~ forever. On Friday night I even had a nightmare in which my mentor (who's an award-winning screenwriter) called in unannounced and said "I have five minutes to spare. Let's get your pitch sorted out." And I couldn't find the papers.

The other reason I haven't blogged since Friday is because tomorrow I am a guest blogger on a poet's blog. A real poet, Anthony Wilson, the person who edited that anthology *Lifesaving Poems* that I've been going on at you about. We'd been having an interchange on Twitter and he asked me to write a guest post and I was bowled over and said "Yes."

But it's not the fact that I will be a guest blogger on a classy blog that's been freaking me out, it's what he said in today's post, flagging mine up:

To mark the start of this new season I am posting a brand new guest blog post here tomorrow morning. It is by the wonderful Sue Hepworth, whose blog is essential reading.
Do stop by and read it.

How can I write a blog post on my OWN blog after that? People who don't usually read my blog will visit. Poets will come. The kind of people who understand every one of the allusions in *The Waste Land* will come. The kind of people who take *A Little Life* to bed, in the same way that I would take a hot water bottle and Garrison Keillor. My regular readers know what an intellectual low-life I am. Visitors don't.

I'm a humble blogger. Sometimes my posts stand re-reading. Sometimes they don't. So if you're new here, and what you've read so far is rubbish, you could try my post on *Perfectionism and all its faults*. That was well received.

SEPTEMBER

September 1st 2015

Today's post

Today I am honoured to be a guest blogger on the poet Anthony Wilson's wonderful blog. I came across his blog in February when I googled "reading poems to the dying." Then I discovered his Lifesaving Poems project and ordered the book. Since it was published in June it has been on my bedside table with my other indispensable books.

This is what I wrote:

Writing my way through bereavement

I don't approve of death. I'm with Edna St Vincent Millay:

I am not resigned to the shutting away of loving hearts in the hard ground.

I don't mean my own death, but the deaths of people I love.

There have been only three significant deaths in my life so far – my father, my mother, and my best friend – so you might think that at 65 I've had an easy deal. Objectively I have. But there is nothing objective about bereavement.

My father died when he was 84 and I was 52. During his last illness, when we knew he was dying, I began writing a journal about losing him, charting his last days and my reaction to them. I continued it for a year after he died, to help me assimilate his death, and the fact of death itself. *We write not to be understood, we write to understand* (Cecil Day-Lewis.) As a former psychologist, it occurred to me as I was writing, that a contemporaneous account of grief might be a useful document – a map of grief.

Here's an extract:

16 May

I don't think Ma wanted to go to the hospital again, but she felt she had to go to thank the staff and take them some chocolates.

We went to the loo before going up to the ward, and Ma washed her hands and face with soap and water, and dried them with paper towels. It seemed a strange thing to do, but then I remembered how when we were little and upset, she would comfort us and then say: "Now go and wash your face, and make yourself feel better."

We went round the corner to see Pa, and he was as far away as I'd seen him. He was like a baby. The orderly had to cut up his food, and he ate it with a spoon: great lumps of baked potato mashed up with baked beans, a meal he would have scorned a month ago.

A small part of the journal was later published in *The Guardian*

I also wrote my father letters. The first was to tell him about his burial, because it was such a "good" day, and I knew that (like me) my father would have noticed every little detail, beginning with the trip up his beautiful and beloved Wensleydale to meet the hearse.

286

….All week there was a succession of sunshine and showers, and a gusty wind. On Saturday it was the same. We kept looking at the sky to see if there was enough blue sky to make a sailor a pair of trousers and there never was.

At half past eleven we took two cars to Bainbridge to meet you. The dale was looking lovely, and the river running a full pot. The rain on the new May leaves made their freshness glisten. There was cow parsley and sweet cicely billowing on the verges all of the way, and the may blossom coated the hawthorns with cream. Lady Hill looked its best, in your honour, with the trees silhouetted against the misty, rainy distance. On the green at Bainbridge the leaves on the big copper beech were fully out, but new enough to be at their richest intensity…

Then later, when I was writing his formal obituary and hating writing it – partly because of all the things I could not say in it – I wrote a piece for the Times about that. Here's an extract:

I could say that he was a successful freelance writer, but make no mention of his sometimes less than happy use of words – that his criticism could be scorching, his rudeness outrageous, or that his acerbic tongue could reduce a sensitive grandchild to a pulp.

Neither could I say how fervently he loved his family, how sure they were of this, how much they valued his wit, intelligence, knowledge and affection, and how much they will miss him sitting smoking in the corner being crabby, and then at the end of the evening asking for a goodbye cuddle.

When my 91-year-old mother died it was different. The whole world felt unsafe. When I tried to write in my journal about losing her I always broke down and had to stop. But I was a blogger by then, and my grief leaked into my blog:

Being bereaved is like being a walking wound. Every part of you is tender. You can't settle to anything because nothing feels comfortable. Sometimes you forget you're a wound and you become absorbed by something outside yourself – like cutting back the autumn garden, sweeping up the leaves, watching three hundred crows wheeling over the field at the back of the house.

Sometimes you go to a familiar place and chat to a friend and forget you're a wound, and you laugh out loud at a shared joke and you think to yourself "I can do this. I can live without my mother and still be happy." And then you leave your friend and walk down the street and you're a wound again. I will know I am healed, I suppose, when all the happy interludes join up and there are no aching times in between. And it is getting better every day.

This year my friend died. She was my best friend for 30 years, my closest friend. I feel lonely without her in the world. I blogged about losing her.

…Mary could be infuriating, embarrassing, and – for the first twenty years of our friendship – invariably late. But outside of my large family [….] Mary was the person in my life I have loved the most…

Apart from the journal about my father, the 'bereavement writing' has not helped. It was just something I had to do. I'm a writer.

What's writing really about? It's about trying to take fuller possession of the reality of your life. (Ted Hughes)

I know now that only time can soften the long empty ache of grief.

September 8th 2015

Anam cara

If Mary was still here, I'd be talking to her about the UK government's inadequate response to the refugees' crisis (punctuation intended) and what we could do about it. And how if I wasn't going to be in Colorado, I might go on *the London demo.*

I'd be telling her that Dave has gone to Coventry for the day, and I have an undisturbed day to think, write, cycle, garden, paint my toenails and pack, and we'd laugh about the glories of an empty house. I'd tell her about this jumper I bought from mail order that's a disappointment, and about how my grandson got on in his first week at secondary school, and how Lux (5) said to Isaac about some marbles she was playing with: "Daddy, I organised these hibernating caterpillars. The blue one is the queen" –

And I'd tell her all the things I can't share with you.

289

I recently came across a Celtic concept *anam cara*, which I really liked. It means 'friend of my soul.' John O'Donoghue explains it in *his book* on Celtic wisdom called *Anam Cara*.

That's what Mary was: a friend of my soul.

September 15th 2015

Away with the fairies

Here in the US I have stepped so far back from struggling to write my pitch that whereas at home I was having nightmares about my mentor visiting me to help, and my not being able to find my pitch papers...last night, by contrast, I had a dream in which I couldn't even remember the name of my mentor.

Life is good in Colorado.

September 17th 2015

Home truths

I come to the States twice a year to see the family. Each time I come, Isaac has a little more grey hair, and the girls are taller and more grown-up. (Wendy doesn't seem to change.) And I was wondering what I looked like to them. So I asked Isaac if he thought I looked older every time he met me at the airport.

"It's not that I *think* you look older, you *do* look older." (He's his father's boy.)

When I was little and went to stay with my Gran, I never thought about what she looked like. She was my Gran. She was old, she was lame (that's what we said back then when someone had had polio and couldn't walk without sticks) and she was huge fun. I loved her, and I loved staying with her. She always looked the same to me, through the years, from when she was 65 to when she died at 92. Or maybe I just didn't think about what she looked like, just as Lux and Cece love me for who I am, not what I look like.

Isaac loves me, of course, even though he notices my wrinkles. Lux and Cece just love me.

The thing is — my wrinkles make me feel less confident, and I'm disappointed that they do. I'm going to the London Screenwriters' Festival at the end of October, where I'm hoping to get someone interested in producing my script. There will be crowds of young vibrant people there with screenwriting careers ahead of them, and then there'll be me. Ten years ago I'd be excited. How do I drum up some confidence and enthusiasm for the coming fray?

September 27th 2015

PItching

I have been reading my book on being a screenwriter, and in the section on pitching to producers, directors and film executives, it says that when you're pitching, you should dress according to the genre of your script.

!!!

Which begs the question – what is my genre and how should I dress?

At the moment I am calling it a comedy drama. Any suggestions?

OCTOBER

October 5th 2015

Hug

I dreamed about Mary, my Anam Cara. I don't remember the dream, but I do remember the hug.

October 9th 2015

"Moving on" from grief

I just read *Grief is the Thing with Feathers* by Max Porter. A difficult read for one who doesn't know Ted Hughes' *Crow,* but powerful and meaningful even so. I want to share with you this brief extract because I have a feeling that someone out there needs to read it today:

"Moving on, as a concept, is for stupid people, because any sensible person knows grief is a long-term project. I refuse to rush. The pain that is thrust upon us let no man slow or speed or fix."

October 16th 2015

Vulnerability, violence and me

I'll start with the context, as it's relevant. I'd had a long, draining afternoon at the hospital that had left me feeling tired and fragile, and the screening of *Suffragette* started at 8.40 p.m., a time when I've usually begun looking forward to getting into bed with a book. (I get up very early.)

So there I was with my daughter Zoë, enjoying the whole experience – a night out with Zoë, her treat of a meal and then the cinema. The film was terrific: an important subject, powerfully told, evocative, beautifully shot, great acting, etc, etc. We got to the scene where a crowd of women is assembled outside parliament to hear Asquith's decision on whether to change the law in their favour. He announces that it isn't going to happen, and the women start shouting in protest, and a bunch of police rush into the crowd and start beating them up, (I think) with truncheons.

It was horrible and I shut my eyes, but I could hear the beating, the scuffles, the screams. Zoë saw my distress, and asked if I wanted to leave. She said it was fine: it was supposed to be my treat from her, my evening out. I didn't want to spoil it for her, so I said no. But as the film progressed, I could see it was going to get nastier – we hadn't even got the force-feeding bit – so I changed my mind, and we left. I was feeling vulnerable and tired, and if I'd been watching it on another day I'm sure I would have stayed.

But it did make me think again about how much I hate screen violence. I'm the woman who got so upset at the pictures of the Gaza bombing last summer that I stopped Twitter showing me photographs. You might accuse me of being an ostrich, but I'm not. I read the news and I do my best to work for social justice and peace. I sign petitions, write to politicians, go on marches, and I boycott Israel.

Suffragette has a 12A certificate, and the British Board of Film Classifications says it has "infrequent strong language, moderate violence, a scene of force feeding." I thought the violence was shocking – but I realise now that my reaction was a combination of my mental state at the time, and the shock of learning about *Black Friday*, when the police beat up the crowd.

I get completely caught up in stories told on screen. I am not a detached observer. It all feels real to me, which is why I steer clear of violent films. I didn't go to see *12 Years a Slave* for this reason: I don't have to watch a film about slavery to know it was obscene. That film has a 15 certificate, and the British Board of Censors labels it thus - "Contains strong violence, injury detail, sex, nudity, and racist terms."

Why is it OK for 15-year-olds to watch strong violence? Why is it OK for 12-year-olds to watch police beating up women?

A friend was bemoaning the fact that her book club always chooses books that are miserable or violent, as if a book can't be literary or important if it doesn't trade in violence and/or unhappiness. We got onto the Man Booker Prize and the fact that the winner is about gang violence in Jamaica, and that the bookies' favourite, *A Little Life*, contains what the *Guardian* says are "the most awful accounts of child abuse, cruelty and self-harm that most people are likely to ever read."

My friend wondered if people can't feel anything if they read something milder. Is this how it is? Is the world so violent and are most people so desensitised to violence that it has to be omnipresent on screen and in books?

And why do I feel as though I am opening myself up to criticism if I complain about this? I increasingly feel out of step with modern culture.

I'm what the Eysenck Personality Inventory calls tender-minded, but I'm not a total wuss. I did read *A Long Long Way*, a harrowing and moving novel by Sebastian Barry about the First World War. I had to take a two-week break in the middle, but I did go back and finish it. The writing was beautiful, and it's an important topic.

Perhaps I have too vivid an imagination. I told you in an earlier post that when a boy I know was 8 he was so upset by the *Paddington* film (which has a Parental Guidance certificate) that his mother had to take him out of the cinema. He'd told her that it was bad enough that the bear didn't have a home, so they didn't need a baddie as well. I asked him yesterday why he'd been so upset, and he said "Because the baddies wanted to skin the bear." He feels stories in his heart. Me too.

And *Suffragette*? I'm really pleased this story of determination and sacrifice is at last being told in such a powerful way for a general audience. I know a lot about protest and the history of protest, but I didn't know the facts about the brutality against the suffragettes. I shall order the DVD of the film, and watch it at home on a day when I'm feeling robust.

I have the vote, and I am indebted to all the brave women who fought for it.

October 26th 2015

Wha' happened?

I booked my place on the London Screenwriters Festival in January, but by the time October rolled around I was so nervous about going I was secretly hoping that a medical emergency would mean a rush to hospital and a cast-iron excuse for opting out. I thought everyone there would be young, hip and slick, and I'd feel like a granny from the sticks. Which I am, actually, but let's not go into that.

I need not have worried: there were people of all ages and at every stage of screenwriting – novices to pros – and fashion was not on the agenda, except amongst the visiting actors. What's more, everyone was so friendly that you could walk up to anyone and start to chat, without them giving you one of those funny looks that mean "Who *is* this woman?"

The festival was a three day event packed with teaching sessions on every stage of screenwriting, from first drafts to rewrites, from pitching to production, and every other stage between. There were also writers telling us about their journeys from their initial idea to the premiere. My favourites in this last category were Stephen Beresford who wrote *Pride,* and Paul King, the director and writer of *Paddington.*

But this is what my dear, regular readers want to know, isn't it? – Did I get anyone interested in my screenplay? Yes. He asked for the first episode as soon as I'd finished the third sentence of my pitch. High five!

October 29th 2015

Sometimes

Sometimes the only person you want to talk to isn't there and never will be there. And the violet dawn and the wind-tossed auburn copper beech can't compensate.

October 30th 2015

My mother

My mother died seven years ago today. It hit me hard.

"She is a procession no one can follow after
But be like a little dog following a brass band."

George Barker

Today I find her in my brothers and sisters.

"What will survive of us is love."

 Philip Larkin

The love she wrapped around us is the love we have for one another. Thank you, Ma.

Let's hear it for love.

Our life is love and peace and tenderness; and bearing one with another, and forgiving one another, and not laying accusations one against another; but praying one for another, and helping one another up with a tender hand. Isaac Penington, 1667

NOVEMBER

November 10th 2015

You can call me a baby if you like

I've got all kinds of medical stuff going on at the moment which maybe I'll tell you about some time.

What I will tell you today is that I went to hospital yesterday for an uncomfortable and intrusive medical procedure. There was no delay in the waiting room, all the staff were kind, respectful and efficient, I was outwardly calm and well-behaved, I was there for an hour and a quarter in total; and I hated it.

I have come to realise that doctors can do whatever they like to me if I am unconscious (and they have done lots), but I loathe it when people mess with my body when I am awake. It has nothing to do with embarrassment. It's the intrusion of my very personal space that upsets me, which is odd when I so often spill my emotional guts on here.

Dave was very caring and indulgent and wanting to cheer me up, let me buy a hot roast pork sandwich to eat in the car on the way home, even though he finds the smell obnoxious. And I went to bed for the afternoon and binge watched *Downton Abbey* on the iPad.

Today I am fine. Today I shall go out on my bike on the Trail despite the wind and the looming skies. One life: live it.

(You have no idea what pleasure I get from using colons and semi-colons on an informal blog. When I use them I always think – *Yay! – it's my blog, and I can do what I like!*)

And now you're not only probably calling me a baby, you think I'm a punctuation weirdo as well. Which is fine.

November 13th 2015

Have you ever felt like a dumbo?

Have you ever listened to a book programme on the radio and heard Mariella Frostrup asking a Russian writer why he had used Old English and current English in his novel, and often both in the same paragraph, and heard him say it was because there was no such thing as time?

Uh?

and again

Uh?

And have you ever been waiting for medical results that didn't arrive, and wanting to check your mobile phone for messages, and unable to find it, rung it up from the house phone, and then on locating it found there was a missed call from an unknown number, and thought *Aha! The hospital and the GP withhold their phone numbers*, and then rang both to see if they had left a message and got a *No* on both counts and been utterly baffled, and then an hour later realised that your own

300

landline has a withheld number and the missed call was you trying to locate your phone?

Durrhhh!

From now on I may just blog in cave-woman grunts.

November 21ˢᵗ 2015

A lump like me

After I'd blogged yesterday, the doctor rang to say there'll be no further action. The lump in my body they found five weeks ago is nothing to worry about. It's fatty and benign. Like me.

It's taken a day to sink in. Waking up this morning without the low level anxiety that's been dogging my days is wonderful. Who cares that there's a wind whipping round the house that sounds like a gale in a badly-funded horror movie, or that there's snow on the grass?

What I'll remember is how pleased everyone was with the news: the love.

DECEMBER

December 1st 2015

Rainy day

I realised some time ago that this blog is more about connection than substance. I say this because some of my blog readers write to me when they're concerned about me. It's pretty wonderful. So these days, if people ask me if you can be friends with someone you have never met in person I would say *Yes!*

Yesterday it rained all day. Yesterday the patchy internet drove me crazy again, and Dave dropped me off at Hassop Station so I could use their Wi-Fi to work. I bought a hot chocolate and sat in a corner with my computer and notebook, and it reminded me how it felt to go out to work. I used to like going *out* to work on winter days.

If I can force myself out of the house when it's raining, things always feel better.

I walked home along the muddy Trail and up the lane, where the drains were blocked with leaves, and I cleared them with a chunky stick. It was huge fun. (You know how I love clearing drains. You know how when I am famous and dead I am going to have a blue plaque on the biggest drain down the lane, saying *Sue Hepworth, writer, cleared this drain every winter 1996* –) When I finally got home, drenched and exhilarated, I said to Dave - "I'm going to get my wellies on and take a spade and finish the job!"

But then I remembered the vacuuming, which also needed doing, and which is no fun at all.

December 11th 2015

What really matters

I've had some difficult Decembers in the past, and it doesn't seem to be related to whether or not it's an OFF Christmas. I know this because I've just been reading earlier Decembers on my blog. Last year, for example, was an ON Christmas, and yet my heart was so dark when I was decorating the Christmas tree that I told a recalcitrant bauble to *fuck off*. The world news was getting me down, and the lack of light, but mostly (I realise now) it was my sadness over Mary's fast failing health. This year she is gone.

I just walked in my study and found a hand made Christmas card from the man who hates Christmas. I love it. The only Christmas we have spent apart in our 45 years was an OFF Christmas a few years ago. My big brother invited me to go and celebrate Christmas with him and his family and I thought it might be the solution to the Hepworth Christmas dilemma. The Christmas was lovely but I was miserable. It didn't seem right to be away from home aka Dave, at Christmas.

December 31st 2015

Oddments at year's end

Thank you, dear readers, for sticking with me through this difficult year. Thank you for coming back, post after post, even when I was a misery. Thank you for all your comments, your emails, and your support.

Tell me...What do you wish people, when you wish them Happy New Year? Do you wish them what *you* would like in the New Year? Or do you wish them what you think *they* would like?

And do you *know* what they would like? Creative writing students are taught to make copious notes on their characters before they begin to write the novel they're planning. I have a list of questions I answer about mine. The last two questions in my long list are:

What does she think she wants?

and

What does she really want?

People wish me good luck with my screenplay and hope I will get it produced, and then they say "Oooh, you'll be rich and famous." Actually, I wouldn't be either. And actually, it's not what I want. All I want is to get my story on screen – to share my characters and their story with lots and lots of people, and to see my characters on screen for myself. It was such an emotional experience having professional actors and a director work on a scene from my screenplay at the London Screenwriters' Festival that if/when I switch on the telly and see my characters, I'll probably deliquesce into a pool of mush on the sofa.

And talking of mushy slush, I didn't mention my saxophone in my review of the year. I realised this week that for the last six months I've been working on two numbers *Here's That Rainy Day* and *Embraceable You* which seems rather apt.

I recently fell in love with a poem that fits my year: *At the moment*, by Joyce Sutphen. Check it out.

I'm wishing you all what you really want for 2016, hoping it's what you really need. Most of all, though - and call me a soppy date if you like - I'm wishing you love.

JANUARY

January 6th 2016

Young, old and elderly

One of my aims this year is to spend more time with young people, children and toddlers. I think their energy and positivity will help me combat the tendency to melancholy I've acquired in the last few years. I never used to be like this. I used to be a bouncing bunny.

Do you think that the world is worse now than it's ever been? Or is it that older people (as a group) have always thought that the world is in a parlous state, and there is dwindling hope that things will ever get better? And talking of older people...

Last rainy day I was on the Trail on my bike, a load of women my age who were newbie cyclists (I could tell by their tentative pedalling) teetered past me in the opposite direction. Then I cycled past two male hikers, who looked older again, and they shouted out jovially "Is there a group of elderly women cyclists on the Trail today?" to which I shouted, over my shoulder, equally jovially, "I wouldn't know. I'm not elderly." They laughed. Really, though. The cheek. I will admit to being older but I certainly won't admit to being elderly until I am 80. No. Maybe 90.

January 10th 2016

In my bones

For readers who don't live in the UK, December 2015 was the wettest since records began, and thus far January has continued the trend. We don't have horrendous floods here in Derbyshire, as Yorkshire does. Our rivers are swollen, and some fields are flooded, but that's about it.

But it has been wet and wet and wet, and the garden is sodden. The patio furniture looks as if it's made of soggy cardboard. And too many mornings it has not been light until after 8 a.m. because the skies have been laden with dark rain and heavy mist.

Every morning on getting out of bed, I've been saying to myself - *at least we aren't flooded, at least we're not refugees, living in the Jungle in Calais*. We have a warm, cosy home that we can afford to heat. We have so much to be thankful for. And then there's the fact that we're still ----- alive!

In the last week, when I've been quiet on the blogging and writing front, I've been thinking. Last year was tough. Mary died in the spring, and I had health worries in the autumn.

The result of my quiet week is this:
1/ lots of ideas for stories, characters and writing projects
2/ a decision about what to pursue this year.

What last year taught me, at last, in my bones, is that we don't know how much longer we have to live, and we don't know how long we'll be fit enough, well enough, to enjoy the things we like to be doing. So I've decided that my word for this year is ENJOYMENT, and that means keeping as fit as I can so I am able to do all the things that I enjoy. This will mean forcing myself out in waterproof trousers on my bike on rainy days. But it also means that I shan't feel like a wastrel if I get to the end of a day in which nothing tangible appears to have been "achieved," but which has been filled with loveliness — people, kids, nature, creativity.

It also means I shan't be beating myself up if I buy an occasional garment in the TOAST sale, such as a biker jacket in boiled wool. I've missed the window for being a rock chick in this life, and I've spent the last year resisting biker jackets of one sort or another, but now I've succumbed. So there.

January 16ᵗʰ 2016

Confession

You may as well know it - I've lost my nerve.

It's been a quiet week and I've been thinking a lot about life, death, losing hope about UK politics, the world, the future, how hard aging is, missing Mary, whether it is worth starting another novel, whether anything will ever come of the screenplay. At times I've thought about posting what's in my heart, but then a voice behind my right shoulder has whispered: "For goodness sake, stop talking about yourself on the bloody blog. Readers want something different. It's all very well doing a review of the year and plans for 2016 at New Year, but now it's time to move on. Get a life! They want to hear about what you're actually DOING, not what you're yearning for, and certainly not what you're miserable about."

I'd like some feedback on this, dear readers. All I know is that my elder brother wants me to blog about anything, but thinks I should steer clear of pics of the grandchildren, and my younger sister doesn't want me to blog about making jam, because she says I've done it to death.

I've had an inner ear infection this week. Perhaps that's to blame. I felt better this morning and went out on my bike on the icy Trail. It was good.

I was cycling through one of the tunnels, and up ahead of me, nearing the other end, were two walkers. All I could see were their black silhouettes against the brightness beyond. They were wearing bulky jackets against the cold. One was carrying a hiking stick, and he had something jutting out horizontally from his neck that looked like the end of a scarf. Had I had a companion, I could have said to them "Look at that guy! From here he looks just like a Ninja Turtle! Look! There's his neckerchief, and there's his sword!"

But I was cycling alone, and I became one of those embarrassing older people who make random comments to total strangers. As I pedalled past them, I called out: "From behind you look just like a Ninja Turtle!" Fortunately they laughed uproariously.

Really. I worry myself.

an hour later - I am already wondering whether to delete this post. That's what I mean about losing my nerve.

January 20th 2016

How to read a rejection

I got a rejection yesterday. It's a funny thing about rejections by email. Your eyes register the name of the person the email is from. You open the email with all virtual fingers crossed, and when it's open, you *do not* read it from the top, oh no. Your eyes skip straight to the sign off, because from the sign off you can immediately tell the tenor of the email.

If, for example, it says "Wishing you every success with your project" you know it's a rejection. So you take a deep breath, and harden your heart, and only then do you allow your eyes to go to the top of the email and read the thing properly. Then you take in all the nice things they say about your writing.

Then you close the email and tell your nearest and dearest.

Then you go back to your computer and forward the offending missive to those (and only those) of your friends and family who will understand fully

> how gutted you are;
> exactly the right way to respond.

What happens next depends on how much you were depending on this particular professional to love your project as much as you do. If you previously thought that they were "the one," you spend the rest of your day "treating yourself" to an extra glass of wine, and then a pudding after tea of Haagen Dazs chocolate ice cream (when you usually eschew all puddings.)

The next day you feel **very annoyed** by the reasons they give that they couldn't pursue your project, even though (and especially because) there was so much about it that they liked.

Then you blog about it.

And the next day you think - *OMG, that was not very professional to blog about it*. Then you think - *What difference will it actually make?* And then, if you had thought this writing professional was "the one," you think - *FFS. I am finished, and nothing further will ever happen to any of my writing.*

And tomorrow I will tell you what happened next.

January 22nd 2016

What happened next

The second day after the rejection you say to yourself - *Well, I have other people considering it. It's not as if he was the only one. And it's not as if he didn't like it - just that it wasn't what he was looking for. Tant pis pour lui.*

Then you practise your sax, drive to your lesson, and there your fab fab teacher has got you some new music which she knows you'll love: *Kiss the Rain*. You do. You admire her new sax, tell her about the rejection (she adores your book and wants to see it on screen and agrees the theme tune should be *It Had To Be You*, and thinks it should be you playing it on the sax.)

Then in the afternoon you meet your friend Liz and she takes you up and around her favourite hill for a wonderful walk. You come home exhausted, and at night you have a two hour fight with the bedclothes and eventually get up and eat 0% fat yoghurt while watching an episode of *As Time Goes By*. Then you go back to bed and sleep soundly and wake up as if drugged, but very thankful for programmes that are so gentle, warm and funny.

And then you remember that yesterday a friend emailed and said her husband, who is not well, was re-reading your books in the middle of the night when he couldn't sleep. And you smile to yourself and think - *Yes. Sex and violence are all very*

312

well, and while at least the former may always be welcome,
sometimes the soul craves other things.

January 25th 2016

Weekend conversations

I met some friends on Saturday for a four hour lunch.

When I first arrived at Ruth's house, Ruth and Annie were discussing Melvyn Bragg's radio programme in which he and two experts had been talking about the political activist, philosopher and revolutionary Thomas Paine. They said "Sit down. We can't break off, or we'll lose the thread."

In the course of the afternoon we covered:
Melvyn Bragg's expertise;
Thomas Paine;
the author of a Paine biography;
the McCarthyites;
the bleakness or otherwise of Alice Munro;
whether or not a short story writer can go deep;
Marilynne Robinson;
Elena Ferrante;
chilblains;
The Archers;
family squabbles;
Jeremy Corbyn's love life;

313

my rejection;

aging;

optimism/pessimism about the future;

whether older people like us have always felt the world was falling apart vs the idea that the world really is falling apart;

what we thought of David Bowie and whether or not he warranted the media coverage when he died;

Bob Dylan and other heroes;

Colm Toibin's *Brooklyn* and *Nora Webster*;

what an old man that Annie saw on the bus was thinking;

why Ruth won't have an answering machine;

how cheering is the company of children;

how we thought about bad news when we were young - maybe scared (e.g. nuclear threat) but certainly not depressed as we are now;

the way the news is reported;

how a constant diet of news is poisonous to the spirit;

the superficial treatment of current affairs on BBC Radio;

which Radio 4 presenters drive us nuts;

whether the real trouble is that we have all been listening to Radio 4 for too many years;

the ingredients of Waitrose cakes;

people who won't face unpalatable facts;

how fed up we are with cooking;

Alan Rickman;

which interpretation of the iChing is the best;

whether we are just a bunch of grumpy old women;

how I am (apparently) in the habit of saying "Well, that's the

last book I am going to write";
how long we've been meeting (23 years).

These are just the topics I can remember two days later. But to sum up, the food we ate was the least interesting part.

Another interesting conversation I had was with my grandsons. Sadly I am not allowed to report on this. But I can tell you that they think I'm improving on their car crash XBox game - *Burnou*t. Yay!

Lastly, I talked to Lux on Facetime who was soooo excited about her wobbly tooth and was beside herself at the thought of the upcoming visit from the tooth fairy.

Melvyn Bragg may be the BBC's answer to Renaissance Man, but I am obviously Derbyshire's Renaissance Woman - I can have erudite conversations about Thomas Paine, Alice Munro, *Burnout* and the Tooth Fairy.

FEBRUARY

February 1st 2016

Golden Oldie

In doing some research for my sitcom, I came across this *Times* piece in the archives which I don't think I've ever shared with you. I hope you enjoy it.

315

Marks and Spencer's U turn: succour for the middle-aged male

This may be the era of the grey pound when trendy fifty-somethings refuse to grow old, and avidly scan the fashion pages for what is hip. But there is a sartorially disreputable underbelly of middle-aged men who are unmoved by new styles, and who wish it was still the 1950's when custard was custard, and middle-aged men were middle aged men, in cardigans and slippers. These are the men whose wives buy all their clothes for them, who would like to wear the same thing year in and year out, and who don't care whether black is the new black, or if bottoms are the new bust, as long as M&S still stock the same trousers as they did three years ago.

Since M&S moved away from "classically stylish" clothes, and began trying to keep up with the competition, wives who could formerly swoop in and re-kit their husbands in half an hour, have been traipsing the high street looking for the middle-aged look that doesn't exist any more.

Granted, Oxfam is a godsend: I recently found four M&S (as new) shirts in my local branch for £2.99 each. And in the past few years my husband has bought three perfectly respectable jackets there.

This is the university educated, middle class professional who reached the age of forty without owning a suit, and who took Richard Branson as his role model in dispensing with ties. Some years ago he had an important job interview coming up, and he temporarily put aside his favourite Thoreau dictum

316

that you should beware of all enterprises that require new clothes: I was dispatched to buy him a suit. Still reeling from the idea that my husband would not be visiting the shop, the shop assistant offered me something as "the most up to date style," and was horrified when I explained that I needed a classic design that wouldn't date, as the item would be worn for interviews only, and would be the only suit my spouse would ever own.

Having finally acquired a suit from M&S, we realised that he had no black shoes to go with it. We found some old beige ones in the back of the wardrobe and transformed them with a bottle of instant shoe colour. But during the interview, my husband was disconcerted to see the panel chairman staring at my husband's shoes, transfixed. The black dye was flaking off the shoes, and revealing the old colour underneath. (No, he didn't get the job.)

Whilst M&S have been chasing hot fashion, there has been an increasing danger of these middle-aged men - children in the market place - losing their way. For the past few years, two pairs of old patched jeans have been sufficient garb for my husband's favourite pastime of DIY. But these got to the stage of being knee deep in three layers of patches, with new rips appearing just above the patch zone. One day I heard pathetic whimpering coming from my husband's deep litter clothes storage system in the bedroom: it was the said jeans begging to be given sanctuary in the fabric recycling bin.

He let them go, and in our local agricultural suppliers he was seduced by a *Dickies* boiler suit in a subtle bottle green, for only £25. Here was a garment he could relate to. It was practical, comfortable, warm, commodious, cheap and had, joy of joy, 9 pockets, three of which were zipped.

But the boiler suit was so new, so comfortable, so smart, he refused to wear it for jobs such as mending the shed roof, because it might get dirty. Instead he would don it as soon as he got home from work, slipping into it as "smart leisure wear." At the weekend he would wear nothing else, and I colluded with him, and bought him another one in navy blue.

I was on the point of persuading him that in fact they weren't classy leisurewear, when, by some freak chance, he spotted a men's fashion article in a colour supplement. This featured a boiler suit by *Kenzo Homme*, at ten times the price of his. He was trendily dressed – the only recorded time since student days.

Last week, something similar happened. The family had at last convinced him that his battered sixties white leather belt (with the white cracking off) was past it, and I was off to M&S for a new black one. Then the photo appeared in the paper: Bob Dylan clutching a Golden Globe award and wearing a black suit with a white leather belt. Apparently, "If it's good enough for Bob Dylan, it's good enough for me."

So, come on M&S. Take the weight from our shoulders, and get back to what you do well: providing clothes for middle aged men who want to dress as they've always done. They can

318

be boring and respectable, and we can have the biggest bit of the clothing budget.

February 8th 2016

I think this is probably a post

I don't know if you've ever been to a Quaker meeting, but they usually last for an hour, and they are silent unless someone feels led to get up to speak. We don't have a minister and anyone is allowed to give spoken ministry. It can be a reading, an anecdote, a thought, a prayer, or sometimes people sing. It can be anything at all except an argument with someone who has already spoken.

Yesterday someone who has been coming to meeting for a couple of years got up to speak for the very first time. She said something interesting and helpful that built on earlier spoken ministry. I thanked her afterwards, over coffee, and she said she had been very nervous, and dithering as to whether to get up to speak, but she said she'd had no option: she just had to get up and speak. That's how you know when to get up - when you are driven by something insistent inside.

I was thinking this morning that writing a blog post, for me, is rather similar. I don't want to write one unless I have something bubbling away in my head that I want to share. That's why I haven't written for the last few days.

I could tell you what I've been doing in the interim - writing, knitting, sewing, cycling, moaning about my aching legs, trying to find cheap travel insurance for someone my age with my health problems, worrying about the 30,000 refugees on the Turkish border - but it wouldn't add up to a blog post.

What might be worth sharing is how I have been feeling since February arrived. Long-time readers know to their cost how for years and years I have hated February. (Even the characters in my books hate February.)

This year, despite the execrable weather, I feel differently. I keep thinking back to this time last year, when Mary was dying. This year the thought constantly running through my head like one of those banner headlines under a newscaster is: "No February could ever be as bad as last year's February." And the next thing I think is: "I am still here, still alive. Mary isn't. I am lucky. I get to see another spring, I get to talk to my kids and laugh with my grandkids, and hear that 3 year old Cecilia said on the day of the Superbowl "I would like to be a Broncos player when I grow up but I more want to do fossils," I get to talk and laugh with Mary's kids, I get to sit in the sun and play my sax and share things with my friends and cycle up the Monsal Trail, and laugh at the hilarious things Dave says, and so on and so on.

And I get to walk round the back of the shed and find a surprise - the têtes-à-têtes I hid round there last May after flowering - already blooming and ready to be carried round to the front doorstep.

320

So I am not going to moan about February again. And if I do, please remind me why I shouldn't.

February 26ᵗʰ 2016

In praise of...

Twice a week I go to a beauty salon and have my hair blown dry. It's cheaper by far than psychoanalysis, and much more uplifting. Nora Ephron

I went to the hairdresser yesterday. When I arrived, I was tired and slightly anxious about something. Nicky came over and sat down on the sofa next to me and looked me in the eyes and asked me how I was, and I don't know I responded, but she, being a sensitive woman who has been cutting my hair for 25 years, could tell anyway. Then she asked me what I wanted her to do to my hair, and got a minion to wash it before the cutting began.

I have been going to Nicky for all this time because she is such a good cutter, but also because she is sensitive, fun, and I can have a conversation with her that isn't about meaningless trivia.

At the end of the trim and the blow dry, when she'd shown me the back of my head in the hand-mirror, as they do, she put down the hand mirror, stood and looked at me in the big mirror with her hands on the back of my chair and said "Right."

And I found myself saying, without thinking, "I've got to get up, now, haven't I?"

I said this because it seemed like such a shame to be leaving the company of someone so amenable (as well as skilful) whom I only see for 45 minutes, every seven weeks. And also because I felt so much more cheerful than when I'd arrived.

"Yes, you've got to get up," she said, laughing. "You're done."

Oh, these wonderful people who are trusty landmarks in our daily lives. Dave and I have a local optician and a car mechanic, both of whom we like and rely on, and it fills us with mild panic that they are both on the brink of retirement.

When I was 15, I remember a friend's mother asking me what I wanted to do when I left school and I said "Something useful." She said "Every job is useful if it's done well." And I, in my idealistic world-changing mode, said with disdain: "What? Even a hairdresser?"

Oh, how little I knew back then.

How would I respond to my friend's mother now?

"What? Even an arms dealer?"

Comment from a blog reader
I've just read this lovely piece because this morning I did something I've long meant to, which is to see if I could find out who had written an article in the Times in 2002. It was

called 'A voyage round my father''.

When my father died aged 89 in 2003, my sister Susan sent me a photocopy of that piece. She had written at the top, 'I saved this because I thought it was a good and lovely piece of writing, and would be a comfort when the time came.' She was right on all counts, and I too have saved the cutting all these years.

So many things struck a chord, not only because our father had his own large store of anecdotes from farming ancestors; a love of Stilton cheese, and a temper that could be wounding when things were being difficult on the farm, but because in his unwavering love for us all, he had created a fine and sturdy family ship.

I still find comfort in that piece of yours, even now when my sister's idiosyncratic hand at the top brings tears to my eyes. (She died three years ago aged 61 of pancreatic cancer.) The ship I sail in now is different: I have my own children and a grandchild; how I hope that the tales I tell them from my own childhood and from the store passed down to me will be family anchors for them, and that no matter how irritating my foibles may be to them, that they will feel that the love steering the ship makes it a good one to be in.

I hope this is not too long to write on a blog comment - I have never done this before. But it comes because I wanted to say thank you to someone who has touched and comforted my life from time to time over the last decade and more.
Anonymous

February 28th 2016

Measures of success

In 2002, the year my father died, I found one of my now favourite books - *Homestead* by Rosina Lippi - in a local charity shop. It made me sad that I hadn't found it until after Pa had died because I knew he would have loved it as much as I did. Since then I've read it every couple of years, and a month ago I found the website of the author and dithered over whether to email her and tell her how much I liked the book I didn't bother.

Yesterday someone tracked me down. They had kept one of my *Times* pieces since 2002, and decided to finally find out who I was, and tell me what the piece had meant to them. The piece was about losing my father. You can read what they said in the comments section of yesterday's post. I read the comment (which arrived in my email inbox) in a hurry in the kitchen in the middle of cooking, and it moved me to tears.

When I look back on the time that I've been writing and think of what it is that pleases me most, it's

my pieces in the broadsheets (most of which were in the *Times*);

Plotting for Beginners (my first novel/baby) being on the tables in Waterstones;

the email I got from a literary agent praising my writing in all kinds of ways, and saying how she adored Sol (one of my characters) but my novel was too quiet to sell;

the success of said novel - *But I Told You Last Year That I Loved You* - after I'd had to publish it myself;

the fact that my mother and siblings liked the private stuff I wrote for them after my father died, and then after my mother died;

that my dearest friend Mary's family liked my eulogy for her;

that one or two people re-read my books because they find them cheering;

the friendships I've made through my blog;

and the message I received about one of my pieces from just one unknown person yesterday.

Now I am going to email Rosina Lippi. But first, here's that *Times* piece about my father.

Voyage around my father

My 85-year-old father died this year. The private family burial was a beautiful occasion, the day so special that the first thing I wanted to do when I got home was to write to my father and describe it, tell him what had happened, how we had been and behaved, what everyone had said. So I wrote him a letter and sent a copy to my brothers and sisters and my mother. It makes us cry but captures the day on paper. I don't know why that is a comfort but it is.

But then my mother asked me to write my father's obituary for the local paper. This task hung over me like a dreaded piece of homework. I did not want to be writing my father's obituary, because I did not want my father to be dead.

Once begun it was soon completed, but not to my satisfaction. The paragraphs about his schooling, his work, his successes and his triumphs described the public man. He sounded like a thoroughly accomplished chap (as he was) but I hated that obituary. The required formal style, and the sensitivity to my mother's feelings, constrained me. I could say that he was brought up a Quaker, but not that for the last ten years of his life he would lie on the sofa every afternoon watching the racing on telly. I could say that he was a keen hockey player but not that he had a passion for Stilton cheese and Craster kippers and home-grown raspberries. I could say that he was a successful freelance writer, but make no mention of his sometimes less than happy use of words - that his criticism could be scorching, his rudeness outrageous, or that his acerbic tongue could reduce a sensitive grandchild to a pulp.

Neither could I say how fervently he loved his family, how sure they were of this, how much they valued his wit, intelligence, knowledge and affection, and how much they will miss him sitting smoking in the corner being crabby, and then at the end of the evening asking for a goodbye cuddle.

The last time I visited him at home I knew he was ill because it was the first time he did not say "I had a shave especially, so I could give you a kiss." This could not go in the obituary either: so much for obituaries.

I don't think I ever described him as "a wonderful father" but so what? He was *my* father and I loved him. All my life I have felt as though I sailed in a sturdy ship, my family, looking down on other mortals whose ships were not so handsome and fine as mine. When he died it was as though someone had blown a hole in the side of our craft.

I am surprised that at 52 I am so shaken by his death. I am not a child. I have a large and loving family. And dying at 85 he was not robbed – *he had a good innings* is the cliché. But I am sad for me, not for him.

As children we would roll our eyes when he told us, yet again, about his great-grandfather's heifer which won first prize in the London Show, and then "was roasted whole for the poor of Chelsea." Now he is gone I see all the dog-eared stories of his farming forebears as weighty anchors to our family history.

Searching for written records of them in his desk I found a photograph of his mother: it could have been me in Edwardian dress. I used to hate being likened to someone else, but this photograph has been a strange comfort. I now feel like a link in a long chain stretching back into the past, and forward through my children into the future. My father may be gone, but he is still a valid link. He may no longer sit at the head of the table repeating his catch-phrase "As good a Stilton as I've tasted in years," but at future family gatherings one of us can say it for him. "Only if the cheese merits it," says my brother. Ah, that critical gene again.

MARCH

March 18th 2016

My daughter in law

It takes two margaritas to get me drunk. I only get drunk twice a year and I am always with Wendy (my daughter-in-law) when it happens. Today in Boulder we had four inches of snow. Wendy was busy and the kids were at school, and Wendy treated me to a pedicure. She paid for an uber taxi to take me to the salon and paid for the pedicure and picked me up afterwards and took me to lunch and got me drunk on margaritas. Everything seems possible when you are drunk on margaritas. For one thing, it's the only time I don't feel old. After lunch we visited the wonderful Boulder Bookstore, half a block away. Cece held my hand very tight to stop me falling over on the snowy pavement. When we got there the kids and Wendy rushed off to the children's section and I stood mesmerised by the bestsellers at the front of the store and nearly bought three, at $25 (before tax) a pop. I wanted *When Breath Becomes Air*, *My Name is Lucy Barton* and Billy Collins' *Aimless Love*. I restrained myself. It was touch and go. Then I dallied with some silly, funny fridge magnets...things I would never think of buying if I were sober. Then I asked at the desk for a book I was looking for and the assistant asked if I would like her to find it for me. "Yes," I said. "Thank you. My daughter-in-law got me drunk on margaritas and I am fit for nothing."

You should all have a wonderful daughter-in-law like Wendy.

March 25th 2016

Missing persons

OK. I've had my three days R and R, my peace and quiet, my catching up on my writing, my lengthy chats with Dave. Now I want my small companions back. The ones who get into my bed for a chat at 7 in the morning, the ones who make me laugh, who practise their English accents - "pyjamas, bananas, tomatoes" - who want to hear funny stories about Dave, whose stuffies litter the house, who like to play hibernating bunnies on the bedroom floor and who like *The Sun Has Got His Hat On* played on the iPad to wake them up for spring, who want me to read the same book over and over, which is fine because it's usually a book I like (e.g. Ahlberg's *Funnybones* and Ahlberg's *Tell Me A Story*), who persuade me to go swimming with them and entice me down the long slide, when I detest going swimming in an indoor pool.

Lux and Cece, I miss you!

APRIL

April 2ⁿᵈ 2016

Facts of life

Lux (5) was explaining to Cecilia (3) how everything moves on and everything dies: "Even I will be dead and gone one day, Cecilia. And all the things that are past are in the memory box. Like my memories of when I was four. That was a happy time. And now I'm five, I have to understand more things and it's harder."

I'm 66 and I feel just the same. But I would like to be five again and get out of bed in the morning and walk downstairs for breakfast without being aware of my body in any way.

It needs focused, concentrated effort to ignore all the twinges that signal its deterioration, as well as cultivating positivity and hope in the face of the current state of the world. That's why having something that absorbs me completely - playing with the children, writing a sitcom, or trying to cycle to the top of Longstone Edge without getting off my bike - is such a blessing.

This isn't meant to be another whinging post, more a recognition of what's involved in being a cheerful older person. I told a friend recently that I was looking forward to being 70 because I'd feel able to sit by the fire and knit or read on a biting afternoon and not feel compelled to do anything more creative or energetic. But actually, I don't think that will be possible because of my mother's genes. I remember ringing her up one teatime when she was 90 and she said she felt awfully guilty because all she had done that afternoon was light the fire, read the paper, and do the codewords.

April 12th 2016

Sibling rivalry

I had a wonderfully entertaining and cheering hour-long phone conversation with my little sister yesterday, in which critiques of *The Archers* and *Neighbours* played only a part. There were a lot of laughs, and various bits of personal stuff. The things I can divulge are... we both think the present Tony Archer is even wetter than the one they had before, and we agree that Kyle should not have flown off to Germany with Georgia, and why on earth did he take the dog?

Back to basics. The chat with Jen started something like this:

JEN: Hello. How are you?

ME: I'm OK. I'm trying to be a stoic like you and Ma.

JEN: What have you got to be stoical about?

ME: I'm OK. I'm fine. Tell me how you are.

JEN: I can't complain.

She and Pete and Kath and me are going up to stay in Wensleydale soon. Jonty lives there and we'll see him, too. I am so excited! Five go camping! Well, OK, five stay in a holiday cottage which is a converted barn on the farm where our grandfather, great grandfather and great great grandfather lived. Cool, or what?

I just emailed a photo of me and my sister Jen in her open top car to Isaac and Wendy and they responded thus…

Wendy: *Look at you two babes! Hot mamas on the road, watch out!*

Isaac: *Lovely picture. You look a lot like gran!*

I think it's clear why I am so fond of my daughter-in-law.

MAY

May 13th 2016

Me and my sax

When I started learning to play the sax at the age of 60, I never wanted to perform. I just wanted to play for me. Then a couple of years ago someone asked me to join a new band and I went to three rehearsals and loved it, but then I realised that if I continued I'd be driving home from Sheffield over the moors in all weathers after late night gigs, and I cried off. I would love to play with another musician in private though. I have just never found that person.

Mel, my sax teacher, is getting married in July and she's asked some of her students to play at her reception - solos. I am one of those students. I love Mel so I've said yes, but I'm petrified.

I have never played in public before. I told her the tune I'd like to play at my lesson yesterday and set about playing it. I've been practising it all week and playing it perfectly at home, but in her music room - with her standing behind me so I could pretend she wasn't there - I bungled it because of nerves: I so wanted her to be pleased.

She said that it's much harder playing for just one person than it is for a crowd, and that I shouldn't worry. Hmm. She's full of encouraging baloney.

I always play better in the morning than the evening, but the open mic set at the reception (during which I'll be playing) starts at 5 p.m. when my intellectual capabilities are at the brink of their inexorable slide into the daily abyss. That means I'll need a rest in the afternoon, then a coffee to wake me up, and just before I go on a glass of wine to relax me. I'm going to be seriously self-medicated. If I feel on the day that it's something I just can't do, she says that of course she understands.

I'd like to do Mel proud. She's been a fantastic teacher. She is encouraging and understanding and has no agenda of her own. She sees herself as an enabler - to get us to enjoy playing the sax in the way we want to do, playing the music we like. And I do. Kudos to Mel!

Wish me luck, you guys. I'll let you know what happens.

May 17th 2016

Bits and bats - the news from Hepworth Towers

It has been a quiet week at Hepworth Towers.

The table tennis table has been on the lawn for a fortnight but we've only played three times because the senior batsman has insisted it's been far too breezy to play. He has also been hassling me to buy a new bat.

He wanted a new bat and said I needed one too, but that I needed to choose my own. I didn't care about bats. I just wanted to play. Could he not just buy me a bat? Any old bat. But he insisted I had to choose my own, because if he got one for me I would complain it was too heavy, or too light, or the handle wasn't comfortable or the colour was wrong. He obviously sees me as some sort of Goldilocks, or perhaps a Princess with a Pea.

Anyway...we went to Sheffield together yesterday and called in at a sports supermarket and although there was nothing classy enough for him to bat with, I bought one. The brand is STIGA - and the name of the bat is FRENZY, and it has FIVE STARS.

Well....you know how Dave always beats me at everything? Last night he didn't. I actually won some games - all on account of the new bat. The trouble is that when he gets his new bat, we'll be back to square one. My edge will have gone, and he will be winning every game again.

The reason we went to Sheffield was to take my old bike to a workshop that fixes up bikes for asylum seekers. The guy in charge came out of the workshop to take the bike from me and said "Thank you," and I told him it was in good working order, but I'd got a new bike.

He was about to go back in and then a thought struck him. "This bike might just suit an asylum seeker who is here right now, working on another bike." My heart fluttered. He leaned inside the workshop and called to someone. How wonderful to actually meet the person who would have my bike. How often do you get to meet a stranger you help? I absolutely wasn't looking for thanks, just the personal connection. The guy came out, he was about my height, and peered at my bike. Then he said "I'm happy with the one inside, thanks." A slim chance. But it was a very nice idea - and I liked the workshop guy for thinking of it.

Some other news is that I washed the porch floor last week and went out somewhere, and when I came home, Dave's two hideous boxes of rammel had gone and the porch looked beautiful. Dave was in his shed sorting through said rammel and later presented me with a new string dispenser made from an old cafetiere plunger.

The last bit of news is that a kind friend, wanting to cheer up a miserable me, is taking me to the ballet tomorrow at the Royal Opera House in London. There will be dressing up, champagne, music, dancing, and Frankenstein. Beat that!

I am so excited!

May 20th 2016

A very lucky country mouse goes to town

When Zoë and Isaac still lived and worked in London, I loved going to visit. They'd shepherd me to where I wanted to go, and take me out to cool new places too, and it was huge fun. They both moved to other places years ago, and since then I've thought of London as a place I don't much like, where I only go when there's a demo I simply have to attend, or an exhibition I'd kick myself if I missed, or a screenwriting festival I want to pitch at, or there's a visiting aging hippie who wants to meet me. I tend to feel alienated, tense and lonely when I'm alone in London.

Thanks to my friend who lives there, I'm beginning to like London again. I got back from there last night. My friend had invited me to stay at her flat overlooking the Thames, and to go to the ballet with her. Oh wow. Frankenstein at the Royal Opera House, along with champagne and dinner. I'd never read Frankenstein nor seen a dramatisation of it, and all I knew of the story was that someone created a scary creature. I'd seen photographs of Boris Karloff as that creature.

I had the most wonderful time. It was lovely to spend the afternoon catching up, and then at teatime to head to the ballet. We had fantastic seats - the middle of the stalls, five rows from the front. I could see every muscle move. I could see the facial expressions of the dancers. I could feel overwhelmed by it. The stage sets and special effects were stunning, and the story was sad and moving. I'm still pondering it. It was a mega treat being there on Wednesday night - all of it. Thank you, Het.

The following morning we walked along the south bank of the Thames to a Mona Hatoum exhibition at the Tate Modern. She's a Palestinian video and installation artist. Her work is political, provocative and often chilling and I'm still thinking about some of the messages in what we saw. One of her many exhibits was a keffeh (a traditional Arabian headdress) woven of human hair. That's the easiest piece to describe. I don't want to go into the many pieces that had an impact on me, but I do recommend the exhibition.

Now I'm back home in green, green Derbyshire. I've been up the Trail on my bike, heard so many blackbirds singing, and pulled out some dandelions on the back path. I love being here. But London was very, very stimulating, and I'm looking forward to another trip some time - perhaps this year - to charge my interest circuits.

I feel refreshed.

May 22nd 2016

Acting on advice

You know that my sax teacher wants me to play a solo at her wedding reception, don't you? And you know that when I play in public I am paralysed by nerves? Well Dave and (independently) my friend Het suggested I force myself to play to as many people as possible between now and the wedding, in order to get past the nerves.

So yesterday, I took my sax and my backing track to Ruth's house where we were having lunch with two other friends. We had lunch, and decided which of Kent Haruf's novels we liked the best, and various similar matters, and then they told me to get out my sax and play. I played a tune and only made one mistake. They were very encouraging; they said it sounded good and if I hadn't pulled a face at the mistake, they wouldn't have noticed. In the middle of my second tune there was a knock at the back door. Ruth lives in a terraced house and you can see through the window who is at the door. It was four burly firemen.

They were calling on everyone in the street to talk about fire prevention because there'd recently been a local house fire. Ruth invited them in and they checked her fire alarms and gave advice, all while Muggins was standing in the corner with her sax.

Guess what happened next?

Yep. They asked me to play, and I did. Would you believe this story if it was in a novel?

I told my 9-year-old grandson about it. "Isn't it funny?" I said.

"I don't know if it's funny," he said. "It's random."

JUNE

June 7ᵗʰ 2016

The fat of the land

The sun is out, and it won't be out tomorrow. I love these lush green days in June when I can eat breakfast outside, play table tennis on the back lawn in my bare feet, and it's objectively too hot to garden until 8 p.m. And even when I've finished watering the sweet peas, it's too nice to come inside so I practise on the slackline in the stillness of the balmy evening. And the blackbird is still singing at half past nine.

June 22ⁿᵈ 2016

Always read the washing instructions

When we bought the sleeping bags for our asylum seeker visitors to sleep in at Quaker meeting, the woman in the shop assured us you could wash them in the machine.

When I collected up said sleeping bags for washing, I checked the instructions on the label. Yes, you can wash them in a machine - an industrial machine. So I went to the cleaners in Sheffield and they quoted me £12.70 per sleeping bag, or, if I did it myself in their large machines, it would work out around £20 for the lot. But the machines were not always free, and as I live half an hour away, I couldn't easily pack five sleeping bags into the car and pop in on the off chance.

So yesterday, I washed and rinsed one in the bath, and spun it in our machine. Then it went on the line. I'm hoping it will be dry enough to pack away in a couple of days. Only four more to go.

As I was swishing it around in the bath, my thoughts drifted to the memory of Dave washing the duvet in the bath. This is what happened. Completely true.

He called my bluff

No sooner had I finished writing an article on my longings for an empty nest (which incidentally the fledgling had checked and edited before I sent it off) than he called my bluff. My 18-year-old cares nothing for the current trend of young adults living forever at home. A friend had phoned and asked if he'd like to share a house with her. His eyes lit up. My eyes lit up. It was hard to know who was the more excited.

He went to his room to pack but then returned to say that his duvet needed washing before he went. The laundrette has just closed down in our local town and now the nearest is 15 miles away, so I rang Sketchley, who quoted me £15.99 and two weeks to wash the duvet.

"£15.99?" said my husband, horrified. He'd just been checking our dwindling Isas and decided we should combine the boy's leaving with an economy drive which would begin with the easy cuts of (1) cancelling *Kerrang,* and (2) shunning supermarkets, now we won't need to buy junk food.

Then he had an idea: "I'll wash the duvet. That will save money."

"But it's a double one," I said. "It won't fit in our machine."

"I'll do it by hand in the fun tub." (A fun tub, dear reader, is a huge plastic tub - three feet high and three feet across - in which builders put rubble, and which my husband uses for his DIY.) But the fun tub was languishing in the shed stuffed with used plastic cartons, which would one day "come in useful," so he decided to use the bath, which is more commodious and also has (of course) running hot water.

He swung the duvet into the bath and started to run the taps, but the duvet behaved like a giant sponge and soaked up every drop of water. He couldn't swish it around to make a washing motion, and had to bend right over and pummel the thing. It was like wrestling with an alligator, with my husband looking less like Paul Hogan and more like an also-ran in a wet T shirt competition.

Even when rinsed and squeezed it was so heavy that my husband - a strapping chap who is as strong as a pair of Charlie

341

Dimmocks - found it hard to pick up. He had to bundle it up and clutch it to his chest like one of the contestants in The *Strongest Man in the World* competition in that event where they stagger for a hundred metres carrying a boulder as big as a buffalo.

The plan was to go down the stairs with it, through the open front door, and outside to the washing line. But he slipped just two steps from the bottom, lurched forwards and squeezed the duvet between himself and the wall, depositing three gallons of water on the hall floor.

And to think I'd been harbouring a fear that life might be a tad dull when my son left home.

Eventually he got the duvet outside and edged it bit by bit over the washing line, which then swooped grasswards in a giant parabola, though miraculously the trees to which it was tied remained rooted. It only took three days to dry.

With the duvet sorted everything else was simple. My son has been moving his stuff in bits and bats, and last night after tea he took himself. We drove three miles through the fog and the dripping wetness of the October night and I left him at the bus stop for his ride into town and his new house.

The empty nest is a strange place. I cannot think of another life event which combines such wildly conflicting emotions. Unaccustomed feelings of lightness and liberation sweep in, only to be edged aside by drifts of haunting wistfulness at the thought of the baby of the family growing up and leaving.

342

I gave him the biggest hug of his life in the hall before we left, because there wouldn't be room in the car for a proper one, while the duvet-washer (aka his Dad) stood with his arms folded and said: "A whole new exciting stage of life."

"Aren't you going to say '*Good luck* with your new exciting stage of life'?" I asked.

"I was thinking about me," said his Dad.

June 24th 2016

AWOL

I was lying in bed last night unable to sleep, writing a blog post in my head about the dearth of sitcoms on telly that make me laugh.

This morning I have woken to the appalling news that we are leaving the EU, and I am too upset to write a post that isn't a rant, and I am sure that you don't want a rant.

As Blackadder said:

"I believe the phrase rhymes with clucking bell."

JULY

July 19ᵗʰ 2016

Sax in public

It was my sax teacher Mel's wedding on Sunday. Do you recall she asked if I would play a solo at her reception? (She'd asked half a dozen of her other students too and told us that we could bottle out on the day if we couldn't face it.)

I was talking to a couple of fellow wedding guests immediately after the ceremony about playing the sax, solo, in public, and how nervous I was, and how it is not something I have yearned to do. I just wanted to play the sax for me. And the woman said "Oh, everyone should have playing in public on their bucket list." I bridled inwardly, thinking, *Surely the thing about a bucket list is that it is deeply personal and there are no universal shoulds or shouldn'ts.* For the record - I have two remaining items on my bucket list - to go camping with my younger brother, and to do a US road trip with my fabulous daughter-in-law Wendy (she of the margarita episode).

Mel's wedding reception was in the evening and I came home to get changed into fitted black trousers, a black top with a fifties neckline (it was a fifties-themed wedding) plus large funky earrings and a leather bracelet.

I thought I looked ace, until I saw the photo of me taken at a distance, when all I could see was a grey haired woman (whose hair wasn't doing what it should have been) wearing reading glasses, which were way more prominent than her funky earrings. This is why I am giving you a photo of the jewellery and not of me wearing them. I always think I look better than I actually do - it's like a reverse of the body image problem that anorexics have, but at least it means I get a little confidence boost.

I waited for my turn to play, shaking imperceptibly and with my heart thumping harder than I can remember it doing before. The last three times I'd practised *Ain't Misbehavin'* at home I had fluffed a bar, the *same* bar.

I am used to speaking in public and am rarely phased by it. I can always make a self-deprecating joke to get the audience on my side. But playing a solo in public is different. There is no space for jokes.

Well....I played! I smudged the same bar, and I lost the timing for two bars in *As Time Goes By*, but I picked up just fine and Zoë (who was there for moral support) said that Joe Public didn't clock a damn thing (ref. *Acorn Antiques*.)

Mel was delighted, which made it all worth it. But I don't want to do it again.

July 20th 2016

Confession

Every time we sit outside on a warm summer evening (which is twice so far this crappy-weather-year) I say to Dave "Ooh, I'd love to sleep outside!" but at that point I'm too tired to go ransacking the shed for the tent, which hasn't been used for seven years, since the family member who declines to be named went round Europe with his friends.

Yesterday it was baking hot from 6 a.m. so I knew it would be a lovely evening, and when I got home from my early bike ride, I found the tent, and ~~Dave helped me put it up~~ I helped Dave put it up, and then I remembered how I can't sleep on the cold hard ground (like the woman in the folk song can when she runs off with the gypsy) because I'm a princess-and-a-pea kind of person, and I persuaded Dave to bring down a single mattress from upstairs.

I took down a duvet and a pillow, and at 10 o' clock I went outside and zipped myself in and settled down to sleep. But it was SO hot last night, that it was hotter and stuffier in the tent than it had been in the bedroom with the windows wide open. And the mattress was not as comfy as the one I usually sleep on, and....

Why didn't I open the tent flaps and get some fresh air? you might ask. I didn't, because I didn't want any kind of creatures, tiny or bigger, joining me in the tent. After two hours of lying in the dark, sweltering, not going to sleep, I decided to give up.

346

I stepped outside the tent into a little more air and looked up at the sky, which was dappled with cloud. It was beautiful. Everything was still and quiet. Then I went inside to bed and went to sleep.

A question I am currently considering is: "Are there any advantages to getting older?" My first response to the question was "Only one: grandchildren." But I think there are more. One is the ability to accept one's limitations and not to be embarrassed or ashamed of them. That is why I am telling you about the failed outdoor sleeping adventure. As I was lying there outside, not sleeping, I decided that I could stay out there and save face and have a terrible night and wake up to the warm sunrise and the fresh air - the best bit about camping - and then be wrecked for the rest of the day on account of lack of sleep, OR I could give up and come inside and avoid laying waste to today. So now I am going to get dressed and pick blackcurrants before it gets any hotter.

And if you're wondering how I am going to fare on the camping trip with my brother (see last post) I will just say that there is more to camping with Jonty than sleeping in a tent. Plus it won't be so hot in August, or probably ever again.

AUGUST

August 9th 2016

PR for peace

Bakewell Quaker Meeting had a silent peace vigil last Saturday for Hiroshima Day. It was wonderfully hot and sunny. We always stand by the pedestrian bridge by the river Wye, over which the hundreds of tourists walk on their way from the biggest car park. They see a bunch of Quakers standing silently holding placards and wonder what's going on. Some try to read the slogans, some walk straight past, eyes ahead, some stop and stare. Occasionally someone will take a photo - one time it was a teacher taking the photo to discuss with her class, and last week it was a visitor from Northern Ireland who thought what we were doing was worthwhile.

Children are generally interested. Some parents hurry them away, wordlessly. Some parents stop and explain what is going on and why we are there and what the placards mean.

Some visitors are struck first by the powerful silence and then realise what is going on. They have told us this.

On Saturday a friend stood with us whose son and family live near Hiroshima. Her daughter-in-law is Japanese and grew up in Hiroshima, and when she found out that on the other side of the globe people were standing in silent remembrance and solidarity   with   Hiroshima   she   was   very   touched.

August 22nd 2016

Two go camping

I've been telling people recently that I only had two things left on my bucket list - go camping with my brother, and go on a US road trip with Wendy, my daughter-in-law.

Then someone asked me what else had been on the list and I couldn't remember, so I scanned my diaries, found the list I made 6 years ago, and discovered there were several other items that needed attention.

Here's the list:
1/ learn to play Misty on the sax   - DONE

2/ learn to walk on my slackline. I can walk half the length of the line — thirteen steps — but not to order. I think it still counts, so DONE

3/ go trampolining*

4/ go on a walking holiday, in Yorkshire or on a coastal path

5/ holiday on a Scottish island

6/ go to the Musee d'Orsay -DONE

7/ have a novel published with a sensible cover (write a novel in the third person – was on an earlier list and I've done that now, though the publisher gave it a toe-curling frilly pink chick lit cover) – DONE

8/ go on a US road trip with someone fun

9/ see the Grand Canyon - DONE

10/ go camping with Jonty - DONE

*I've been told I probably should not trampoline because I have an artificial knee, so that item is, I suppose, null and void.

That means I still have 4, 5 and 8 to do because this last weekend I went camping with Jonty, with whom I haven't camped since he was a toddler. I haven't camped at all since I was 14.

Rain was forecast for our three days, and I texted Jonty to ask if he wanted to postpone the trip. He texted back "You can wimp out if you want to, but I'm still going." So we did, and were rewarded with an hour of sunshine on arrival. As soon as we'd put up the tent and had a cuppa it started to rain, and it was showery all weekend, but it didn't matter. It was good fun. Getting away from everything, and having the time to talk properly when we never usually have the opportunity, was wonderful. And I loved lying in the tent wrapped in two sleeping bags listening to the weather as I fell asleep.

Poor Jonty, though. Out of the five of us I am the least practical, so he got a raw deal. Any of our other siblings would have been better at pitching and dismantling the tent. He was very patient, even when he said on packing up, "Fold it over the roof!" and I could no longer tell which part was the roof.

Thank you, Jonty.

SEPTEMBER

September 1st 2016

It's a mystery

When we bought our house twenty years ago our garden was wild and overgrown. It was a hot June that year and the escallonia front hedge - fifteen foot high and eighteen foot deep - was budding with tiny pink blossoms, with vivid cerise dog roses trailing over it. The front garden was a charming haven with unmown lawns knee high. You could imagine finding an old bench in there and settling down in a sunhat with a cool drink, and reading a favourite book. Bees went in and out of the hives in the garden. The back garden was thick with nettles, brambles, dandelions and convolvulus.

After we moved in we got rid of the bee hives because the bees were annoying, very annoying. Dave helped with the heavy work of clearing, and landscaping, and I spent long days gardening. In those days I could garden for six hours before I was tired. (Now I can manage two.)

A few years ago we chopped down the front hedge because the escallonia was sad, damaged by a bitter winter, and we revelled in the view of the fields beyond.

It's a lovely garden now but it lacks the charm it once had. I think it lacks the charm.

When I go for a teatime bike ride on the Trail there's a spot where I often stop and sit, overlooking a deep valley. I sit amongst the wild flowers and grasses, and revel in the silence. The only sounds come from sheep and birds. I sit and mull over problems, or plots and plans, and think it would be great to sit there all day in the wildness and to sleep there at night. I feel more at peace there than I do in my garden. Why is that? It's not just because when I'm sitting in the garden I can see weeds that need pulling up, or a shrub that needs pruning, or a lawn that needs mowing. It's something more, and other than that.

And if sitting in the wild country makes me feel so peaceful, why did we ever tame our garden?

September 3rd 2016

Being old, successfully

I recently set a writing exercise for a group of people, 90% of whom were over 50. They had to answer the question: "Are there any advantages to getting older?" I was amazed at how many of them came out with abundant and optimistic lists of reasons to say "Yes!"

I was surprised, because I could think of only six, and four of those are my grandchildren. My other two were seeing my children grow into adults I admired (as well as loved); and having the mental space to really appreciate tiny, everyday pleasures, such as my pillow, or a summer evening bike ride on the empty Monsal Trail. I could go on forever with this list.

I'm still thinking about the question.

Assuming we have enough money not to worry, and we are healthy, being old successfully - i.e. staying happy - is still a tricky thing to master. Death is all around us, and we're aware of how tenuous is our grasp on life, so we want to use our days in ways we won't regret. How we spend our days is how we spend our lives. And in order to retain our health we have to pay daily attention to keeping fit, eating well, not drinking too much. We need to keep cheerful and not complain about our aches and pains - or in my case, my tiredness and lack of energy. And we need to stay involved in the world and its concerns, up to date with latest trends and developments so as not to become old fogeys, always doing new things and going new places so as not to be boring and bored. (Mixing with young people helps with all of this.)

It's hard work and it's a skill to practice - being old successfully.

OCTOBER

October 3rd 2016

Still in transition

Have you noticed, those of you who are gardeners, how hard it is to sit and relax in your garden, when you can see weeds that need pulling and jobs that need doing? And yet if you're in someone else's imperfect or untidy garden, say that of a holiday cottage, you can relax just fine?

I've just spent two weeks in a house with a 4-year-old, a 6-year-old, two very active parents and a cat, and I can say without offending said parents that there is clutter in that house. Even so I could relax. I came home on Saturday to mowed lawns (to please me), vacuumed carpets, an empty laundry basket, no washing up, and a fridge full of yoghurt. I am forever grateful that I live with a house-keeperly man (yes you, Dave!) but I was struck on arrival, yet again, by our clutter.

Admittedly, Isaac and Wendy's house is bigger than ours, and the rooms are bigger, so the clutter doesn't take up so much visual space. But I don't think the size of anything is relevant: it's just that clutter in someone else's house doesn't annoy me, just as long as it doesn't get in my way. In a similar vein, doing the washing up in someone else's house can sometimes be pleasant, whereas at home it is always a chore.

I can see that clutter, the clearing of clutter, hoarding, and a superfluity of objets d'art on display are a continuing area of disagreement at Hepworth Towers. We have different views: there is no right or wrong, and there is no way out.

October 6th 2016

Visibility and vanity, and a happy heart

I've been woozy with jetlag and missing my girls, but I don't want to dwell on that. I want to talk about my hat.

Are you a female over 60 with grey hair, and when you venture out do you feel invisible? Buy a hat.

Isaac and Wendy bought me for my birthday and I had to wear it on the journey home from Colorado because I already had hand luggage so I couldn't bring a hatbox. I managed to store it in the overhead locker without damaging it, but all the time in the airport, charging from one terminal to another, hanging around in waiting areas, queueing to board, I wore my hat. And I noticed people looking at me - all kinds of people - young, old, men and women. I was visible for the first time in years!

OK, they may have been thinking "What the hell has she got on her head?" but there were no rude comments, no nudges, no winks. And when I asked the stewardess on the flight to Manchester if she would help me find somewhere to store my case, and she took it from me, I watched her. She took several minutes to make a space for it, stored it away, and shut the locker. Then she went back and opened the locker and checked the address label to see who I was. Did she think I was someone famous? Poor sap.

On Tuesday I wore the hat around Bakewell (with some trepidation) and no-one looked at me. Why was that? Answers in the comments at the bottom.

October 9th 2016

A suggestion

It's been a hectic week of highs and lows, and I am sitting in bed this morning wanting to blog, but feeling too stunned. I'll share one thought...

If you can no longer bear reading the news because it is too upsetting or appalling or disgusting, find one small, practical, real, local thing you can do to make the world a better place and concentrate on doing that. It really helps.

October 13th 2016

Citizens of the world

Last week was my first week back from abroad, and on Saturday we had an event that I've been helping to plan since August. Bakewell churches were hosting a group of women and children asylum seekers and refugees on a day trip to

Bakewell. We had activities planned for them inside and out, two home-made meals, and transport to and from Sheffield, where they've been given accommodation (our nearest city.) On the Thursday night before, I got very little sleep, worrying about if it would all go to plan, and generally fretting - would they have a nice time? would they? would they?

On Saturday morning I was so nervous I was thinking of ringing up my co-planners and saying I was ill and couldn't come, sending Dave to deliver the food I'd cooked. I am a friendly person, but talking to people I don't know, starting from scratch, is hard.

But I went, and I was the one to wait on the main road to greet the visitors as they stepped down from the small coach we'd chartered. The volunteer from Sheffield was the first to step off the bus with a warm smile, a hearty thank you and an outstretched hand, and she was followed by our visitors - all smiling. My heart lifted, and I relaxed. It was going to be OK.

It was more than OK. As soon as the children got to the Quaker Meeting House they launched into the games and activities we had waiting for them. And the women accepted hot drinks and wanted to talk and get to know us, just as we wanted to get to know them. Everyone in Bakewell who took part enjoyed the day, and felt privileged to meet our visitors, to hear their stories, and to make a connection.

I have hesitated to tell you about it lest you think I was parading my do-goodery. But it's not, and it wasn't. All of those planning the event have been touched and are touched

357

every night by the news of people fleeing the horrors of war, starvation and persecution. What could we do to help besides collecting clothes to send and giving money?

I am sure you feel the same, and I'm telling you about it in the hope it will inspire you to think about what you might offer.

This initiative, which we plan to repeat, is a very small local practical thing. It won't change the world, and it won't help anyone to start a new life. But it is a sign of friendship and warmth and support, and offers a day away from a daily life of hardship, living in basic accommodation on scant resources. (Asylum seekers are not allowed to work and get £5 a day to live on). In post-Brexit times of racism, jingoism and insular thinking, it is a way to show our common humanity. It was a wonderful, memorable day, and now we are torn between inviting our new friends back, and inviting new ones on a future visit.

October 17ᵗʰ 2016

Real life for writers, and a question

I've not told you anything about my writing life lately, have I?

Last autumn I was intensively pitching my TV comedy drama based on my novel *But I Told You Last Year That I Loved You* to TV production companies. I had interest and very nice comments from one company, but then they said it didn't fit with their oeuvre because it was pre-watershed i.e. family-friendly.

It was a huge achievement to get them to even consider it, because most film and TV companies refuse to look at unsolicited scripts from writers. They only want material submitted via agents. You know that old conundrum that you can't get a job until you have some experience in it to put on your CV, and you can't get that experience because you can't get a job? Getting an agent as a screenwriter is rather like that. You have to have a body of work - screened work - to show them, before an agent will take you on. And you can't have original work of your own even considered, never mind screened, unless you have an agent.

So this is the background to what follows.

While I was away in Colorado in September, I received this email from a production company to whom I had written *last November*:

Dear Sue,

I understand that you contacted my colleague xxxx xxxx with the pitch for your comedy drama But I Told You Last Year That I Loved You. Apologies for the delay in responding to you, but xxxx has gone away on maternity leave and your pitch has been passed onto me to respond.

Whilst I thank you for considering us to help develop your idea, I'm afraid we don't accept unsolicited ideas and would encourage you engage an agent to represent your interests going forward.

Whilst the premise for your comedy drama does sound very promising, I'm afraid it is not something that I would be able to develop further as two quite similar comedy drama ideas in development.

Sorry to not have more positive news, but do be encouraged that there does seem to be something very distinctive and heart-warming about your idea and I wish you every success in adapting it for TV.

With very best wishes,

Yyyy

What is remarkable about this is that someone even bothered to respond - so yyyy deserves full marks for that. But 10 months later? Since I wrote to these guys I have adapted the same material into a situation comedy.

This is real life for writers. You sweat over your writing, redraft it, rewrite it, get feedback from trusted readers, rewrite it, tweak it, then sit down to submit it to publishers, agents, film companies, whoever. Then you wait for weeks months for some kind of response.

Then you get a blank rejection, or hear that something similar is in production.

You squawk in frustration, kick the door post, go out on your bike, dig the garden, watch junk TV, go to bed, wake up and consider whether you have the emotional energy to launch another marketing campaign, and decide you would rather crawl on your hands and knees to Bakewell and back. You do all the jobs on your to-do list, including the dreaded one labelled 'tax return' - as if you ever earned enough to pay tax - and go out on your bike again. "I'll start next Monday morning." you think.

So here I am. It's Monday morning and the sun is shining with rain forecast for later. I have gardening to do and I'm getting twitchy because I've not been out on my bike for four days. My dearest friend died last year. Others close to me are ill or have died. Life is short, and there are plenty of other writers out there with great work to offer. Is it worth continuing to spend my time on pitching mine?

Answers in the comments box below, but please don't wait ten months because I could be dead.

October 19th 2016

Mary and the pictures

I used to go to the pictures (aka the cinema) with my friend Mary. And actually, only with Mary. That was what we did together. That and talk - on the sofa, in the kitchen, in cafes, on park benches, on the phone. At the end of the film, Mary insisted on sitting until all the credits had gone up and the lights had come on. We wouldn't talk about the film until the next day on the phone. That's what we liked....to process it on our own before discussion.

There was, however, one memorable time when we went at her suggestion to see a gritty and depressing Mike Leigh film. I can't recall the title. I've expunged it from my memory. It was an early showing and we sat in the cinema cafe for a drink afterwards. I'd hated the film so much because of the unrelenting misery, that I couldn't hold back, and said: "What on earth would possess anybody to want to see a film like that? Why would YOU want to see a film like that?" My voice was supersonic, high like a tiny bat's voice (if bats could speak). It behaves like that when I'm upset or angry or excited.

Mary laughed. I can't remember what she said, but during the following conversation she did have a realisation that, unlike her - who would relish a film with subtitles about abortion in Romania - I go to the pictures to be entertained, uplifted or moved, not to be harrowed. I don't mean I like lightweight, vapid films. I want something substantial, just not harrowing. So films like *Twelve Years a Slave* are out and ones like *Witness*, *Pride*, *Billy Elliot* and Richard Linklater's *Before* films are in. Mary wanted films that made her think and feel, but hated violence, like me. After that episode, when we were fixing up our next trip to the pictures she would sometimes say things like "There's nothing suitable for you this week. I've checked." And we'd laugh.

I'm thinking about all this at the moment, because I went to see *Born* to be Blue, a film about Chet Baker, the brilliant (drug-addicted) trumpeter. It was well acted and interesting, gritty and tough. A film for Mary. I went because of the jazz angle, and came home wanting to get out my sax. I didn't. It would have woken Dave.

And I'm thinking about Mary because there is a film that I want to see and I don't want to see, and I know for sure that Mary would be going if she were still here: Ken Loach's *I, Daniel Blake*. It won the Palme d'Or at Cannes, and it's about what real life is like for hundreds of thousands of people in the UK in 2016.

The New Statesman critic said: "The greatest virtue of *I, Daniel Blake* is its patience in confronting painstakingly the incremental humiliations visited on the neediest in society." The Guardian critic said: "...a drama of tender devastation that tells its story with an unblinking neorealist simplicity..."

I just watched the trailer. It made me cry. The trailer made me cry! See what a wuss I am.

I love you, Mary.

October 26th 2016

Those determined not to see

I did it. I went to see *I, Daniel Blake*. I went with Mary's younger daughter. I was armed with two

363

handkerchiefs, but as it turned out, I only needed one. That was for the most memorable scene, set in a food bank. It was devastating and it was by far the most powerful moment in what was a hard-hitting film.

Before I went, I read the British reviews on the website *Rotten Tomatoes*, and noticed that the right wing papers gave the film a lower rating than the liberal and left wing papers. And I thought "Hmm. Typical. They don't like the message, so they're dissing the film."

Now I'm thinking about the film and puzzling over my reaction, and wondering why it doesn't match the wave of feeling on the net. I think it's partly because I had steeled my heart to avoid collapse, partly because (as a writer) I had a few personal tiny doubts about some of the acting and some of the script - who do I think I am? This is the great Ken Loach! - but mostly I think it's because the film didn't tell me anything I didn't already know and have been fuming about for several years.

I used to volunteer in a Citizens Advice Bureau which helps people with a wider range of problems, including wrestles with what was then the bungling bureaucracy of the welfare benefits system. Since I worked there things have changed: the benefits system has been redesigned to be punitive, inhumane, unbending, humiliating, and it is also financially even meaner. Added to this, the poisonous newspapers in this country have whipped up ill-feeling against benefits claimants so that the majority of the public thinks that benefits fraud accounts for 24% of claims, when in fact the figure is 0.7%.

I know how the system works now because I read *different* newspapers and because of things I have heard from friends. In my day there were no food banks. Now these are an indispensable safety net, and they are run by charities, not the state, which is shocking. But what is more shocking is that over ONE MILLION people in the UK needed emergency three-day rations from food banks last year. *I, Daniel Blake* shows why, and makes it clear that this need is due to circumstances beyond their control.

The screenplay for *I, Daniel Blake* was written after research, in which the writer spoke to people claiming benefits, and to anonymous sources in benefits offices. Everything that happens in the film has happened to at least one person in real life, and the way the system is portrayed in the JobcentrePlus is realistic. So the truth of the film is beyond reproach.

I don't feel qualified to express misgivings online about the film itself (qua film), so I won't. It's an important film and delivers a message people need to hear, and that is all that matters. I just read a disgustingly cynical and snide piece about the film by Toby Young in the *Daily Mail*, where he peddles the usual *Daily Mail* lies. He queries whether someone who has had a heart attack and whose doctor says he must not work would be turned down for Employment Support Allowance. This does happen. It has happened. There is plenty

365

of documentary evidence. *Dying people have been told they are fit to work.*

As long as the politicians in this country shut their eyes to the suffering their policies cause, and as long as poisonous (and worryingly popular) papers like the *Daily Mail* vilify benefits claimants, there will be a need for films like *I, Daniel Blake*. I so wish things were different.

NOVEMBER

November 6th 2016

This isn't that minute

from the film - *While You Were Sleeping*

01:10:50 You work hard, try to provide for the family, and then, for one minute,

01:10:56 everything's good.

01:10:58 **Everyone's well. Everyone's happy.**

01:11:01 In... In that one minute, you have peace.

01:11:07 Pop, this isn't that minute.

Wendy has put it on Twitter, so I feel able to share it with you.

Wendy, beloved daughter-in-law, dear friend, loved like a daughter, sharer of good times, welcoming, indulgent and patient host of mothers-in-law, generous and thoughtful sender of videos of Lux and Cece opening their birthday presents that I paid for and Wendy went out and bought after consultation, expert maker of Bloody Marys and margaritas, expert drinker of same, fun-time companion, sad time companion, fantastic wife and mother, inspiring and compassionate yoga teacher, all of the above and so much more that I can't think of at 6 in the morning but I will think of later and be annoyed that I didn't put down....has breast cancer.

She reads my blog and the comments below, so if you'd like to send her a message, please do.

And here, 5,000 miles away, I am going to be rock-like (don't scoff) and to try hard to be the best support someone can be from so far away. I'm channelling my emotions into stocking the freezer, because they are all coming over for a Thanksgiving visit before Wendy starts her treatment.

She's a peach.

November 30th 2016

Missing, but always here

I think about Mary every day. It's a fleeting thought. It's a - "I wish she was here to talk to, I wish she was here to tell about

X, to ask what she thinks about Y, to share a laugh about such and such." She is like when I notice the moon coming up, or Venus appearing in the cold winter sky. I miss her and then move on. Or she is like someone walking briskly across a screen I am watching. She's like a bead on the thread of my day. There's no telling when she'll appear,

but appear she does.

I am fortunate to have had such a friend.

DECEMBER

December 6th 2016

Everyday post

Some news for regular readers - Wendy has her surgery tomorrow - Wednesday. She is having a double mastectomy and reconstruction. (This is not private information, oh sibs who think I sometimes overstep the mark.)

We hold her in our hearts.

The second thing to say is I am better from the virus.

Yesterday I went for a long walk on my own, setting off from the house. It was very healing. I climbed up to the top of Longstone Edge which runs behind the village. It was raw and very misty, but also bright. Even at midday the frost was still sharp where the sun couldn't reach.

I met no-one on the top, and no-one on the descent and it was wonderful. But I realised I should have taken my mobile phone with me, because if I'd fallen, I might not have been found until Dave alerted the search and rescue helicopter. That would have been bloggable.

I moan about living here in the winter, but on still days when there is even a smidge of sunshine, it's heaven.

December 9th 2016

The tree

Wendy is doing OK. She had her operation two days ago and hopes to be home by tomorrow. Thank you for all your good wishes and prayers. We appreciate them so much.

I've been wondering about whether to bother with a Christmas tree this year, even though it's an ON Christmas. The family aren't here on Christmas Day - I'm going to Zoë's house - and it feels like a huge indulgence, with so many people (even in the UK) with not enough to eat, never mind not being able to afford Christmas presents for their kids. Some of our family have charity donations instead of presents; maybe the next step was giving up the tree and making decorations from stuff in the garden? Was it OK to buy a tree just for my pleasure? Last year's tree that I planted in the garden after Christmas has not survived.

Well, I've bought one and I loved it even before it was decorated. That is how much I love the tree.

December 13th 2016

Change of plan

There's been a change of plan.

Dave is going to have an OFF Christmas here, and I am flying to Boulder to be with our family there. Things are tough for them right now, with Wendy having a really difficult recovery from her operation, and I'm going over to try to help. Amongst other things, this will involve driving on the wrong side of the road in snowy weather in an automatic car. Eeek.

When things aren't quite so frantic remind me to tell you about the time I drove out of San Francisco on my own all the way to Yosemite and back ON MY OWN: one of my proudest achievements. I'll see you when I see you, or rather, you'll read me when you read me.

Happy Christmas!

December 24th 2016

Christmas bulletin from Boulder

I have wanted to blog before now but have not had clarity of mind at the same time as energy at the same time as opportunity. Now I am snatching a moment to say:

Wendy is up and about and feeling much better - which is wonderful.

There is no time to write anything else. The hordes will return in a minute.

Happy Christmas to you all from Boulder!

December 31st 2016

Snapshots of my current life in Boulder

losing my best cashmere jumper for three days, thinking it's gone forever, and then finding it being used as a doll's under-blanket

Cece sitting on the downstairs loo down the corridor shouting out, à propos of nothing: "I love you, Sue!"

the pedicurist telling me she likes my socks and my responding that I bought them at McGuckins (a well-known Boulder independent hardware shop) and feeling like a local, wondering why the baked potatoes aren't cooking at 200 degrees, and Isaac reminding me that they cook in Fahrenheit over here, not Centigrade

seeing a bobcat in the garden - halfway in size between a domestic cat and a labrador - and finding out they are vicious, eat deer as well as rodents, should be avoided as urgently as one would avoid a bear (which I saw in the garden last year) and that animal control should immediately be alerted

playing game after game after game after game of Guess Who (fortunately I like Guess Who)

eating the tastiest Christmas turkey I have had in years

seeing seven deer calmly grazing in the garden (on a different day from the bobcat's visit) mastering the vast washer, the immense dryer, the dishwasher, learning which day the weekly milk is delivered and where to store it, but failing to realise that the temperature one cooks things at should be not only in Fahrenheit, but also altered for the higher altitude

loving the way the children say "aminals" not "animals" and hoping this continues for another couple of years

being so pleased at a delivery of ready-made food from a friend of Isaac and Wendy's and then when warming it up, managing to burn it (though the majority of it was edible); oh dear, it seems that anything to do with cooking over here has been my Achilles heel

taking an afternoon walk in crisp air under a blue sky with a view of the mountains, wearing my sunglasses

being so delighted at learning how to use the complicated television controls that I do a victory dance, waving my arms around and puncturing the paper lampshade with the remote

watching the Ellen DeGeneres show (during the aforementioned pedicure) where a novice screenwriter is picked up in a Starbucks and asked by Ellen to say what the screenplay is about in three words, and thinking OMG a one sentence logline was hard enough, and watching enviously as she is invited onto the show to have a scene acted out by Ellen and Tom Hanks, and then when they ham it up, feeling grateful it's not my screenplay they are massacring drinking wine during the pedicure and moving on to a Mexican restaurant with Isaac and Wendy and getting sozzled on just one margarita and wondering if alcohol makes you drunker quicker at higher altitudes (Boulder is a mile high)

realising with some dismay (at my insularity?) that the kids telly programmes I enjoy the most are either English or Irish....oooh, oooh, apart from *Paw Patrol*

Wishing you all a Happy New Year from Boulder!

JANUARY

January 7th 2017

Home

I am home, sitting in bed drinking Yorkshire tea: it tastes better than it does in Boulder. I have opened the presents that Santa left by the bed, I have opened the pile of Christmas cards left on my desk (no of course Dave doesn't open them - you know what he thinks of Christmas) and on my bedside table I have this year's homemade Christmas card from the OFF Christmas fairy.

Yesterday morning was a blue time for me: a time of push-pull, mixed emotions. Getting ready to leave is always hard and not just because of the slight anxiety about making the plane, and the 19 hour journey ahead. After three weeks away I was so looking forward to being home and seeing Dave, and at the same time, it was a wrench to be leaving my lovely and loving American family. There had been such heavy snow that the schools were closed so it wasn't just a hasty goodbye after breakfast. When it was time to leave, 4-year-old Cece hugged me and said "I will never forget you." Lux came out in the knee-deep snow to wave me goodbye as my taxi drove away.

It was the right time to leave. I can't tell you how wonderful it's been in the last few days to see Wendy returning to her buoyant, sassy self. Next week she starts her chemo. We wish you strength, courage, stamina and ultimately, astoundingly good health, LRH.

FEBRUARY

February 12th 2017

I love to dance!

I went to a party last night. It was for a friend who was turning 70. His 'kids' had planned the surprise party with exquisite care, and he loved it.

I loved it too. After a month of anxious concern about politics here and abroad, I got to dance. The last time I danced was two years ago at my nephew's wedding, which is too long ago when I love to dance. Actually, no. The last time I danced was in my pyjamas with Lux and Cece in their kitchen. I LOVE TO DANCE!

Last night a small rock band played oldies like *Blue Suede Shoes*, *La Bamba* and *That'll be the day*, and the hall was filled with 60 and 70 year olds, all having a fantastic time.

60 and 70 year olds don't care what they look like when they're dancing: they want to enjoy themselves. Next week they might be seriously ill, they might be dead. And what's also nice is

that offspring of 60 and 70 year olds tend to be past their teenage years, and are no longer embarrassed by their parents' dancing.

For the first time in weeks I woke up happy. It was the best medicine. I now feel energised for all those letters I've got to write to the Prime Minister.

There's only one way to beat the sadness of life - with laughter and rejoicing.
Rohinton Mistry

February 14th 2017

How you feel is how you feel

Some people, kind people, don't understand that the way to be a friend is to sit alongside a sad person, and to accept their feelings....to accept their feelings as valid.

Some people, kind people, think the way to be a friend to someone who is sad is to try to persuade them to see the bright side – "Cheer up - it's not the end of the world!" "Cheer up - think of all the things you have to be grateful for!"

If you do that, the sad person feels misunderstood and even more alone than they did already.

Let's learn to accept how other people feel, no matter how uncomfortable it is for us, because it's the best way there is to comfort them.

Yesterday it was Mary's anniversary - two years since she died. I felt happy. I was still in the dancing zone. It was a bright sunny day after a week of yukh. I considered this - that I was feeling happy - and thought - *Well, I am not going to feel sad or feel guilty about being smiley on Mary's anniversary. I miss Mary everyday. Everyday. There is a big Mary-shaped gap in my life that no-one else will ever fill, and if I don't feel sad on this particular day, I know Mary wouldn't mind, so why should I?*

Grief is a thing which varies from day to day and there's no making sense of it, no pattern to depend on so you can protect yourself. It hits you hard and unexpectedly sometimes and then it recedes.

February 20th 2017

It's time to make a pact

You could say that February has been a minor bête noire in my writing - both in the blog and in the books.

For example....

'February that year was muddier and greyer and more miserable than usual'
from *But I Told you Last Year That I Loved You*

'February's always grey and cold. You look out of the window feeling desperate for fresh air, and then you look up at the leaden sky and change your mind.'
from *Zuzu's Petals*

'The price is February. The grey days, the looming mists, the dripping rain, the faded grass, the inescapable mud and the long dark nights: I hate them all.'

from *Plotting for Beginners*

And lastly, from *Plotting for Grown-ups*:

'Talking in bed circa 3 a.m…

Me (surfacing from sleep, quasi-drugged): "Kit, Kit, Wendy wants me to go on a Senior Citizen day trip to Iceland with her, all inclusive for £10, with a good lunch. Do you think I should go?"

Kit (as if I am not talking gibberish): "What date is it?"

Me: "9th of Feb."

Kit: "Definitely go."

Me: "Why definitely?"

Kit: "It's a vile month, so you should do something to take your mind off it."

This man is perfect for me:

a/ he takes my dreams seriously

b/ he appreciates the horror that is February.'

And then last year on the blog it changed (February 8th 2016):

'This year, despite the execrable weather, I feel differently. I keep thinking back to this time last year, when Mary was dying. This year the thought constantly running through my

379

head like one of those banner headlines under a newscaster is: "No February could ever be as bad as last year's February." And the next thing I think is: "I am still here, still alive. Mary isn't. I am lucky. I get to see another spring, I get to talk to my kids and laugh with my grandkids, and hear that 3 year old Cecilia said on the day of the Superbowl "I would like to be a Broncos player when I grow up but I more want to do fossils," I get to talk and laugh with Mary's kids, I get to sit in the sun and play my sax and share things with my friends and cycle up the Monsal Trail, and laugh at the hilarious things Dave says, and so on and so on.'

I have felt differently this year too, except last week, missing Mary, I sank back into the old ways and I tweeted:

"February is a very trying month."

Several people agreed, but Roopa Banerjee tweeted:

"I like the hidden hope in February. The gradually lengthening day, the daffodils, the slight lifting of gloom."

And I decided that the lengthening days are what I am going to concentrate on in future. Because it is pretty wonderful when it gets past 5 o' clock and it's still light enough to see the snowdrops.

The other thing is what I say in the para above from my blog last year..."I am still here, still alive."

...which ties in with what I said last week –

"60 and 70 year olds don't care what they look like when they're dancing: they want to enjoy themselves. Next week they might be seriously ill, they might be dead."

...which ties in with a quote from the Quakers' Advices and Queries no 30. which used to puzzle me until last year –

Accepting the fact of death, we are freed to live more fully.

The years of active life I have left are numbered, and I am feeling that, rather than just knowing it intellectually. And to dismiss every February as a month to be tolerated, is dismissing a twelfth of what I have left.

So today I am making a pact with February, as Ezra Pound did with Walt Whitman:

I make a pact with you, Walt Whitman -
I have detested you long enough.

MARCH

March 14th 2017

Wendy's progress

When I meet a friend these days, as soon as they've asked how I am, they want to know about Wendy. And I'm guessing that you'd also like an update.

Wendy is doing OK. She has to have six chemotherapy treatments three weeks apart, and she'll be having her fourth tomorrow. For the first week after she's had her treatment she feels terrible, and spends a lot of time in bed. After the last treatment, she went to sleep on a Friday and woke up on Sunday. During the second and third weeks after the chemo she feels pretty awful, needs to rest, but is fit enough to be up and about and to teach her yoga classes.

Her matter-of-fact approach to the awfulness that is cancer and its treatment is an inspiration; and she's willing to answer questions from anyone honestly. She lost her hair, couldn't find a wig she liked and is happier to be bald than to wear a headscarf.

In May she will have three solid weeks of radiotherapy and I am going to stay and act as family backstop. It's a long haul for all of them, but they are getting through, and Wendy says that it gives her strength to know that people all over the world are rooting for her. So, thank you my lovely, warm-hearted regular readers.

March 21st 2017

Toasting my big sister

You know how you plan a day walking with someone and when you wake up it's raining, and the rain is set to continue till three o clock, and the someone says "I'm not going out in that! It's horrendous! We'll get soaked!"

My big sister isn't like that. She's game. She's laid back. She's up for it.

So we donned our boots and our macs and we set off through the woods in search of Mill Gill Force. We walked along muddy tracks, along puddled stone paths through fields, up steep slippy hillsides, across squelchy bogs, over tree root after tree root, alongside green velvet walls - oh you should have seen that moss!

Till we got to the falls. They were worth the trek, though the camera lens was damp and the picture not so sharp.

By that time, Kath was wet right through to her pants (underpants to you Yanks) and the track ahead promised only a slide into full frontal mud, so we turned back. At which point I fell over. Thwack. The strangest thing was that I didn't swear, I didn't even yelp. Is my big sister's stoicism rubbing off on me? At last! It's only taken 60 years. And here's a tip - fresh moss is a very efficient cleanser - of hands and coats.

All I really want to say is that if I had been with a lot of other family members - no names, no pack drill - they would have moaned at the rain, at the wind, at the wet. They would have turned back. Some would not have set out. Kath set out and never complained, and the trip was exhilarating and fun. Thanks, Kath.

MAY

May 22nd 2017

Monday musings

I woke up from a dream in which I was being interviewed at the Jobcentre. I was sitting between the family member who declines to be named and a man whose CV was handwritten on four small post-its. Because of the cuts they were interviewing three of us at a time. The interview was friendly and relaxed, even convivial. This was not the real world.

May 31st 2017

Postcard from Boulder

You're honoured. I've come in from the quiet hammock to say Hello.

Wendy had a three-hour nap today, so as far as I'm concerned the day has been a success. Now she's at the pool with the girls and I've been lying in the hammock on this warm sunny teatime, catching up on emails, reading the news, looking at the trees, drinking wine and eating crisps.

It's been a busy day with Lux - a knitting lesson, a bike ride to the park, a game of baseball, lunch, beads, reading a chapter of *Ramona the Brave,* and chat. So an hour in the hammock is just the ticket.

Yesterday Lux and I went to the pottery painting studio, which was, as they say, aces. She designed and painted a fabulous plate as a surprise for Cece, who has not yet broken up from school.

On Sunday we had another success: we made a rocket launcher from a kit. For all of you who remember the Pom Pom Puppies Fiasco (which I have tried unsuccessfully to link to, because I am working on Isaac's spare laptop and I can't for the life of me work out how the hell you right click for copy without a mouse) - let me inform you that this time I followed the instructions and achieved success. So there: I am not an utter dummy in the craft department.

JUNE

June 27th 2017

It's good to be home

Boulder is beautiful with its wide tree-lined streets and its ubiquitous bike paths and its views of the Rockies, but here it is home. The spring grass was green in Boulder and the trees were fresh and thick, but here it is lush, the verges overflow with wildflowers, the trees are varied, and the deer don't eat my fruit or flowers. The runners and cyclists on the Boulder trails are serious and intense, keeping fit, stretching themselves. Few of them respond to a good morning or hello, even though generally Boulderites are warm, chatty and hospitable. The people on the Monsal Trail - although they are retiring Brits - seem to find it easier to greet a friendly passer-by.

I'm finally over my jetlag and am tackling the pile of admin that's built up on my desk over the last three weeks. I've also just picked my gooseberries, and am picking strawberries every day. Soon it will be the blackcurrants. My sweet peas are yellow and sickly and I've just dosed them up with sequestered iron. My blackbird still sings at 4 in the morning. It's good to be home.

JULY

July 6th 2017

Current status

I have just one plum on my plum tree because of sharp frosts when the blossom was out; my raspberry bushes refuse to flourish; my sweet peas are pathetic - I don't know what they were doing while I was away in Colorado for three weeks, but they weren't growing; and my strawberry patch is infested with grass again.

Yesterday my legs ached on the briefest of bread and butter bike rides, and at 2 p.m. I shlumped, like Mr Bix's borfin. There was no alternative but to lie on my bed and watch an episode of *Neighbours* on the iPad. My sax calls to me, begging me to find the energy to play it and the slackline is thinking of leaving home on the grounds of neglect.

And yet, and yet, I am loving the summer. Ploughing up the Trail with my weary legs I was euphoric. It's fabulous here! At this point in the year I see the benefits of all the rain we have to put up with month in month out. Everywhere is so wonderfully lush, and the verges of the lanes and the Monsal Trail are spilling over with an ever changing variety of wild flowers. Last week I counted 17 varieties on just one ride. This week among the buttercups and clover there are orchids.

The other reason to be cheerful is that thanks to Dave's inspired dismembering of our dead washing machine, we now have our very own firepit, made from the large metal drum.

He has promised to take the detritus to the tip today, but he's kept a bucketful of other components, in addition to the 'firepit,' including the motor, some 'wonderful springs,' and the domed glass from the door, which he has cleaned up and says makes an excellent fruit bowl.

I just asked him if he minded my putting this bit of news on the blog and he said "No. Why should I mind?" Then two seconds later he said "Perhaps you could ask your readers to send us their unwanted washing machine doors."

Dear readers, please don't.

July 11th 2017

Celebration!

Wendy had a double mastectomy last December, began four months of chemotherapy in January, and yesterday completed six and a half weeks of daily radiation therapy. It has been a long, hard row to hoe and she has done it with stoicism and cheerfulness. She is awe-inspiring.

July 12th 2017

Ancient authors at night

10 p.m.   turn out light and go to sleep.

1 a.m.   wake up for a pee, get back into bed and brain remembers tasks for the following day that should have been done yesterday. Switch on light and email self with subject line only - 'pay house insurance, get flea stuff for cat, ring Tracy and pay the bill, collect beads, buy bubble machine for children on next refugee hospitality day.'

1.30.   unable to sleep.

2 a.m. still unable to sleep and remember another item so forward email already sent with 'order repeat prescription' added.

3.30 a.m. wake up for another pee. Brain refuses to settle and suddenly a scene that I've been wondering how to write pops into my head. Not only are the two characters there and I know exactly what they are doing, their precise conversation is issuing forth as well. Wake up and write as much as possible in dim light with no glasses, just enough detail so I'll be able to pick it up in the morning.

4 a.m. still unable to sleep and not sure I'll wake up before Dave sets off for Sainsbury's so send him an email with items to buy I forgot to tell him last night.

4.30 a.m. still unable to sleep but it's light now. To wake up or not to wake up? Decide not and shut eyes and doze till 6.45 a.m.

July 17th 2017

Missing Mary

It's the most beautiful sunny morning here in Derbyshire. I'm sitting in bed looking at the sun on the lime trees and missing Mary, my best friend, my Anam Cara, who died two and a half years ago. The feeling swept in last night and is still here this morning.

But…

'The sun rises in spite of everything.'

Derek Mahon

AUGUST

August 10ᵗʰ 2017

Various

It's good to be well again. Antibiotics are wonderful, even if reading the list of possible side effects sends you witless, and you have to forego your one glass of wine a day at teatime* because alcohol is not allowed.

Dave was out for the day on Tuesday and I worked on the novel. Guess what? I wrote for 5 hours and produced 3000 words. It was amazing. Dave came home and laughed and said maybe I'd open my laptop the next day and find everything I'd written was drug-induced gibberish. Also he said it was like the scene in *The Mighty Wind* when Mitch gets his Mojo back and starts writing at 200 words per minute.

Fortunately the words weren't gibberish. They were a pretty good shitty first draft (a technical term used by writers.) You know I said I am writing this book in a different way from all the others? Usually I plan the whole thing out and this time I am flying by the seat of my pants.

When I started it I knew the theme and the setting and not much else. I'm seven eighths of the way through now and I've got to know the characters along the way, as well as how the plot works out. Until three weeks ago I didn't know how it was going to end, but one day it came to me in a flash. And when this conclusion arrived it was all so obvious, because hints had been dropped in the text much earlier on.

Right now, a character from twenty years before the novel started has turned up on somebody's doorstep and I have no idea what is going to happen. I'm just waiting to hear what these two characters say to each other and then I'll know where to take it next. It's so exciting!

After this, I have to decide how it ends - happy or sad. It's a momentous decision. I have never before made an ending sad. Hey, maybe I'd stand a better chance of having a best seller if it was sad - you know how darkness rules these days...

*Teatime   -
When I was in the States I had an interesting conversation about tea and teatime. A native I was talking to was puzzled by the double use of the word - tea meaning the drink and tea meaning the meal. Then we got onto the fact that there is afternoon tea and high tea, and then I explained that people in the midlands and north don't have dinner in the evening, they have tea, and that a relation in the south calls her evening meal supper. By the end of the conversation, the American was more bamboozled than enlightened, and I hadn't even explained that in our house at midday the terms lunch and

dinner are interchangable.

August 23rd 2017

It's a fine thing

It's a fine thing to have a sister. It's even finer to have one who cares about you and puts sweet peas in your bedroom and cooks you roast lamb one day and fish pie another, and who has a summerhouse where you can sit and write, and a kitchen where the afternoon sun shines through the stable door as you talk about everything and nothing, and then you slope through to the sitting room to watch *Neighbours*. I am enjoying this convalescence lark.

August 31st 2017

One of those nights

Did you ever have one of those nights where you go to bed tired and at a reasonable hour and you wake up at 1.30 a.m. after disturbing dreams and go to the loo and then you can't get back to sleep because your brain won't stop flitting about so you listen to an episode of *Book of the Week* on iPlayer and then another and another because it's so good and then you go to the loo again and try to go back to sleep and can't, and you spend the rest of the night in alternating bouts of dreadful dreams and trips to the loo and when you finally open your eyes to see the pale morning light of 6.25 creeping round the blinds and feel like death and need more sleep you decide to wake up because you can't stand any more appalling dreams. I just had one of those nights. It was hateful.

I'm sure that after a third mug of sugared Yorkshire tea I'll feel better.

OCTOBER

October 3rd 2017

Domestic trivia

I am going away on Saturday with one brother and two sisters to stay in a cottage in Wensleydale which is five miles from where our other brother lives. We go up en masse, sans partners, and have a jolly good time. We remember what it is we love about each other and we rediscover our petty irritations. To outsiders we appear to be similar - and probably annoying - but within the family we are distinctive. We each have our role. I am the soppy unpractical one.

But I do make nice cakes, and I emailed the other three to ask them what kind of cake they would like me to take. Please would they vote on the following: a chocolate cake, a coffee and walnut cake, or a moist, tangy lemon drizzle. Guess what? They all chose a different one.

October 17th 2017

Converted

What do you think of SatNavs? Do you use one?

Dave has no innate sense of direction, so when he was given one a few years ago it revolutionised his journeys. He loved it so much that for the first two weeks he had it switched on and talking to him all the time, even when he drove the three and a half miles into Bakewell. Well, you know Dave.

On our first long joint trip to a foreign place (somewhere in Gloucestershire) Dave had it plugged in and programmed and I sat with the road atlas on my knee. I like maps. I like to plan out the route before I go and if necessary write myself notes and directions. It became clear on this maiden voyage that my idea of the most sensible route did not match that of the SatNav - or 'Jane' as we called her then. This led to increasing frustration and animosity between me and Jane, and me and Dave, so I surrendered to both of them. We got there just fine, of course.

Since then I have always spurned the thing for trips on my own to new places. Last night I had to be somewhere in Sheffield that I had never been before. I had to be there for 6 p.m. so I was driving through the rush hour and the venue was in the middle of one of those fast moving one-way systems. There were arrows on the google map showing direction of travel on some of the streets but not all. I looked at the map in the morning and again before I set off and memorised a visual image. Yes - you know what happened - I went sailing past where I needed to be. Do you recall that scene towards the end of *Little Miss Sunshine* where they can see the hotel they need to be in but have no idea where the bloody entrance is, and in the end they just drive through a barrier and go hell for leather across a place they really really shouldn't be? It was not like that.

I ended up parked on a street within a few minutes walk of the venue but I didn't know which way to walk. Fortunately I have a tongue in my head. I got there just fine. But that was in daylight. The meeting finished at 9 o'clock and it was dark. I found my way back to the car but had NO IDEA and I mean NO IDEA which way to go. That part of Sheffield is alien to me and it is very near a dual carriageway that leads straight to the M1. I didn't want to end up in Leeds. So I plugged in Jane and tapped HOME and followed her directions. With her help, I got within sight of a familiar landmark - Sheffield University Arts Tower. As soon as I reached it, I switched Jane off.

I shall never be rude about her again, and next week when I have to do the trip again, I shall programme in my destination. So I guess I'm converted, but only in extremis.

November 13th 2017

How to keep sane when the world is falling apart

Don't watch or listen to the news. Read it just once in the morning. This means your horror/despair at the state of the world is not renewed throughout the day.

Find something immediate, local and practical to do to make the world a better place. This should be something that suits your personality, your interests and your deepest concerns. Focus on this work.

Give money to the good causes that tear at your heart.

Write to your MP about your political concerns, even if your MP's views are far removed from your own. (But this is a tricky one. Sometimes the satisfaction I feel after writing to my MP evaporates when I receive his complacent deflecting replies, and I feel even angrier than I did when I first wrote.)

Clear the dead leaves from a gully that's blocked down the lane. See the water flow unimpeded and feel the satisfaction. It's fun playing with water, and you have made a difference, if only minimal.

Watch *Neighbours* or some other mindless, harmless telly – twenty minutes a day. It takes you away from the real world and lets you unwind.

Listen to your favourite piece of calming music.

Pick up litter.

Practise a skill you are trying to master.

Play with and talk to children. Their joie de vivre and innocence are refreshing, and inspire hope.

Indulge in bracing, aerobic exercise: release some endorphins!

Get out in the fresh air and under the sky for at least an hour every day, but more if possible. Associate with trees. They are calming and healing and strong and beautiful.

'When we are stricken and cannot bear our lives any longer, then a tree has something to say to us: Be still! Be still! Look at me! Life is not easy, life is not difficult. Those are childish thoughts…Home is neither here nor there. Home is within you, or home is nowhere at all.

Herman Hesse

DECEMBER

Thursday, December 7th 2017

Oh dear oh dear oh dear.

I went to a book group last evening to chat about my novel about autism, *But I Told You Last Year That I Loved You*. The people there were either psychiatrists or trainee psychiatrists, and although they were friendly and welcoming - of course! - I have to admit I felt a little intimidated.

When I got home, I told Dave how I felt, and that the next book on their list is *Metamorphosis*, and he said "Well, at least you turned up. They won't be getting Kafka."

Good old Dave.

December 12th 2017

Re-writing

It feels as though Christmas at Hepworth Towers is being rewritten. You know how people always say to you in December "And what are you doing for Christmas?" To me they always say "And is it an ON Christmas, or an OFF Christmas?"

Last year it was ON, but it had to be abandoned after I'd decorated the tree, because Wendy was not recovering well from her op and I zoomed off to Boulder to help Isaac look after the family. And Dave dismantled the tree, and we lent it to our friend Liz, and he had the best OFF Christmas he's ever had. But we can't switch this Christmas to ON, because Zoë and family are away alternate years, and the family member who declines to be named will also be away with his fiancée.

Last weekend one of my grandsons saw a charity appeal leaflet on the kitchen table that had a photo of an old woman on it and the caption NO FAMILY, NO TREE, NO CHRISTMAS, and asked "Is that you, Sue?" and then gave me a big hug. Oh dear.

If the snow and frost retreat, I'll be digging up my tree and bringing it in, and it will be in the sitting room, not corralled to my study, because I had to abandon it last year. Don't tell Dave this, but apart from the tree I care less and less about the ON/OFF thing. We are both still here, alive, well-fed and warm. And I'm thankful.

Being here with just Dave on Christmas Day will be lovely. And I'll be with all the family (bar Dave) on the 23rd for feasting and games at Zoë's house. I have it all.

I hope you all have the kind of Christmas you long for.

We live in dark times.

Here is the thought I'd like to leave with you for 2018:

It is better to light one small candle than to curse the darkness.

2018

JANUARY

January 2nd 2018

It's not so bad

I'm turning into my mother. I give people pots of homemade jam when I visit, and I blithely ask forthright questions of medics such as *And what is your job title? and How do you qualify to be that? and You speak beautifully - so clearly I can hear every word. Was speaking included in your training?* ...all questions I put to the nice young man who tested my hearing before Christmas and said I had age-related hearing loss and was entitled to a free NHS hearing aid.

I can still hear my 91-year-old mother on the night before she died asking the doctor inserting the pic line into her chest to explain the procedure, and then asking him how many times he had done it before. It's not so bad being like my mother. But I would like to have inherited her stoicism.

I'm also like my mother in that when I wake up in the morning I feel like death on a biscuit until half past nine. Yesterday, however, it was New Year's Day and our ritual at New Year is to go to bed at the usual time and be woken up by the fireworks across the field at midnight, curse about it, and turn over and go back to sleep, but then be out of the house by 8 a.m.

Since we moved here we've been going down to Bakewell to feed the ducks on the river while everyone else is still asleep. It's beautifully deserted and the low beams of sunshine light up the weeping willows and the gulls wheeling above. But now it's not allowed: there's a sign up that says it is bad for the ducks. So yesterday we drove to Monsaldale and climbed onto the Monsal Trail and said hello to the view from the viaduct instead.

Happy New Year, dear readers.

January 18ᵗʰ 2018

Bulletin from the house of jetlag

Isaac, Wendy, Lux (7) and Cecilia (5) are visiting from Boulder during this filthy, dark and freezing January weather. That's why I've been quiet. If there are 45 minutes in one block when I can be spared, I would rather hide somewhere and zone out to *The Good Wife* than marshal my remaining brain cells in order to blog.

It's so wonderful to have them here - I really can't express how wonderful - and I thought things were going swimmingly as far as jetlag was concerned. There was a visit in May 2013 when Lux was almost 3 and Cece almost 1 when we had to have a 24 rota for a play and sleep schedule for everyone, as there was only one hour in the day when everyone could be depended upon to be asleep - midnight to 1 a.m. - and only four and a half hours when everyone was awake - 3.30 to 8 p.m.

This time they arrived Saturday lunchtime after an overnight flight on which some sleep was had, but not much, and then they all crashed out at 8 p.m. and slept right through. That's what Lux reported when she bobbed downstairs with her bright eyes and her joie de vivre at 9 a.m. on Sunday. And that's what I continued to believe was happening. They are all sleeping upstairs, and I am sleeping on my study floor downstairs. Plus, as you know, I am going deaf. The only mystery was why Isaac and Wendy continued to look as drained and wrecked as when they'd first arrived. I found out eventually that people are not sleeping through. There are actually stretches in the early hours (the graveyard shift) when the girls are awake and ready for action, eager for fun. Oh dear.

At this stage of the visit (5 days in, and they leave in 2) it's a case of endurance for I and W. Dave and I have lots of fun with Lux when she gets up at 9. Cece, who was found asleep and camping on the landing on Tuesday, tends to wake late morning like her parents.

The problem with a January visit is that although we live in a tourist area, everything is closed this month - even Chatsworth adventure playground. But we have boxes of Lego, the ever popular collection of 300 yoghurt cartons, and the gutters and marbles for marble runs. We found a trampolining place in Sheffield that was a big hit.

402

And the kids are properly kitted out for winter weather, now they live in Colorado and not California. They are as cheerful as Inuits on trips to the park in Bakewell and the village rec, and enjoy the puddles as much as if they were toddlers. They'll go on the climbing frame and then after ten minutes Lux will shout 'Puddle break!' and they'll go and smash some more ice on the huge deep puddles on the grass. Colorado is a dry state: even the snow is dry, which is why it is good for skiing and not making snowmen. But we - oh yes - we have plenty of puddles.

January 20th 2018

Back to Colorado

They've gone. They went an hour ago, at 5.35 a.m. The house has never felt so quiet. I am back in my own bed, Dave is on the sofa downstairs doing a crossword, the cat is re-establishing her territory, and the washing machine is turning. It's another quiet Saturday at Hepworth Towers.

The giant puddles in Bakewell park will return to being unloved and unremarked, the Lego will return to the attic, and the soft toys will return to the girls next door.

I might stay here in bed all day, only getting up to put on another load of laundry.

It's been exhausting, and soooooooo worth it.

And I miss them already.

FEBRUARY

February 2nd 2018

Have you ever...?

Have you ever finished knitting a scarf for your grand-daughter and realised it will probably be far too thick around her 5 year old neck, and in fact you realised this (without admitting it to yourself) half-way through the process but you didn't pull it out and start again because you wanted to get the thing finished within the week?

Have you ever spent an hour cooking dishes from store cupboard basics without all the necessary ingredients and ended up with two nutritious meals that are tasteless, but you will have to eat them because you don't want to waste the food?

Have you ever written a blog for eleven and a half years and run out of things to say but not wanted to say to your readers you are taking a break because when you've done that in the past, you've always thought of lots to write about the following week but no-one read your posts because they thought you were taking a break?

Have you ever wondered if your time for sharing happenings and thoughts and ideas with the world has come to an end because you have morphed from an opinionated extraverted writer into a quiet person who has private thoughts she doesn't want to share, unless they are disguised and put in the mouths of fictional characters?

Have you ever been (just a bit) fed up?

Have you ever looked at a photo of yourself and thought: "My God! I have really thick ankles!"

February 13th 2018

The jigsaw

It's three years today since my dearest friend Mary died. It's like having an important and irreplaceable piece missing from the jigsaw of my life. No other piece will fit in her place, and the gap spoils the picture. It's no longer complete.

Lying in bed this morning, thinking about this image, I developed it and thought about my parents, who were like the corners of the jigsaw, maybe most of the edges, giving the puzzle stability, protecting it from the edge of the table. But they are both dead, so there's no longer anything to stop me falling over the edge, except perhaps my brothers and sisters, who are vital parts of the picture - the lighthouse or the beach, the café or the cliffs.

There are other missing pieces besides Mary - my grandmother, other good friends who have died - and the gaps spoil the jigsaw too, but these pieces were lost some time ago and the gaps feel almost part of the picture now.

My friends are there in the picture - the flag, the clump of sea thrift, the lone oystercatcher, the sandcastle, the rowing boat.

Towards the centre are my immediate family - Dave, Zoë, Isaac and the family member who declines to be named. Then there are their partners and my grandchildren. Every one of these pieces are those very, very, favourite bits of the jigsaw - the vivid red scarf, the seagull sitting on the pirate's hat, the child's small hand resting on the mother's knee.

I don't know if this image works or if it sounds silly. But I do know I miss Mary, and that I'm dedicating my new novel to her.

February 16th 2018

Shower the people you love with love

Yesterday was bright and sunny.
Today is bright and sunny.
Sucks to the rain, sleet, ice, mud, bitter winds and grey skies of February.
Today's post is more cheerful.

I woke up from some nice dreams this morning at the perfect time - the sky was light enough to draw the blinds but the sun was not yet up. It's peeping over the horizon as I write. I can see it through the bedroom window.

Last Sunday when Quaker meeting finished I walked across the room to say hello to a friend who's been away for a month, and who I haven't seen since December. Before I could say anything like "Welcome back!" or even just "Hello," she gave me a big hug and said "I've missed you!" It was such a heartening thing to hear. It made my day, and I realised later that it touched me so much because I've been feeling embattled and discouraged.

In bed this morning something in the nice dream I'd been having, made me think how good it would be to be able to attend you own funeral and hear what people said about you. In a Quaker funeral or memorial service there is no minister (just like in Quaker meetings) although an elder will introduce the meeting. After that, everyone present is free to get up and speak about the person who has died. It's a warm and wonderful occasion, as well as sad.

Let's not wait until people are dead before we list why we liked them or loved them, or what it was about them that made them special, or why we are grateful to them, or how they have helped us. Let's tell them now. Everyone needs encouragement. Everyone needs to feel loved.

Saturday, February 24, 2018

Style

I go to have my hair cut every seven weeks. At this week's appointment I was restless and looking for change. I toyed with the idea of having it coloured, but decided that with my hefty dose of wrinkles, it was too late to be having turquoise streaks in my hair. It's not my age, it's the wrinkles. (Despite the fact that when I was flicking through a Poetry catalogue this week, looking for something to wear at the upcoming wedding of the family member who declines to be named, Dave said: "Shouldn't you be looking in a catalogue for biddies?" *Get back in your shed, Dave!*)

Back to the hair salon...I sat waiting for my hair cut, flicking through *Marie Claire*. I love waiting because it's the only time I ever look at a women's mag and *Marie Claire* appeals to me with its intelligent writing and its focus on FASHION. Where else would I find out how to build a capsule wardrobe? The trouble was that before I began, I had to categorise myself as a Modern Romantic, A Minimalist or a Statement Maker. I plumped for Minimalist but was appalled at the suggestion of trousers priced at £250, as men's straight cut indigo jeans from Sainsbury's (£14) are my current favourites. But then Nicola arrived and asked what I wanted me to do this week and I said "Something different." I trust her. She's been cutting my hair for 27 years, she knows my hair, and she's a good cutter.

She cut it beautifully. It's a really pretty cut.

But

...isn't it a shame that just as you can take stuff back to M&S and get your money back if you decide you don't like it, you can't go back to the hairdresser and ask her to put your hair back because actually, you don't like it this short? Hey ho. Worse things happen at sea.

February 27th 2018

Yearning for youth

I went to see a production of *West Side Story* on Sunday at Buxton Opera House. It was performed by a cast of local young amateurs, and directed by an award-winning director. It was fabulous. I enjoyed it so much that at the end of the show I felt like storming backstage so I could thank the cast in person. Now the mere thought of it raises my spirits.

It took me back to being 17 and in love. It was a weird feeling. The cast were exactly the right age for the parts, and that made me yearn to be young again. I'm always wishing I wasn't this old, but on Sunday I wanted to be young enough to run around the stage and dance like they were doing, to be slim and lithe and have my thick brown hair back again, and my eyelashes, to be getting ready for a date with a boy I really really fancied like Maria when she was singing *I feel pretty*.

February 28th 2018

The least from the east

On Monday it was so cold when we walked eastwards down the Monsal Trail to Hassop Station for a BLT that the wind burned my face. I clung to Dave with one hand and covered my face with the other. But the snow itself had not arrived. It did its pathetic best for 24 hours and on Tuesday we woke to a light dusting on the hills.

Why had there been warnings on the national news of terrible snow? Yet again, we thought, it's the London-centric media being hysterical. It reminded me of this piece I had in the *Times* some years ago.

Go chew on some northern grit

The current fuss about the BBC's new weather forecasts suggests that those of us who live in the wild and woolly wastes north of the M25 have hitherto been getting sufficient attention paid to our weather. But the bias against the north has existed for years.

One winter night, Leeds was completely cut off by a severe snowstorm and hundreds of commuters had to find somewhere to sleep in Leeds, but the BBC said nowt. By contrast, whenever there is a even a whisper of snow over Primrose Hill the national newsreaders begin to tremble with excitement. And if the snow actually settles to more than half a centimetre deep, you can be sure it will be the scariest of the six o'clock headlines.

I lived in Sheffield (you remember Sheffield - England's fourth largest city) for twenty years and several times each winter there was sufficient snow to stop the city buses. We made no fuss. We put on our wellies and walked. But if a sprinkling of snow stops a London commuter train, and poor Londoners have to trek half a mile up the track, the whole of the British Isles gets to know about it.

The television weather team – who are presumably looking at maps all day, and should know better – have always been guilty of a south east bias. The weather person will point out chilling charts with a concatenation of cold fronts encrusted with isobars laying siege to the entire country north of the Wash, and then they will smile and say happily "But it's going to be a fine dry day in London and the south east." Oh, that's all right, then. That's what matters.

Outside the capital we have grown so used to the hysterical reporting of minor meteorological squalls in the south east that we now take it all with a pinch of northern grit. Five years ago, when the terrible floods first swelled in Kent and Sussex, in London's back yard, some northerners paid it little heed. "There they go again, crying over a few blocked drains." Only when the news became swamped with reports of floods in the south west did we take it seriously. (Although a cynical ex-London dweller did suggest that the only reason the floods in the south west made the news was because so many media types have second homes in the west country.)

Weather reporting is only one example of south-east bias. At the time of the fuel protests, a friend pointed out the folly of starting them in the north west, because only when fuel ran out in London would anyone in power take notice. By the Tuesday of that first week we (in the Peak District) could find no unleaded petrol locally. The next day bread and milk was rationed at our nearest supermarket. Meanwhile, the national news reports were of the pickets at the refineries and not of ordinary people having difficulty getting fuel, getting food, and getting to work.

On the Thursday my daughter rang to say she was coming up from London for the weekend, and was amazed to find we could not spare the fuel to pick her up from the station. Only by Friday, when petrol stations in London ran dry did the media and politicians give full attention to the implications for the ordinary worker in her Nissan Micra.

There are six times as many people living outside London as in it. Will someone explain why – apart from politics – national news reporting concentrates on what's going on in the capital? Of course London being the capital deserves a special status. But London isn't the United Kingdom, and those of us who live outside are not lesser mortals living in places devoid of newsworthy events. We don't eke out a sad existence scrabbling for cultural scraps that have fallen from London's high table.

My Derbyshire weather is at least visible on the new BBC map. The Scots must feel dispossessed. But this little squall over the BBC's biased weather map will soon settle. As far as general media coverage is concerned, the regions will never come in from the cold.

Current status: yesterday afternoon we got respectably heavy flurries interspersed with bright skies, and Liz and I went for a walk on the Monsal Trail. It was exhilarating and fun, and this morning we woke up to real snow.

APRIL

April 12th 2018

Choices

My suitcase is open on the blanket chest to receive newly washed clothes for my trip to Boulder next week, and unfortunately Lux reminded me on the phone on Sunday to pack my cossie, which means I'll have no excuse not to go to North Boulder Rec swimming pool with her and Cece. Oh, the things we do for our beloved grandchildren, that we would do for nobody else.

How do you feel about packing? I find it hugely difficult because of indecision. How many shoes? How many woollies, and which? How many pairs of jeans? Which of my two posh options for going out on the town? An essential item is my joggers for snuggling up on the sofa with the girls when we watch the telly.

And on the subject of clothes...I have a question for my female readers.

Last week a male writer of commercial fiction said he could write from a woman's point of view, and gave an example which I should really show you but it would take an awful lot of tedious searching. Suffice it to say it was crass, and focused on the woman's thoughts about her breasts and a man who was watching her. This caused a lot of well-deserved mockery on Twitter, and then Laura E Weymouth tweeted a series of tweets on the subject of how women feel about their clothes. this was the first:

"Similarly, 90% of our thoughts regarding clothing revolves around (SURPRISE) how comfortable/functional it is. Yes, sometimes we want to look nice. But mostly we just want pockets and no uncomfortable chafing."

I don't agree AT ALL. I'd say that 80% of my decisions about clothes revolve around whether I love the look of them, whether they suit me, whether they are flattering, and whether or not they're modern. The other 20% might be about comfort, and while pockets are useful if they don't spoil the line, they don't come into any decision about whether or not to buy an item. I mean, really! What's your view?

A social researcher friend of mine who has done research on older women's attitudes to fashion has a similar attitude to mine, but she says we are probably a specific "sub cultural group."

It reminds me of that question some of us used to think about when we were young: Would you rather be clever, beautiful or good?

I have a new question: Would you rather be comfortable, beautiful or stylish?

April 21st 2018

Letter from Colorado

Last night in bed after an evening out with Wendy, I wrote a really entertaining margarita-infused blog post in my head. Sadly it's evaporated this morning.

But it was a great bar we went to last night, with the best tacos I've ever had, and excellent margaritas. And you know how I feel about margaritas. The bar was humming, full of people relaxing after work on a Friday evening. It felt very friendly, and we had a charming barman called Griffin, who gave me their margarita recipe:

1.5 ozs Tequila
1.5 ozs Lime Juice (fresh, of course)
1 oz of orange liqueur
1 squeeze of pure agave.

So now I know, and so do you.

April 22nd 2018

Postcard

I have discovered (thanks to Dave) that there is far more alcohol in my favourite Colorado tipple - a margarita - than there is in a glass of wine. I am surprised, and somewhat disconcerted, and am considering whether or not this will affect my habits on future trips. Already decided: no.

Yesterday we went to town and the girls wanted ice lollies from Le Pops, a gourmet ice lolly shop. Yep. This is Boulder.

Cece was trying to persuade me to have one: "Go on, Sue. It tastes as if fairies are dancing in your mouth and having a party."

So I did, and as I ate my salted caramel lolly dipped in melted chocolate and covered in sprinkles, I wished I had Cece's powers of description.

MAY

May 29th 2018

Worse things happen in the Mediterranean sea

I was talking to someone the other day who was depressed, and after he'd told me how he felt, he said "But I have nothing to complain about - there are so many people in the world who have REAL troubles."

What he said was true, but if you're depressed, counting your blessings doesn't help. It's in this same spirit, however, that although I burned the roof of my mouth 6 days ago and it's made me miserable, I've not yet blogged about it. You know what a wuss I am. You know how I long to be a stoic, but am the least stoical person in my family.

Do you know the film Annie? Do you know that bit when the orphans are singing It's a hard-knock life and Miss Hannegan says "And we're not having hot mush today" and all the orphans smile and cheer, and then she says "We're having cold mush"? Well, lukewarm mush is what I've been eating for days and I'm bloody sick of it.

But back to those REAL troubles. I heard the BBC4 programme *Ramblings* on Sunday and it made me cry. Clare Balding was walking in Surrey with a group of asylum seekers who are former detainees of the Gatwick Removal Centre. Walking with them was a group of volunteers from the Gatwick Detainees Welfare Group.

I am well-informed about the appalling way the Home Office treats asylum seekers - yes, it's still a hostile environment - but hearing on radio about one man's horrific and arduous journey from Eritrea to the UK brought it home ten times more powerfully than reading about it in the newspaper. The last part of his journey was from Calais to Dover and he travelled under a truck.

JUNE

June 4th 2018

Me and him and the tip

Because of interruptions from a certain person, I've been trying to write this blog post for an hour.

This morning there were ten items on my to-do list and I was trying to decide which to tackle first when Dave appeared at the kitchen window and waved his arm about in a table tennis movement. The table has been out in the garden for over a week and so far we've managed one game, so I decided to seize the moment and play.

Then I came into my study and shut the door and had just begun to write when he knocked on the window and frightened the life out of me and said "Can you tell me exactly what you want me to take to the tip?" which is a request that could not be ignored. I've been wanting him to go to the tip for over a year.

You know about his shed, don't you? I wanted to take a photo to illustrate, but it's been embargoed. Suffice to say his shed is so rammed full of 'stuff' that he often has to work outside it. And this 'stuff' leaks out onto the patio area in front of it, and bits of rammel get left there when the job is finished and the tools have been put away and the man who works in the garden is in the kitchen eating his yoghurt. And said rammel (which includes jam jars of unlabelled noxious liquids) stays outside the shed for months and months reducing that part of the garden to an unsightly, distasteful mess. And I can't clear it away because if I do, I am bound to throw away something that would have "come in useful later."

So...when he appears at the study window saying "Can you tell me exactly what you want me to take to the tip?" it takes precedence over everything - even a literary agent emailing a response to my novel. Yes. Even that. Pretty extreme.

Well I've given him a list of what to take, and now I'm going to do some writing. Then I'll tackle the rest of the list.

Aarrgghh! another question – "Would you like me to take all the green stuff that won't fit in the recycling bin?"

June 16th 2018

Wheelbarrows and yoghurt

I've complained to you before that the garden is getting too much for me to cope with because I don't have the energy it requires any more if I want to save some for cycling. Well, Dave has been remodelling part of it - digging up stuff and levelling it into lawn. He's been at it all week, as well as driving over to the house of the family member who declines to be named to work on landscaping *his* garden.

Today we buy the grass seed and sow it. Dave bought a new orange wheelbarrow to help with the landscaping and he loves it so much that on the day it arrived brand new, he wanted to bring it upstairs to the bedroom at bedtime. That's my man. Dave's energy levels are incredible: it must be because his diet is 70% yoghurt. I am not exaggerating - I once wrote a piece in *The Times* about his yoghurt addiction.

Anyway, you know how I sometimes post pics on here of my garden? Well, they are carefully crafted so you don't see the scuzzy bits, the shocking bits, the parts where convolvulus is rampant and the bits where gravel paths have all but disappeared under overhanging unpruned shrubs. I am hoping that after the changes I will be able to take a photo of any section and not feel ashamed.

And here is the piece about the yoghurt:

He who sups with the devil should have a long spoon

If a medical researcher ever discovers that yoghurt is carcinogenic then my husband is doomed.

His passion for yoghurt began in 1971, when he began to dabble in hazelnut yoghurt, made by *Ski*. He was just becoming hooked on the stuff, and therefore thinking that he ought to stop eating it, when *Ski* ran a special offer. If you sent them six yoghurt carton lids they would send you a teaspoon with a long handle, a design which enabled the yoghurt fancier to scrape the last trace of yoghurt from the distinctive cartons, which were shaped like miniature cooling towers. Dave cannot resist a bargain, nor can he resist interesting tools, and what is a long handled spoon, after all, but a tool?

Unfortunately he had never heard the saying "He needs a long spoon who sups with the Devil." All too soon we had twelve long handled teaspoons; and Dave was a yogaholic.

When we moved to Sheffield two years later, he switched to natural yoghurt. He says he abandoned the hazelnut variety because it was too fattening, but I know it's because it only comes in 150gram cartons. Longley Farm Natural Yoghurt is available in larger cartons and is powerful stuff - a Class A yoghurt that gives him a high like no other.

At one point he decided he was spending too much money on yoghurt and started to make his own, first in the warming section of our Rayburn and then in a yoghurt maker. But soon he could not make it in sufficient quantities, and we had to supplement it with Longley Farm Natural Yoghurt (LFNY) from the deli down the road. Reintroduced to LFNY, Dave remembered its superiority and he gave up making his own.

By 1979, he was slurping a 450gram carton of LFNY daily. I had to go to the deli every day, because if I bought more than one carton, then more got eaten.

When we went on our annual holiday to Northumberland, the week was taken up in the pursuit of LFNY. Visits to the beach, tours round castles and boat trips to the Farne Islands were interleaved with yoghurt hunts.

We found a source in a Bamburgh greengrocers, and another - though only in small cartons - at a caravan site near Dunstanburgh Castle. But they didn't have enough. There must be dealers in Northumberland with supplies big enough to feed Dave's habit but we never managed to map out a definitive, reliable network. In the end, we resorted to buying a week's supply from the deli and taking it with us.

By 1984 Dave had persuaded the deli to supply him with catering cartons of LFNY. Each of these cartons, made of tough white plastic, with a bright orange screw top lid, has an integral handle. A good job, as these caterers cartons contain 5 kilograms of the stuff.

In 1994, when we moved to the Peak District it was my job to ask the man in the village shop if he could get us two 5 kg cartons every week. He made no comment. He was a discreet man. He got it from the driver every Tuesday afternoon and stashed it safely in the bottom shelf of his fridge behind the counter, away from prying eyes.

Dave moved onto consuming three catering cartons of LFNY a week. Every Monday morning the last carton was cut in half and licked clean (and not by the cat) and he had more than 24 hours to wait for the next delivery on Tuesday afternoon. Sometimes I would make an emergency dash down to Bakewell's Monday market on my bike, where it was possible to buy LFNY, though the price was high.

Sometimes the Tuesday delivery failed to arrive and I scoured the Derbyshire Dales for shops that stayed open late and stocked LFNY, an odd 150 gm carton, the normal size for normal people.

If on a Tuesday we were not home until after the village shop had closed, the shop man swathed a carton in carrier bags and hid it behind the old milk churn outside his shop, for us to collect.

At Christmas when the shop was closed and Dave had to pre-buy his LFNY in bulk, and yet I also needed extra fridge space for family entertaining, he kept his extra cartons cool by floating them in the water barrel behind the shed. One year he put them in the pond, tethering the carton handles to the garden seat.

When he was working away from home and staying in hotels, the LFNY went with him. The 5 kg carton is too big to fit in the minibar, so he filled the bath with cold water and stood the carton in there to keep it cool.

You might think that I am an indulgent woman. Not true. If you could have seen Dave on Monday nights vainly searching the fridge for a hidden cache of liquid snow, your heart would have melted too.

And if you could have seen his pleasure on a Tuesday afternoon when he unscrewed the orange cap and discovered that this week the LFNY was prime vintage, so thick that it was difficult to shake it through the spout, so thick that it came out with a glug and swirled in the dish, and kept its shape, just like egg whites whisked for meringue… you would understand.

In the days of the LFNY 5 kg cartons, I planted my sweet pea seeds in adapted ones, filled with compost and Dave would say: "Good job I eat yoghurt when you need so many sweet pea pots."

"Yes Dave, only £19.80 a week. What a bargain."

(Actually, I still use them for my sweet peas so maybe it was a bargain.)

JULY

July 13th 2018

The end of the line

When I was six, I wanted to be a trapeze artist, and when I was 60 I wanted to walk a tightrope. The nearest thing available was a slackline, so Zoë and family gave me one for my 60th birthday and Dave fixed it up on our front lawn with sturdy wooden posts and supports.

This was some years ago, since when I've been spending more of my time outdoors on my bike than on anything else. The slackline has been neglected, and this spring Dave pointed out that after 8 years, the polypropylene band would be weakened by exposure to ultraviolet light and would be unsafe. We took it down, and I felt sad. I had only ever managed to walk half the length of it in one go - 13 steps - though I could balance on it on one leg for 20 seconds or more.

Dave kept asking me when we were going to pull up the wooden posts that had supported it, and I kept saying – "Not yet. I might buy another slackline." But last week I accepted that just as the back garden has needed remodelling to take account of decreasing energy and increasing bike rides, buying another slackline would be a waste of money.

When he pulled up the posts, two of them snapped, so saying goodbye on safety grounds was a good call. Even so, letting go is hard.

But my genes go on. Seven-year-old Lux had trapeze lessons on her holiday in the spring and she showed amazing natural talent.

AUGUST

August 9th 2018

Out of the heat

In my future, the memory of this summer will not be of my country falling yet further into an abyss of maladministration, racism, insularity and poverty, or of the world on fire, it will be of the wedding of Jaine and the family member who declines to be named.

In the EU. Hoorah! Specifically, in Croatia.

It was a small family wedding - 17 people including the bride and groom - and it was perfect. Beautiful and perfect. Forgive me for not giving you all the details...it feels too personal.

I will say this: if it's your youngest's wedding day and you're in a foreign country and the temperature is an unbearable 36 degrees C, and you're so nervous you can't face breakfast, Wendy has the answer. There we were sitting in the hotel lobby lapping up the aircon, waiting to check into our rooms so we could change, and she ordered champagne and tea. Two flutesful and a cuppa later and I was a new woman.

The only thing that made the end of a week spent with all my kids and grandkids bearable is the cool of England. It was too hot for me in Croatia. Jaine kept coming up to me and saying "Are you feeling a bit cooler now, Sue?" and I kept saying "No." Thank God for Wendy and her fans, which she passed around most generously.

But I would have gone to Timbuktu and survived the heat of the Sahara to see them get married. It was so special in so many ways. Of course, one way to keep cool is to get your teenage grandson to push you around the pool on a giant flamingo. But that was the morning after.

August 31st 2018

In which I contemplate the future assisted by a guest blogger.

Me first, and then Dave.

Yesterday morning Dave walked into the bedroom at 6.15 a.m. and said "I'm glad you're awake. I want you to help me find my keys. I've looked everywhere. I'm really worried!"

Dave's inability to find his keys is legend. He is not the tidiest person (ahem) so I thought OK, better get up and get this over with and then I can get my Yorkshire tea and come back to bed and drink it in peace.

So I got up and looked everywhere obvious. No joy. I looked in places not obvious. Still no joy.

We verbally retraced his steps of the previous teatime when he'd arrived home on his bike from an optician's appointment in a village 11 miles away. Was the front door locked so he'd need his keys? Or had he walked straight in? Neither of us was sure.

Having searched and fussed again for another five minutes, the theory was that either his keys were in the optician's car park for some reason, because he'd felt hassled when he'd finished his appointment, or they had fallen out of his shoulder bag on the journey home.

He was going to look for them and couldn't wait for me to get washed and dressed, so I hastily pulled on my jeans, and a

427

jumper over my pyjama top and took my mug of tea with me in the car. Dave set off, and I kept my eyes glued to the kerb of the far side of the road for eleven miles. The keys have a bright green lanyard attached to them which I had always thought excessive, but now was secretly pleased about.

But we did not find the keys.

It was 6.45 a.m. by now and we'd arrived at the car park outside the doctor, optician, physio, dentist and gym. The keys were not in sight, and I went in the gym to leave Dave's name and phone number in case someone handed them in. Then we drove home and I scanned the roadside again for eleven miles. No keys.

After breakfast I phoned the optician, doctor, etc, and left name and number and details of the keys. Then I shopped and baked a lemon drizzle cake because Zoë was coming over for the day with the boys (the fabulous grandsons I am no longer allowed to picture on the blog, let alone name). Half an hour before they were due, Dave set off on his bike to the optician's, to retrace his journey one last time, to make absolutely sure the keys were not to be found. I thought this was a waste of time. Hadn't I already looked on the road twice? Didn't he trust me?

I carried on faffing in the kitchen and opened the dresser drawer to get out a clean tea towel and guess what? There were the keys. WTF were the keys doing in the tea towel drawer? There is a hook for the keys. Why would ANYONE put the keys in the drawer that contains tea towels and dishcloths and nothing else except a secret stash of barley sugars (ahem)? The keys have never ever seen the inside of that drawer before. Believe me, it is as strange a place to put the keys as the cat's litter tray.

Zoë and the boys arrived and I told them the tale. The fabulous grandsons were amused. Zoë's expression was rather more complex as she contemplated the implications. I asked the younger FB if he thought Dave would be cross or relieved. He said "I have never seen Dave angry. Does Dave get angry? If Dave gets angry I'll have to change my view of him."

"Yes, he gets angry," I said, "but not very often. I think he'll be relieved. Also, he got in another bike ride today and he didn't think he would because you were coming."

Dave arrived home, and his only obvious emotion was relief. It wasn't just expressed relief about the keys, it was silent relief that he was not responsible, because we both knew - without even saying it - who had absentmindedly put the keys in the drawer and it wasn't him and it wasn't the cat. We knew it was me, because I am the only one who is tidy and PUTS THINGS AWAY.

This, dear readers, is the future.

As a special bonus, Dave has given his account of the saga. Hold onto your hats...

There is always something a bit cock-eyed about Thursdays.

No real surprise then to find us out just after dawn yesterday, Sue in pyjamas clutching a cup of tea, and me at the wheel, furrowed but determined, both with eyes glued to the kerb between here and the opticians where things went wrong.

Things had not begun well. I got up around 0400 as usual, messed about a bit, and then set out to feed the zoo next door while its owners are basking in Wales. I could not get out of the house. My keys were nowhere to be found, and I am the world's worst looker-for-lost-items. But no, they were not there: not on the hooks marked "keys" where they occasionally live. And not in any recent pockets. Not in any piles of washing, or tossed into the porch. They were not there, and the large green can't-lose-me lanyard was not there either.

I roused Sue, who camps on the borders of coma most of the morning, ready to slip across at a moment's notice. Nothing short of a cattle prod gets her going before 1030 at the earliest, and she isn't even interested in the latest astronomical news until late morning. In short, she is virtually dead before noon.

But she recognised the keyless panic, and boldly got up in the faint light to hunt for the keys. It did not take long to decide that the keys were not there. I mean, really not there, as in lost, and not as in 'you will have left them in your pockets.'

Cut to Wednesday, the day before. I had an appointment at the opticians, 10 miles away, but Paul at the garage suddenly needed the car to ease it gently towards scraping through its MOT, which it failed last week. So I set off on the bike in the sunshine, with bag full of useful things like keys and bike locks slung over one shoulder.

430

All good. A bit of a palaver at the opticians, and I came out after a couple of hours slightly dazed and pre-occupied. I unlocked the bike (so the keys were there) and cycled off. I had meant to go the long way home to get a decent ride, but it was late and I headed for home, making a short detour to add a few miles.

That was the last known sighting of the keys.

So back to Thursday and the pyjamas. We retraced my exact route, all eagle-eyed and keen as mustard. Sue was even awake. Nothing. Zilch. No keys.

The family was coming on Thursday, and I was detailed to construct more medieval weaponry with grandson minor. But before they arrived, I felt that speeding in the car had not done the job, and I needed to ride the route on the bike to get a slower and closer view. I set off, and did the trip, but disappointingly, no keys leapt from the verge or anything else.

On the last hill before home, I was surprised to be overtaken by my car, with S at the wheel, and grandson minor bellowing something out of the window with his usual grin.

Meeting them on the drive minutes later I began to explain the abject failure, but was interrupted by Sue who said that the keys had turned up. Calloo, callay. The keys had turned up.

But where had they been hiding? In the tea-towel drawer.

What you need to know here is that only tea-towels live in the tea-towel drawer, and over a period of 22 years living here, no key has ever seen the inside of that drawer. And I go into the drawer only when I have made oatcakes and need a clean tea-towel to drape professionally over the cooling batch. No, I have no clue why I do it.

Later, much later, with no intervening accusations as this is a no-blame zone at least in theory, S wondered aloud why and how she had put them in the drawer as she would not usually do that.

And it remains, dear reader, a mystery. And for the moment, the keys remain safely on the hooks. I feel like patting them smilingly every time I go past.

Is this what the future will look like?

SEPTEMBER

September 6th 2018

My life

Someone commenting on a recent post, in which I bemoaned my EXTREMELY wrinkled face, told me to "Get on with living your interesting, full and satisfying life and stop worrying about pointless things."

I did respond in the comments section - twice - but I can't get that phrase 'interesting, full and satisfying life' phrase out of my head. It keeps cropping up in all kinds of situations. Take

432

this morning, when I woke up feeling like all writers do from time to time - that I was a big fat impostor, that I was kidding myself that I could ever write page-turning plot, and I should give up, and concentrate on the rest of my 'interesting, full and satisfying life.'

Is my life interesting, full and satisfying? Is this what it looks like from the outside?

From the inside, I know I am very fortunate. I have good health, a lovely home, a great family (Dave is included in this word though he would argue that he doesn't count as family. I know! Take it up with him.) I have good friends, and I have enough money so I don't have to worry, though the price of domestic heating oil is currently causing some alarm at Hepworth Towers.

No-one outside can tell if my life is satisfying, but as for interesting and full...I had always thought that mine was a very quiet life. I do the same bike rides over and over, we rarely go out in the evening, and these days, my domestic and admin duties seem to take up far more time than they ever did, and they are neither interesting nor satisfying. I have a couple of trips down to London a year, one up to Wensleydale, and two to see the family in Boulder. That's about it.

Yesterday I woke up thinking - Oooh, Dave is out all morning, so I can write. Then I went downstairs to get my first mug of tea and walked in the kitchen and there were the plums that we picked the day before: five pudding basins full and the laundry basket also overflowing with plums.

These are from our one tree. And it's not all of the crop. They needed processing - stewing so Dave can eat them with his yoghurt, jamming to give away, making into crumbles for freezing, and dispersing amongst friends and neighbours.

Dave has worked as hard as I have on them and we've more or less cracked it now. But the freezer is full and we have four large containers of stewed plums in the fridge for Dave to get through before they go off.

So...I have fun. I am happy. I like my life. But I still don't like my wrinkles. Does anyone? Honestly?

OCTOBER

October 3rd 2018

The world, the universe, and trees

Dave does not do indifferent. He is either outraged - as in this morning's justified rant against Trump's latest unspeakable behaviour - or he is euphoric - such as about new discoveries in astrophysics.

In the latter case, he erupts into the room and waves his arms about in febrile excitement, while hyberbolic sentences pour out of his mouth. Unfortunately, when I hear phrases like 'billions of light years' my brain goes into meltdown. I cannot imagine what such humungous numbers mean, nor do I understand how they relate to me. When I tell him this, he explains that the immensity of the universe is a comfort. It makes him realise that his troubles and his life are insignificant.

Everywhere there is trouble - here, in America, Syria, Gaza, Indonesia, Eritrea, and more and more and more, and the politicians in so many places make things worse. Life would still go on if there were no politicians, no government. The trees, the rivers, the clouds would still be here if there were no governments.

I love to be outside in the warm, cold, breezy, whatever air, and to see the trees. Trees are such a comfort. Yesterday, Liz and I went for a replenishing walk along Bradford Dale. Before we climbed the hill and left the dale, Liz introduced me to one of her favourite trees, a sycamore. It is old and has a wide and sturdy trunk and leans asymmetrically over the water. It is not a perfect shape, I mean in terms of the platonic ideal of a sycamore tree. But it is beautiful - really beautiful. And it has ferns growing in its bark. I don't mean at the base, I mean 6 feet up, and again at 12 feet up. It's a nurturing tree. You'd feel safe if this tree was your home.

I have started to grow some trees at home. Currently they're seedlings. I have a pine, a holly, a beech and an oak. When they're robust enough I'm going to plant them alongside the Trail. It's some kind of contribution. Perhaps one of them will be a comfort to someone in the long long future.

435

October 15th 2018

Leaving an Aspie at home

The day before I flew to Boulder - which is where I am now - Dave and I had the conversation we always have before I leave the country. For the record, Dave and I have been married for 48 years.

Dave: "If I die while you're at Isaac's, you mustn't think of cutting short your holiday and coming home. You must stay there. There would be nothing to come home to - just a cadaver, which will go in the fridge. Though I don't know why they would bother when it's going to be burned anyway."

Me: "You're crazy. Do we have to go through this again?"

Dave: "It's important. I don't want your trip to be spoiled if I die. There really is no reason."

Me: "I will do what I think, Dave. You'll be dead. It'll be up to me."
(*Thinks: there is absolutely no point in trying to explain AGAIN how upset I'll be.*)
Dave: "But I don't want you to come home before you need to."
Me: "Fine, fine. Now, can we talk about something else?"

The next day when I was waiting at Heathrow for my flight to Denver, we had a chat on the phone.

Me: "What have you been doing? Been out for a bike ride?"
Dave: "No. I've been cutting up that wood and stacking it."
Me: "Great. Which woodstore did you put it in? Was there room for it?"
Dave: "It's in the orange wheelbarrow in the sitting room."

October 30th 2018
What I miss

It's good to be home.

Cece always says very sadly: "Why do you have to go home? I don't want you to leave," and she hugs me tightly, and I say to her, "But I miss Dave."

There are other things I miss when I'm in Colorado:

my other 'kids' and grandkids
my own bed
the view from the bedroom window
Dave's oatcakes
the taste of tea made at home
sitting in the sunshine in our bay window reading the
Saturday paper
my garden
the Monsal Trail
cox apples
Bramley apples
shop-bought puddings that aren't drowning in corn syrup
wholemeal bread not containing sugar

playing Scrabble with Dave

talking to Dave

my friends

my study

my laptop - Isaac always kindly lends me one of his while I'm there, but the environment is so different and I don't have easy ordered access to my files and my emails, so my writing life feels hampered

my sax

what I don't miss is the slug that's taken up residence in our porch

There are definitely things I miss about Colorado when I'm here:

the family, of course

Wendy's bike, which is so different from mine and such fun to ride, with its upright riding position and cruiser handlebars, but which would not be fun on these Peak District hills

the multi-use trails in Boulder that go in every direction

the bike lanes, and the courteous attitude of drivers towards cyclists

the vast open spaces

the views of the Rockies

the Flatirons

the sunshine

the blue skies

cycling to lunch with the family and eating outside in the sunshine

the Boulder Bookstore

being able to go into any cafe and find at least three kinds of salad on the menu

being able to order just about anything on the menu in any combination at any time of day in any café, and not being told stuff like "we don't serve lunch after 2" or "you can't have a full breakfast after 12" or "you can't have coffee while you're waiting for your lunch" or other British restrictive eating-out nonsense

American bacon and burgers, separately or together

the girls' cuddles

going out to breakfast with Wendy

watching Seinfeld with Isaac

and last but not least - margaritas!

NOVEMBER

November 16th 2018

Still not a stoic

Have you ever said to someone who asked you how you are: "I feel old" and have them respond "It's better than the alternative" (i.e. death) and felt like socking them in the jaw?

I would like to be a stoic, but I can't seem to manage it. Last night I was awake for three hours with aching legs and feet.

November 20th 2018

On the nose

I am not good at writing subtext in my dialogue. For non-writers, subtext in dialogue is the underlying meaning or motivation behind something someone says. When you write something straightforward with no subtext it's called writing on the nose. When I was working on the screenplay of *But I Told You Last Year That I Loved You,* a friendly writer critiquing it for me said the dialogue was "too on the nose."

After much thought I realised that if you live with someone with Asperger syndrome for 50 years (in my case, Dave) and you have other people in the family on the autism spectrum, you learn to talk in a straightforward and unambiguous way, otherwise you are misunderstood. Even then it can be tricky, because some of these Aspies look for subtext that isn't there and read all kinds of things into what you say that you really did not mean. But that's another problem.

In addition to being programmed over the years to be straight-talking, I am basically a frank person, and am sometimes criticised for being too frank by certain members of the family - ironically the two main critics are the ones who often look for subtext that isn't there.

But the crucial thing with my screenplay difficulty was that the story is about a marriage in which the husband has undiagnosed Asperger syndrome, so the long time wife had learned (as I did) to talk without subtext. What's a girl to do? it's a conundrum.

Subtext in dialogue is a huge problem for me, and it's one of the things I am currently wrestling with in the rewrite of *Friends, Lovers and Trees*.

Now, something for everyone - whether or not you're a writer. I came across an idea on a blog yesterday. It's the reverse advent calendar. I am a little late with this, as you're supposed to start one at the beginning of November. You collect an item every day of November - an item for a foodbank - and then hand it in at the end of the month, so the items can be given out by the foodbank in December. Isn't it a cracking idea to do with children? I would do it if I had kids still at home. As it is, I just put something in the foodbank collection basket every time I go to the Co-op.

441

November 30th 2018

What it feels like from the inside

Today, I have a guest on the blog - Dave.

Doing social

Having Aspergers means that I rarely have a sense of what is going on.

Early on I learned – don't ask me how – that the best I could do to understand the world was to conduct constant and exhaustive analysis. I have done this habitually all my life. It may take days, weeks, months, and even years on some occasions. There are things I am still analysing after 40 years and somehow the committee of brain cells is not satisfied yet.

Many of these analyses have a life of their own. They are fired often by puzzlement. Feeling bamboozled is fairly familiar. Feeling lost.

An example – a trivial example – of such analysis is Having People Round. They may Eat, Visit, or perhaps just Chat. Everything is OK until they leave. I ask Sue 'Was that OK? Were they alright?' and then, whatever her answer, plunge into analysis. I search for nuance, study body language, remember what seemed significant moments, trying to figure out if the evening went well. The thing here is that I simply have no circuits to tell me how it was, whether they were OK or not. I have absolutely no sense of it, and have to try to arrive at a conclusion by means of relentless analysis.

442

To normal people, this process is at best aberrant, and at worse plain nuts. They have an intuitive feel for whether some social occasion has been OK. They don't need to ask anybody. The question seems absurd. To them, whether someone enjoyed themselves or not is obvious, like asking them if the sky is blue, or what colours mix to make orange. It is not something they think about. Ever. This always feels like amazing magic to me: some spell I never mastered. One of very many.

Analytical thinking was useful at work, when it was explicitly useful. Leading a group through the foothills of analysis to the peaks of understanding was something I could do with ease. But nobody at work knew that the same process was constantly clicking over covertly in my head. It is incessant. It is exhausting, but I can't stop it. And if I ever did stop it, I would have no understanding at all of what is going on around me. Analysis is the best I can do.

Sometimes there are intuitive insights which make me feel like an idiot savant. I can sometimes pick up on odd emotional undercurrents, and can stumble upon the hidden issues to unlock problems. This can be mistaken as being smart, when it is merely an accident of circuitry.

In particular, my radar has always been tuned to the wavelength of distress. I have never handled happiness well, and cannot detect it confidently in other people or myself. But misery? That's another story. I seem able to see the tapestry of misery with all the subtlety of a Farrow and Ball paint chart. I

443

seem able to home in on people's hidden sadness in a way which often takes them aback.

Why is this? Well, I do not know, of course. It was true when I was a child, and is still true now.

This random and bizarre combination is all I have to try to understand the world. No wonder I feel so often out of place, puzzled, adrift.

I am hopeless at 'doing social'. I often wonder aloud to Sue whether people I know might be considered friends, or if she thinks they might think of me as a friend. I was never sure, am still never sure. People are at best a mystery, and occasionally a nightmare.

Doing social was always a problem. Living in a shop, there was a clear boundary between the house and the shop. You stepped through a door from a private world into a public one. In the public one there were likely to be hordes of strangers: customers, reps, deliverymen, all of whom you were supposed to talk to. I remember always feeling tense before stepping through the door that led from the safety of the house into the shop where strange customers might be lurking. It often felt like us against them, though none ever got through the door to the house and actually invaded.

When 'visitors', 'strangers' actually got into the house, it was usually at my mother's invitation. She even invited relatives to visit. When they came, much to my mother's delight, my father, grandfather and I saw thought of it as an alien invasion. Relatives were inconvenient, verging on hostile. We withdrew

444

into our respective shells like alarmed tortoises. There were a few exceptions: relatives with favoured status. We never invited anybody: relatives had nothing to do with us. We tolerated them to please my mother. I think she found this difficult.

I never understood relatives, and could never find common ground with them. It was hard to even figure out how they fitted together. They always felt like a problem that was just too difficult to solve. After my mother died in 1971 it was an opportunity to slip out of sight of many relatives, and her funeral was the last time I ever had any contact with most of them. I do not know whether they are alive or dead, but either way they do not trouble me now.

The family motto was "God gives you relatives. Thank god you can choose your friends."

The thing was that we did not choose many. My mother had a bunch of them. She visited them, and they came to see her. I think she probably needed the light relief.

My father had a friend. Jack Brownhill had improbably furry eyebrows and appeared very infrequently. He had been best man at my parents' wedding, and after that came around like a comet maybe once every two years. It wasn't a close friendship, but it was the closest my father had. Jack Brownhill and my father both look bewildered on the wedding photographs, though that might have been due to the fancy dress. I have no idea who Jack Brownhill actually was.

My grandfather had a tiny group of friends who never visited, though he went to see them. They were previous colleagues from work, and all of them female. He – and I – always got on more easily with women than with men. Neither he nor I were competitive, and both of us were vaguely cerebral, probably feeling safer in our heads than out in the company of people.

As a kid, I had friends at primary school. I even did Susan Sloboda's maths in exchange for her doing my sewing. My stuffed Bambi still has Susan's tiny seams punctuated by wild blanket stitch where I took over. My sewing looks like the webs spun by spiders after being given marijuana. But I was taken home ill from the end of school leaver's party. It was the social stress that made me ill, rather than the jelly and buns.

Secondary school was a nightmare of Kafka-esque proportions from the first day to the last, and 'friends' there were never more than acquaintances really. The school used surnames only, so I guess that friends were the people whose first names I knew. The main task at school was to protect myself from the school's desire that we should all fit in with what were odd rules of behaviour. I did this by being difficult when I was there, and by being there as infrequently as was possible. I was often not there when I was actually there – playing truant inside the school. I have been playing truant all my life.

I did A levels at 16, and went to university when I was just 17. I was socially inept, hideously immature, ill-at-ease, but good at Latin. It was not a promising prospect.

The university wanted me to go into hall. This was a deal-breaker as I simply could not face spending time in the company of so many strangers. I wrote to say that I would not be going to the university at all if I had to be in hall, and so I ended up in digs with a dozen other misfits, oddballs and eccentrics. They were delightful, though Sue always felt we were faintly creepy as a bunch.

University was the best period of my life. By light years. There were very few, if any, rules. Nobody seemed to care very much what you did, and there was no pressure of any kind. I failed to turn up for any departmental meetings, parties, meals or wine tastings, and did not go to graduation.

I missed not only lectures, but whole courses of lectures. I read voraciously and discovered delight in so many areas of learning. I bought astonishing numbers of books and had VIP status in the bookshop as a result.

As an adult I have studiously and creatively avoided groups of people wherever they gather. Shops, parties, weddings, sports, festivals, collective bonhomie of all kinds. I am most alone in groups of people, and feel existentially threatened. I have been to three weddings, one of which was my own, but could not face going to my wonderful children's weddings. There are many reasons for that, but social events are something I welcome as much as the invitation to have flu for a month, or have someone push wires under my toe-nails. I break into a sweat at social events, feel my pulse rate and blood pressure rise, and can't wait to get away.

447

To other people, it seems incredible that I have this debilitating lack of social feel. It is unbelievable to normal people that anyone can lack this basic capability. I look un-ironed but otherwise almost normal. My behaviour is a little eccentric, but not wildly enough to have me barred from public spaces. But there is just no circuit in my head which can tune in to how happy people are, whether they like me, whether they are having a good time, whether they are satisfied.

Analysis, analysis, analysis … there are usually several simultaneous analyses continually running in my head. No matter what I am doing, however absorbed I am in some obscure woodwork or music, committees of brain cells are beavering away trying to find answers to impossible and often trivial questions.

I cannot tell whether people are angry or upset. This is true of myself, too. It is hard to distinguish between them. I try not to get into that whole territory, as it feels rather scary. On occasions when I have been angry, I feel out of control and unstoppable. Martial boggled at the rhino displayed in the arena. He commented that it was slow to anger, and hard to provoke, but once aroused it was ferocious beyond belief. The Romans were awe-struck that a rampaging rhino, suitably goaded into action, tossed anything in its path. Its fury was indiscriminate and implacable. I know how it felt.

Until really recently, and decades after her death, I always thought of my mum as volcanic. She seemed to me to have two settings: calm and explosive. There was no mid-setting, and she moved unpredictably from pacific to violent without warning. It was scary and made me feel a bit insecure. Now I see that she must have had infinite gradations of gently increasing annoyance. The puzzle for her must have been that I ignored the warning signs and ploughed on regardless. It must have been so frustrating and inexplicable. But I simply did not notice any warning signs, could not read them, did not even see them. I simply went on with whatever nefarious thing I was doing, and kept on enthusiastically until she exploded, much to my complete surprise. And much to her huge incomprehension. How could I be so wilfully annoying ?

No relevant circuits, that's how.

I am colour-blind. My rainbows, wonderful, glorious, and moving have only two distinct colours really. I see yellow and I see blue, and maybe am aware of another colour, though I don't know what it is. Not for me the ROYGBIV version which I know exists for other people, but never see. It's just the same with emotions. You have to work with whatever you have.

DECEMBER

December 3rd 2018

The wife's tale

Dave, who has Asperger syndrome, wrote the last post on here about how he feels in social situations, and someone suggested I write my side of the story. Here is a slightly amended version of something I wrote for the National Autistic Society's magazine, which was at that time called *Communication*.

An odd marriage

It hasn't been an easy marriage. And I know that Dave would say the same. But it has been a long one – 48 years. After huge difficulties – especially in the early years - we're still together, still good friends, and I'm happy. Very happy.

It's a little difficult to write about one's marriage honestly without saying things you'd rather not share with the world at large. Perhaps that's why I wrote a novel - rather than an autobiography – about a woman married to a man with Asperger's syndrome. The novel, for those of you who haven't read it, is *But I Told You Last Year That I Loved You*. The main female character (Fran) doesn't know her husband (Sol) has Asperger's syndrome, and only realises this towards the end of the book. She has been married to him for thirty-something years and finds him hard to live with, awkward, stubborn, pathologically unsociable, with inconvenient food fads and obsessive interests and addicted to routine, but at the same

450

time honest, loyal, caring, reliable, creative, fascinating, and always with something interesting to say. She also finds him very very funny.

If I had known in the early days that Dave had Asperger's syndrome, it would have made things so much easier. I can't remember now all the adjustments I had to make, but I learned to go to parties on my own, often to go on holiday on my own with the children, to travel abroad on my own. He would not eat with the children and me: he ate different food at a different time. Perhaps I've managed because I have a robust self-confidence, and because I don't mind people thinking we are odd. And I have learned to see things from his point of view. For example, if he finds parties painful, anxiety-provoking experiences, wouldn't it be mean to insist he come with me?

There are still some problems. Dave sometimes misinterprets my reactions and emotions: he often thinks that I'm angry and hostile, when actually I'm upset. At other times he can't appreciate the intensity of my feelings if I am speaking calmly, without obvious signs of distress. I may have to get to the point of tears for him to grasp how I feel. It's different if I am physically hurt, when he will respond immediately with sympathy and care.

Another issue *for me* is his apparent inability to accept that my feelings can change. If I tell him one time that, for example, I don't like a person, he doesn't seem to allow me to say later – "Actually, now I know them better, I think they're OK." He

451

will forever say "I know you hate so and so." Note here that he doesn't say "dislike" but "hate."

Things are either black or they're white. If he makes something and brings it in from the shed to show me and I say "It's very nicely made, but it's not my *favourite* thing you've made," when he later shows it to someone else he will say "Sue hates it."

It was only a few years ago that I found out the reason for Dave's unusual behaviour and outlook on life. Someone else in the family was diagnosed with Asperger's syndrome, and Dave and I researched the disorder, and it all became so obvious that we wondered why we hadn't thought of it before. It explained EVERYTHING.

Does it make any difference to me now, knowing about Dave's Autism Spectrum Disorder (ASD)?

What helps at this late stage is knowing that the little things he makes a fuss about are genuinely upsetting to him, and he's not just being a drama queen. He was upset that the monitor of his new computer was black, when he'd ordered a white one. Black upsets him. He went on and on about this problem, which appeared trivial to me. *OK so you don't like black! Get over it!* But to someone with ASD this kind of thing isn't trivial.

He finds patterned fabrics visually disturbing, so we have plain furnishings. He has an unusually sensitive sense of smell. Narcissi and hyacinths make him unbearably nauseous, as do the smell of many foods I like to eat – blue cheese, parmesan, fish pie. I just asked him for some other examples

452

of domestic smells that upset him and he said "Gangrene." Thanks, Dave.

Even the pluses have their downside. Dave's honesty, which I value immensely, has made my strong self-confidence necessary for survival. One morning I woke up very late. When I eventually came downstairs, Dave said: "You've been asleep for so long, I was beginning to think you were dead."

"Didn't it occur to you to come up and check? Weren't you worried?" I said.

"It would have been fine. I know how to get rid of a cadaver."

He said this in all seriousness. Fortunately, I found it hilarious.

And then there are the "compliments."

Dave: "From this angle your nose is rather reminiscent of the twisted spire in Chesterfield."

Sue: "Can't you say something nicer than that?"

Dave: "But I like the twisted spire. And don't forget it's a tourist attraction."

I found this last comment so comical I put it in the novel. For me, his unusual take on life is refreshing, challenging and interesting, as well as often funny. Here's another real-life conversation I used in the novel, word-for-word:

"I've conceived a strong antipathy for my dark blue underpants," he said.

"*What?*" she said. "But they're exactly like your light blue ones. M&S. Exactly the same design."

"The dark ones seem sinister, ideological, repressive. They're less willing to negotiate than the pale blue ones. I don't want to be bullied by my underpants at this age."

All marriages, whether or not to someone with ASD, have their difficulties, their irritations, their times of frustration. What it boils down to is this: *How much do you love this person?* and *How much do you want to stay married?* Each person has to decide whether the balance between what they are putting into the marriage and what they are doing without in order to stay in the marriage, is worth what the marriage gives them. Dave is honest, loyal, caring, considerate, supportive, incredibly helpful, a wonderful home-maker, reliable, creative, engages me in fascinating conversation, and makes me laugh.

That's more than enough for me.

p.s. I need to emphasise that I am no saint: there has been mutual aggravation in this relationship. So I assume that just as I think it's worth it, Dave does too.

December 7th 2018

Cottage cheese, anyone?

I started 'dieting' in the spring, and as a result have managed to drop a size in Sainsbury's men's jeans. A style icon, that's me. I have lost enough weight for people to notice and say

"Sue, you look so slim!" I have no idea how many pounds I've lost as I don't ever weigh myself, and if the doctor insists on weighing me, I always look away.

By 'dieting,' I mean cutting out biscuits, cakes and puddings, and having cottage cheese and tomato on Ryvita every day for every lunch I eat at home. That's it. Breakfast and tea as normal. I've had occasional lapses but managed to keep up the pattern now for 7 months.

Now, however, the short dark days and the cold are taking their toll. And every time I sit down and look at the plate of Ryvita and cottage cheese my heart sinks and my digestive juices drain away in disgust, shrieking "No! No! Not again!"

Yesterday I got back from a bike ride urgently inserted into the gap in the rain, and was so hungry that I rebelliously stuffed my face with beans on toast. And then, half an hour later at 2.15 (not even a mealtime) I microwaved the out-of-date Christmas pudding that has been staring me in the face every time I've opened the store cupboard door since January. It was delicious.

For tea I had fish and chips.

Today is a new day. It's not that I want to lose any more weight, I just don't want to pile it on again over the winter months. What's your secret slimming tip?

December 18th 2018

Frugality plus inventiveness can be a trap

When people see all the beautiful things Dave has made - furniture, stained glass, carvings, Christmas decorations - they envy me. They also envy me because he is so good at FIXING things. I am a lucky woman. I know this. However...there is a dark side to all this talent: his eagerness to create things from bits and bobs when one would much rather go out and BUY said object.

Take yesterday. I came home from Bakewell market and complained to Dave about the heavy shopping, and how I was wondering about buying a shopping trolley - a trendy one (if 'trendy shopping-trolley' is not an oxymoron.) He said "Oh, you mean one of those tartan ones."

"No! No! Something modern!"

"You don't need to buy one," he said. "I'll make you one. Something robust and capacious."

My heart sank.

"What you need is one like window cleaners used to have," he said. "I could use old bike wheels. I've got two in the shed."

"I have no idea what you're talking about, but NO."

"Yes, yes," he said. "Google an image of a traditional window cleaner's trolley."

I did. It had large wooden cart wheels with a platform on top.

"That's it," he said. "But there should be a big box on top."

"And just how am I expected to get that in the back of the car to bring it home from Bakewell?"

"I'll make you a ramp!"

You may laugh, dear reader. I would if I didn't live with this man.

Anyway, this conversation reminded me of a piece I once had in the *Times* which I don't think I've shared with you before:

Make do and ~~mend~~ spend!

Do you ever look with dissatisfaction at your furniture and wish you could start again? You don't want to submit to the horrors of trial by makeover, but you would like to junk that ugly lumpen armchair your mother-in-law gave you, or that trendy-in-the-seventies standard lamp reminiscent of a salon hairdryer? After we lost all our things in a fire, and the emotional ashes began to settle, we had that chance to start again. But even with a lump sum and an empty house the task was arduous for a couple with no experience of buying new furniture.

We married as impoverished students, and as the years passed most of what furnished our house before the fire was not so much chosen and bought, but inherited, or just somehow acquired. Objectively speaking we had some good stuff, such as the three handsome grandfather clocks my husband Dave had inherited. But I could have counted on the fingers of one hand the items of furniture which we actually went out and bought in a shop. This was a result partly of lack of funds at the appropriate time, but also of an abhorrence of waste, a make-do-and-mend philosophy, a drive to recycle and reclaim wherever possible, and the inability to look a gift horse in the mouth.

In our young and untroubled student days when we were able to afford a Land Rover but not new furniture (why was that?) we had been asked by some newly married friends if we would take to the tip a "hideous three piece suite" which a parent was foisting upon them to be helpful. Well, the suite turned out to be beautiful - art deco, upholstered in blue velvet, with walnut veneer arms – so we took it home. It became one of my favourites, much coveted by the more discerning of my friends, but much reviled by my modernist husband. It was followed by similar items, which friends wanted to get rid of and which I wanted to give a good home to. At one time in the sitting room of our first small flat we actually had three sofas.

It's hard to buy new things when recycling is in your genes. I remember going off to camp for the first time with a home made rucksack my mother had recycled from an old gaberdine mac, with zips reclaimed from long dead trousers, and a cord from a pair of tattered pyjamas. She would make us bedside tables and dolls houses out of orange boxes, and even long after she had anyone needing dolls furniture, she found it excruciating to throw away those tiny plastic catering tubs when emptied of jam or UHT milk - they made such

458

wonderful wash-basins. Her one thousand and one ways with a pair of old tights is so well documented that we can't see a pair adrift in a hedgerow without my husband saying "your mother must have been here again." Her favourite use was as twine for tying up my father's raspberry canes in the autumn.

And my grandmother was the same. She made a superior picnic blanket out of an old tweed coat, and dusters out of old knickers ("every gusset a memory" – Victoria Wood.) Her better underwear was not suitable for dusters, being made from an old silk parachute. The tights-recycling gene manifested itself in her case in the knitting of them into peg bags.

As for Dave, his recycling tendencies verge on the pathological. Once, to get rid of unwanted junk, we hired a skip with the couple next door. The two men would each wheel a barrow full of old rammel through their respective gates to meet at the skip with mutual cries of "Don't you want that? Can I have it?" followed by the swapping of treasures and the wheeling of full barrows back up the two garden paths.

So you can see that the fire did us one or two favours: I am delighted to be rid of the hundreds of beads from a dismantled car bead seat, the spherical light shade made out of Sainsburys High Juice plastic bottle caps, and a mound of worn bicycle tyres.

Make-do-and-mend is a trap. In one of my Dave's joyful austerity periods he mended my daughter's glasses with string

459

and then sprayed it gold to match the glasses: she has never forgiven him. He also resoled his shoes with an old car tyre. Even now, when anyone needs anything at all, from a bird feeder to a roof rack, our long flown children will say with ghoulish delight "Don't worry - Dave will knock you one up out of an old bike tyre!" Don't get me wrong: I love the huge set of wind chimes made from wardrobe rail which now adorn our hall; and the aerobic ankle weights he fashioned from a piece of old lead piping are great.

But recycling requires raw materials, and even Dave was flummoxed by an empty house. On receiving the insurance cheque it was extremely difficult to break away from frugal ways and actually spend money on large items of furniture, particularly when we viewed them as once only purchases which had to last us the rest of our lifetimes.

And even though we had been married for 25 years, the profound clash in our tastes only became apparent when we were choosing new things. It was a case of traditionalist with a penchant for period style meets radical minimalist who thinks that form should always follow function. What possible middle ground in clothes storage is there between someone who wants an Edwardian chest of drawers in satinwood, and someone who prefers a stack of wipe clean plastic boxes? Or between someone who yearns for a kingsize cast iron bedstead, and someone who hankers after hammocks?

Yet another problem was Dave's aversion to shopping. I thought I'd found the solution by using mail order. But catalogue sofas with apparently perfect proportions, when transposed to our sitting room looked like sofas on steroids. We returned them, and for 18 months we sat on the floor.

We have now managed to buy most of the furniture we need, but it has been a novel and a gruelling process. And after having a lot of detritus forcibly taken from us, we are definitely more discerning in our recycling. But what's that lurking behind the new sofa? A carrier bag full of old tights?

December 24th 2018

Hope and love

Things are tough out there, aren't they? Stormy, scary, poisonous, and desperate.

But let's not give up on hope. Hope and love.

Thank you for staying with me throughout the year, dear friends. I hope you have the kind of Christmas you wish for. At Hepworth Towers this year it's ON, so I can't stick around here sharing poetry and dawns no matter how much I love you, because *Perks must be about it*. Happy Christmas!

JANUARY

January 1st 2019

New Year's Resolutions for others

Happy New Year, dear readers! 2019 is not for the fainthearted, but in the history of the world I'm sure there have been worse.

Here, to give you a boost, is a piece I had in the *Times* some years ago...

When you're dead I'll read in bed

At the beginning of January three things happen with an unfortunate synchronicity.

First, you get a desire to purge domestic detritus.

Second, peri-Christmas pressures make trivial niggles with your partner get out of proportion, leading you to consider clearing the domestic decks in a rather more drastic way.

Third, there is a problem that links the two above – that of wanting to throw something away but your partner saying that you can do it only over his/her dead body.

I have no neat solution to the problematic intersection of the above. However, my husband Dave and I have devised a game to dispel some of the tension it engenders. It is based on the idea that no matter how happy and settled you are with a person there will still be some things that you look forward to when they are no longer around.

The best time to play the game is when the winter seems interminable, and family members are getting chronically fractious, like schoolchildren after two weeks of wet playtimes. We have found it especially invigorating on those gloomy January afternoons when we have attempted a post-prandial walk and only managed to get as far as the end of the road before an icy downpour has propelled us back home with our dripping anoraks stuck to our soaking jeans, which are stuck to our cold wet legs.

We call the game *When you are dead,* but if you find this title in poor taste you can always re-name it (less pithily) *In my next life I shall marry someone who.*

"When you die," says Dave, "I'll rip out the phone."

"When you die," I respond, "your 25-year-old cycling jersey will be the first thing to go." It has more runs than the Australian cricket team and is now more mends than original. Yet before putting it on for a bike ride he stretches the darned thing out on the kitchen table to show me the latest holes and pulled threads, and says pathetically 'Couldn't you mend it, just one more time?' A less indulgent woman would have made the "mistake" long ago of mixing it up with the bag of jumble bound for recycling.

"In my next life" say I, "I shall marry someone who doesn't complain when I want to read in bed."

463

"In my next life," says he, "I shall marry someone who doesn't rush off to answer the phone when they're in the middle of talking to me."

Another version of the game is *New Year Resolutions for others*. Thus Dave's resolution for me would be that I would throw away old food rather than leaving it to skulk in the back of the fridge. Last week he thought he saw a novelty fabric cucumber behind the egg box, because the mould on it had the texture and sheen of velour.

He would also like me to desist from clearing away his tools from the kitchen when he hasn't finished a job, and to restrain myself from returning his half-read books to the bookshelves in random order. Also to do some mending – starting with his cycling jumper.

My first resolution for him would be to take off his muddy shoes at the door - as the children do – rather than keeping them on, forgetting to wipe them, and then treading mud all over the carpet, followed by his saying in a puzzled tone, as if the effect were as mystifying as the marks on the Turin Shroud, "I seem to have got some mud on the carpet."

I would like him to stop soaking his bicycle chain in paraffin on the draining board in one of my Pyrex dishes; to finish off an item of food before starting on a new one - loaf of bread, bottle of milk, cucumber, whatever; and to stop using the answering machine to screen every single telephone call – even when it's a bank holiday and the only person we are expecting to ring is my sister.

464

You may see recurrent themes emerging from all this dissent, and that explains the intractable nature of the problems, and why the game is such a boon. Living with someone long-term is like Dr Seuss's Crumple-horn, Web-footed, Green-bearded Schlottz, 'whose tail is entailed with un-solvable knots.'

And I still think the original name of the game is best - *When you are dead.* I felt a great sympathy with Lady Longford, who, when she was asked if she'd ever thought of divorcing her husband, said – "Divorce never, murder often."

January 18th 2019

The flesh is weak

A friend said to me in an email yesterday: *Don't know about you, but endless political turmoil is so very unsettling in almost every aspect of daily life. No matter how much you try to keep it at arm's length, there's an underlying agitation.*

That's exactly how I feel this week. I can't settle.

But let's try to think about something else...

How do you feel about veganism? The only time I've considered it in the past has been when I've heard the cows in the adjacent field crying for their calves.

Things are different now. We've had a couple of vegans in the family for a year now, and every time I have thought about cooking for them I've felt annoyed. I know, I know, this is most uncivil of me. It's not as though I eat a lot of meat. And it's only

465

a step further than cooking for vegetarians, which I've been doing since 1971. It's just...what the hell do you do for flavour when you can't use cheese?

Anyway, two weeks ago I heard a short radio programme about sustainability and saving the planet, and it made such a good case for veganism that I was completely persuaded that it was the right way to eat. I have not become a vegan - come on, I was brought up on a mixed farm in the 50s - but it has made me completely sympathetic to their requirements. I still feel irritated by the things I can't use in recipes, but I don't feel cross with the vegans themselves. I admire them for doing the right thing.

I decided that although I'm not willing to be a vegan myself yet, I would move towards it and cook some vegan meals for myself every week. (I don't cook for Dave. His Aspergers makes him graze, and anyway most of his diet consists of yoghurt. And before you ask, I'd rather not answer questions about his diet right now. It's not relevant.)

I started the new regime by making some beanburgers which were easy to make from store cupboard ingredients, but they were tasteless.

This week I tried again. I had four large flat mushrooms languishing in the fridge salad drawer that needed eating, and I made some mushroom and nut burgers. I made up the recipe. They were amazingly tasty, but then I had found a small lump of vegan 'parmesan' cheese in the fridge, left there by a vegan at Christmas, and I'd grated that into the mix. I also added soy sauce. They tasted great, and something I might even choose on a menu.

I was feeling pretty pleased with myself and wondering what I would try to make next, and maybe I could be a vegan one day, when I popped into the Co-op to buy some hummus and came out with said hummus and a ribeye steak.

I ate it last night. It was delicious.

But I'm not giving up. I'll try more vegan stuff next week.

FEBRUARY

February 19th 2019

On not blogging

My brother on the phone at the weekend: "You haven't blogged. Why haven't you blogged?"

Me: "I've got nothing to say."

Him: "Well, put some nice photos on, then. Get outside with your camera and take some spring flowers."

Me: "I don't want to just put photos on. I was thinking of baring my soul."

Him: "Oh no. Don't bare your soul."

Gales of laughter.

MARCH

March 15th 2019

Fun in Boulder

Last week I went for a hugely enjoyable 18 mile bike ride with Isaac, and today I had a fun trip out with Wendy: breakfast out, a pedicure, and then a drive into the mountains.

Some time ago, a woman on Goodreads reviewed *Plotting for Beginners* scathingly, saying it was unrealistic that a woman of 50-something should behave as Sally Howe does. I have long wanted to tell her that it was based on how I felt at that age and she was entirely mistaken, but it's infra-dig for authors to respond to 'reviewers' about stuff like that. If she'd seen Wendy (42) and me (69) last Monday, driving in the Beetle with the top down and loud rock music blaring from the radio, with Wendy and I singing along, and waving to people as we passed, that reader would no doubt have needed smelling salts.

March 23rd 2019

Letter from home

When Isaac and the girls waved me goodbye as I went through security at Denver airport, I had an ache in my chest. I don't remember it being that bad before.

But then I arrived home to Dave, the green grass of spring, and the leaf buds on the hawthorn tree. It was wonderful. There was also the blessed silence after the hellish travel.

Aye, but it's good to be home for the spring. In Boulder the grass is brown and dead and there aren't any blackbirds.

Wendy said excitedly last week "I saw a hock in the garden!" and I said, puzzled, "What's a hock?"

"You know," she said. "A bird of prey."

"Oh, we don't have hocks in the UK."

Isaac said: "She means a hawk."

March 26th 2019

Spring

Yesterday morning as I drove down to Bakewell in the sharp spring sunshine, I was hit by a seasonal melancholy. The light was clear and unforgiving, the daffodils on the verges were searingly lovely and the world was saying "In your face, it's spring!"

I don't know what it is about daffodils in this particular angle of sunlight, with mistiness on the far horizon, but it makes me feel sad. I came home and told Dave and he knew just what I meant. So did T S Eliot -

April is the cruellest month, breeding

Lilacs out of the dead land, mixing

Memory and desire, stirring
Dull roots with spring rain.

Yes, I know it's not April, but it *feels* like April.

Later, in the afternoon, I was pottering in the front garden sorting out the raggedy pots of tête-à-têtes, when a local farmer drove past in his Land Rover, with his window down and his Jack Russell terrier on his knee and the spring felt human again, friendly.

March 30th 2019

Working it out

I am still wrestling with the idea that I am going to be 70 this year, and wondering what it means for me and my life. Perhaps it doesn't mean very much, just as passing from December 31st to January 1st means little, though people mark it as the start of a new year, with new aims and purposes.

When I was about to turn 60 I felt the same, and asked various friends who were already that great age how they felt and if they were approaching their lives any differently. That resulted in my taking up the sax, and having a slackline in the garden.

So far I've only asked one wise friend about being a 70-something - someone who happens to be in his 80s and is still active politically, socially and physically. I explained I wanted to do something 'useful' to help people, and he said I should start by considering what brought me joy. Then think about what are my main concerns, and see if I could bring the two together.

I don't think it's going to work. What brings me joy is being outside in the countryside, either walking or cycling or gardening, and being with friends and family, while my main concerns are refugees and food poverty.

I asked a member of the family who is in his thirties about what I should do, now that I will not be writing another novel, and he said "Have fun." When friends are seriously ill, and others have already died, there is an argument for seizing the day and packing in as much fun as possible before I too become infirm.

Yesterday I told Dave that when I got back from an early morning errand I was going to drive into Sheffield to buy some knitting wool, but when I got home from the errand the sky was so blue and the sun so bright and I knew it was the last day before the Sheffield school holidays began and the Trail would for two weeks be full of visitors, so I went out for a long bike ride instead of going to town. I didn't regret it. But I was knackered, and couldn't do much for the rest of the day but sit around in the sunshine.

Old age feels like a balancing act - between enjoying what your savings can buy, and keeping enough for possibly decades of rainy days; between having fun, and helping other people;

between taking it easier because you're older, and pushing yourself every day to keep fit.

I've said it before and I'll say it again: old age ain't for cissies.

p.s. I just had a lovely Mother's Day card saying -
"Hope you can rest on your laurels a bit after 48 busy years!"

APRIL

April 3rd 2019

Sartorial ecstasy

One day when I was staying in Boulder with the family I was looking for my boots in the shoe rack and came across some bright blue tennis shoes and I fell in love with them.

I tried them on and joked to Wendy – "These shoes obviously won't suit you, so I think I'll have them."

"Of course!" she said. "I ordered them online and when they arrived I knew they weren't for me, and saved them for you."

I don't believe her: I think she bought them with me in mind. She's that kind of girl. And she never wears blue.

Do you have an item of clothing that brings you joy? Something that lightens your heart as soon as you put it on? That's how I feel about these shoes. I catch sight of them on my feet and I can't help smiling.

You may recall that a month ago I said I was going to treat myself to something from TOAST which was far too pricey but which I was buying as a 70th birthday treat? (Don't worry, this 70th birthday fixation will be over by Christmas.) It was a pair of dungarees. I bought them and they were too wide and too short so I sent them back, but in Boulder's famous hardware shop, McGuckins, I found some I loved, which were a third of the price. I ADORE dungarees. I had three pairs in the 80s - bright yellow, bright green and bright turquoise - but we lost them in the fire and I have always mourned them.

I asked Dave if there was anything he wears that makes him feel unreasonably happy and he said yes, his light brown carpenter dungarees (we are so made for each other) and his leather jerkin. He rocks his dungarees but I loathe his jerkin, which amongst other faults, is two sizes too big. I hate it, but now I understand what joy it brings him, I shall not complain when he wears it to walk down to Hassop Station with me.

Sartorial joy is rare and should be honoured and celebrated.

April 24th 2019

Passing moods, whims and must-haves

Do you ever think out of nowhere about a very specific item of food that you haven't had in ages and feel you've got to eat immediately or you'll die?

473

I had that feeling yesterday about a scone. I could have baked a batch, but as the family have left home and Dave doesn't eat them, it would have been excessive. I only wanted one. So I went to Chatsworth Farm Shop and bought one and I had it with butter and homemade blackcurrant jam, and it was just as delicious as I imagined it would be.

MAY

May 30th 2019

Losing it

I know that some of you are in the same age bracket as me, so I want to ask you...Can you feel your capacity for short term memory ebbing away?

My brother rang this morning, asking if we'd finished the weekend crossword. What was the solution to 2 down: Sneaky, as most female athletes are essentially? (15)

"Oh," I said breezily, "I can't remember now. I'll fish the paper out of the recycling and email you the answer."

I fetched the paper which I had tidied away yesterday, and was amazed to see we had not finished the crossword. We ALWAYS finish the crossword, and if it's too hard, we leave it out on the coffee table or the kitchen table until we have. When I tidied it away yesterday I assumed we'd completed it. I had no memory whatsoever of breaking off and our saying to each other we'd finish it later.

And here's another thing... Have you ever had a discussion with someone about something and reached a decision about a task that needed doing and then two days later when you came to do said task, you'd forgotten what was decided?

Have you ever had an engagement in your diary for three months and then when it came to the day itself, forgotten all about it?

Yes, folks, I'm on the way out, and it ain't pretty.

JULY

July 6ᵗʰ 2019

Deterioration

I didn't realise how fond I was of my keys until I lost them.

Before I continue, I need to explain that apart from an incident last August which I told you about, I am not known as a key-losing person: that has always been Dave's province.

However, when I got home from my recent holiday in Cornwall, I couldn't find my house keys. They had no identifying label on them so it wasn't a security worry. It was annoying and inconvenient, and it made me worry about the soundness of my mind.

But I also felt sad. My mother died in 2008 and we sold her cottage in 2010, and yet I kept the cottage key on the keyring.

Then there was the fob. It looks like a random bit of chunky red plastic, but it's claim to fame is that Isaac made it for me in CDT at school when he was a teenager. He is now 46.

My friend Het, with whom I'd been staying in Cornwall, scoured her house and came up with nothing. She rang the local post office and Land's End to enquire if anyone had handed in the keys, which I thought I might possibly have lost while walking along the coastal path. I rang the lost property offices of the trains I'd been on. All came to nought.

Dave said he remembered my saying before I went away that I had put them in a drawer to keep them safe. I didn't recall saying that. Was his memory playing tricks on him too? Whether or no, I looked in every drawer in the house: nothing. I searched all the bags I had taken to Cornwall several times: nothing. I was resigned to not seeing the keys again. And then yesterday Dave borrowed my rucksack and emptied it out at the end of the day and there they were.

I am ridiculously happy to have them back. I feel hugely relieved that I am not the sort of person who loses house keys outside the house. But I am also faintly disturbed, because this kind of thing is just going to get worse, isn't it? I have just now realised that my blouse - which I wore to go to Bakewell this morning - is inside out.

Dave says we need a checklist to work through before we leave the house, and I think he might be right.

Top and bottom covered in clothing

All clothes the right way out

Hair brushed

No smears of toothpaste round mouth

Facial hair plucked

Shopping list in pocket

Note left to absent partner as to intended destination and time of departure

Windows shut and locked

All doors locked

Keys safe

Hey ho. We were young once.

July 11th 2019

Boob talk

I've been reminded of my mastectomy this week through a conversation with someone on Twitter, and it made me dig out this piece I had in *The Times* in a different lifetime.

Boob talk

"The worst thing about your mastectomy, as far as I'm concerned" said my husband, "is forever finding your falsie in the fruit bowl." OK, I admit it, sometimes when it's itching a bit I do take it out and leave it in the receptacle closest to hand. And while I'm not upset by finding such a good friend in unexpected places, other members of the family are not so keen on reaching into the magazine rack for the Radio Times and getting a handful of pink blancmange instead.

We wouldn't have this problem if I'd had a reconstruction after the mastectomy. It was five years ago and feel I got off lightly because I had no other treatment. And although I've had occasional cysts, which do cause a bout of the jitters until they are diagnosed and dealt with, I've had no recurrence of cancer.

I did originally discuss reconstructive surgery with my breast care nurse, a fellow mastectomee and someone who also shared my sense of humour. She entertained me with the trials of colour matching fake nipples, and with stories of swimming on holiday and being startled at the sight of her freedom-

478

loving prosthesis, having escaped the confines of her cossie and approaching her atop a wave.

Yesterday at my annual check up the doctor asked me if I'd ever thought of having a reconstruction, something no-one had mentioned since the mastectomy. I explained that I wasn't keen on having alien bodies implanted into my own body, which with advancing middle age looks alien enough (on those occasions when I'm feeling robust enough to look at myself in the mirror with no clothes on.)

The truth is that I have adjusted to being an Amazon. The only real drag is having my falsie escape at inopportune moments. Like the time I was painting the gloss in our new house while the builder and plumber were in the adjoining room. I was on my knees doing the skirting board when my falsie slipped out and was threatening to fall out of the bottom of my rugby shirt. How could I grab it and hide it before anyone came in, when I had paint all over my hands and there was nothing in the room but a tin of paint, a bottle of white spirit and a grotty old duster?

I don't feel the need for a reconstruction. I always used to be proud not of my bust measurement but my flat stomach, and I yearned to be like Audrey Hepburn, not Dolly Parton. Also, I am 51 and have been married forever, and my husband has never been a boob man. Before the operation and since, he has been everything I could have wanted a husband to be. The surgeon was tactful and skilled and all the nursing staff were sensitive, but it did take time to accept my new …well,

479

lopsidedness. Now I am used to being asymmetrical, and having a scar instead of a breast, if neither I nor my husband care, why should I want a reconstruction?

When I asked him about it again today, he said "Reconstruction? Isn't that something on *Crimewatch* where they make a passing resemblance to a former reality and hope viewers' imaginations will supply vital missing details?" Then he asked how they would make the new boob sag incrementally over time to keep pace with the old one. He pictured me at sixty as part Lolita and part Nora Batty.

The doctor did talk about alternatives to having bits inserted. It was possible to take fat from the belly, she said, and use that to reconstruct a breast. Now she was talking. I could return to the lost era of the flat stomach. But was a reconstruction operation a price worth paying?

Then I had the idea. Women who have had breast surgery are offered free counselling and plastic surgery on the NHS, on the grounds of helping their adjustment and speedy recovery. If some kind of plastic surgery is going to make them feel better, does it matter what it is? Maybe they should be offered a voucher for non-specific surgery after a mastectomy, so they can have liposuction, or a new nose, if that is going to improve their body image and boost their self-esteem. Maybe I'll write to the Health Minister about it. If the scheme is adopted, I'll keep the falsie and go for the tummy tuck.

SEPTEMBER

September 6th 2019

Embraced

When we lived in Sheffield, and the family member who declines to be named went back to school in September, I would cycle up to the Mayfield Valley (the beginning of the Peak District) and pick blackberries. It was a marker, the beginning of a new chapter.

Yesterday I was getting ready for my sister visiting, and was cleaning. I HATE cleaning. I got to a point when there was still a lot to do but I couldn't stand it any longer. It was a fine blustery day, so I got on my bike and cycled up the Monsal Trail. It was the end of the afternoon so there were very few people about. In any case, the summer holiday crowds had vanished. It was heavenly.

The margins of the Trail were edged with dried leaves, and the wind was chilly enough to require an extra layer of clothing, and it was clear the autumn had arrived. Surprisingly, I didn't feel wistful. I relished it, but not because I want the summer to end or that I like the autumn. It was rather that I felt overtaken and embraced by the natural world and it's unstoppable, overarching 'plan.' With all the tumultuous politics going on right now - down there in London - it was refreshing and comforting to be in a space where none of that was relevant - at least for two hours. I relished the breeze, the clouds, the

481

sunshine, the shadows in the valley, the open views - it was magical. I came back
on a high.

I love living here.

OCTOBER

October 25th 2019

Life and love and time

Yesterday we went to a funeral at the village church. We arrived half an hour before it was due to start and there were only three empty seats. Dave had to stand, and he counted 90 other people also standing. I was moved to see how many people were there to celebrate the life of a man who was much-loved in the village, a farmer two years older than me.

Roger was friendly, good-hearted, intelligent, fun, warm, sound, and so much more. He was born and bred in the village and wrote a regular farming column in the village newspaper.

We sang *Plough the fields and scatter the good seed*, *Morning has broken* and a local man sang a solo of *A Farmer's Boy*. The Bible reading was from Corinthians about the supremacy of love and someone read a poem called *God made a Farmer*.

We walked back up the lane under a cloudy sky feeling melancholy. Dave was ahead of me because I was looking for photographs, but it was fruitless because the light wasn't right. But in the late afternoon the sun came out and I went back outside and onto the lane and got some beauties.

It was a sobering afternoon, and has left me feeling that I don't want to waste a moment.

NOVEMBER

November 16th 2019

Letter from home

Despite the desperate political news, and the terrible floods, I've had some good times this week.

OK, so we've been stuck inside unable to cycle and driving each other nuts, but one cold wet afternoon, desperate for fresh air, I went out armed with a stout stick and cleared the gullies on the quarter mile lane at the end of ours. Why people don't want to clear gullies opposite their houses is a mystery. All that fun on their doorsteps and they leave it to someone on a neighbouring lane. Yesterday I drove home past them in pouring rain, and the road was awash with water again because the gullies were again clogged with leaves. Honestly! Don't people realise how satisfying it is to clear mud and leaves and grit from a grate and to see and hear the rainwater gushing down it?

DECEMBER

December 20th 2019

Early mornings at Hepworth Towers

Every morning for the last three months, Dave - who gets up hours before me - has come into the bedroom while I am drinking my first mug of Yorkshire tea in order to recount the latest outrage from Trump. I wish he wouldn't.

For one thing, it is not a good start to the day, and for another...it doesn't matter what awful thing Trump does, he can no longer surprise me. I say this to Dave, but still he tells me. Every morning.

On Wednesday Dave went out before I was awake, and when I woke up I breathed a sigh of pleasant freedom, thinking I'd have a Trump-free morning. What bliss...able to begin the day with no news from here and no news from there. We have sufficient problems on this side of the Atlantic without dwelling on the US horror show.

I got out of bed, switched on the fairy lights on the weeping fig in the bedroom, and fetched my tea. Then I picked up my iPad to check my emails and found an early morning email with an attachment from Dave, entitled 'Nuts!' Inside was a domestic message, and then 'What do you think of the letter?'

He had attached a copy of a letter from Trump to Nancy Pelosi, beginning thus:

Dear Madam Speaker,

I write to express my strongest and most powerful protest against the partisan impeachment crusade being pursued by the Democrats in the House of Representatives....

There was I, thinking I'd escaped the morning bulletin on Trump, and here instead was a *six page bloody letter* to wade through. Reader, I didn't.

Yesterday, Thursday, I woke up at 5 a.m., too late to go back to sleep but also too early to switch on the light, so I thought, 'Ooh, I know, I'll listen to the next episode of *The Railway Children* on BBC Sounds.'

I found this delightful programme by chance. A young actress [sic] is reading *The Railway Children* in 14 entrancing episodes. It's a wonderful antidote to everything OUT THERE.

Yesterday's chapter was entitled *The Amateur Fireman* and featured a part of the book I'd forgotten, where the children rescue a baby from a burning barge. It was so exciting! I was on the edge of my pillow! It was far too exciting for a gentle musing doze, and at the end of the episode I switched on the light, over-heated and charged up for the day, and it was still only half past five. It took me some time to recover.

I've just realised that a biographer could use this as a vivid illustration of something about me, but it's only 6.52 a.m. and I am still drinking my first mug of tea, so you'll have to decide what it is.

December 26th 2019

On being 70

I turned 70 this year and it's OK. If you're not there yet, be encouraged!

I hated being 60. I was miserable at 60, and 70 is so much better. I was telling this to a 59 year old friend at Quaker Meeting yesterday and he said, jokingly, 'Is that because you don't have to worry about what you're going to be when you grow up?'

It sort of is.

I feel as though I've arrived. This is me, warts and all, or, in my case, wrinkles and all. Take me or leave me.

I was recently in the supermarket with my two teenage grandsons and embarrassed them by explaining to the young and pleasant check-out man that it is much easier for the customer if, when giving change, you proffer coins first into the palm, and then notes. Said check-out man responded graciously. It *was* Waitrose.

As we left, I told the younger grandson "I know you find it embarrassing but the great thing about being old is that you don't care what people think of you."

"I wish I didn't care," he said. Of course when you're a teenager, what other people think is crucial.

Later in the morning, he said "Actually, Sue, you do care what people think." He calls me Sue, as they all do. "When you buy something new to wear, you always ask Mum what she thinks of it."

He'd got me. "You're right. But I don't care what people I *don't know* think of me."

The other nice thing about turning 70 was the party. It was wonderful. I mean it was *really* wonderful. The last time I had a birthday party was when I was 40. That was a fancy dress party and people had to dress up as what they wanted to be when they grew up. This growing up thing is obviously a big thing for me. I realise that only now as I write this post.

Isaac and Wendy and the girls came over from Colorado for my 70th birthday party, and of course my local 'kids' and grandkids were there, all my siblings and spouses came, plus one niece, and lots of old friends. I got to dance with three of my four grandchildren (one a 15 year old boy - dancing with him was one of the highlights of my night - but along with his brother I am no longer allowed to name or picture either on the blog, and more's the pity, because I would dearly love to show long-time blog readers who recall them from ten years ago what these fabulous teenagers look like now).

And there was a surprise cake made by a friend and relation-in-law, Chris Oxley. She put on it tiny edible replicas of all my books, sweet pea packets, sax, sax music, my patchwork and my laptop. I am still in awe of it. We ate the cake and the icing but I've kept everything else.

I only had the party so I would have a chance to dance, but having all the immediate family together plus old friends and the way everyone helped to make it happy - that was what was special. I went to bed that night thinking "If I die tonight, I'll die happy." Maybe that's what turning 70 is about for me. If I die now, I'll die happy – with my life, you understand. Not with the state of the world.

Heartfelt thanks to:

My blog readers for their support and friendship across the void.

Jan Hill and Valerie Dalling who independently and enthusiastically suggested I publish my blog as a book.

Pauline Wainwright for spending her time reading the text, and for comments and suggestions.

Kath Sharman and Peter Willis for reading part of an earlier draft.

Chrissie Poulson and Heather Noon for reading some of the text, and for their encouragement, helpful suggestions and patience as I worked on the project.

Isaac Hepworth for producing the front cover.

Zoë Hepworth for the cover calligraphy.

News International for their agreement to my publishing pieces originally appearing in *The Times*.

Dave Hepworth for formatting the text and for providing some of my choicest bits of copy.

Poems which I have permission to post on the blog but not in this book:

The thing is   by Ellen Bass   February 22nd 2012

http://www.suehepworth.com/2012/02/when-you-have-no-stomach-for-it.html

Let's celebrate   by Mandy Coe February 19th 2015

http://www.suehepworth.com/2015/02/those-moments.html

Ridge Walking by Char March December 18th 2015

http://www.suehepworth.com/2015/12/untitled.html

At the moment by Joyce Sutphen December 31st 2015

http://www.suehepworth.com/2015/12/oddments-at-years-end.html

Everything is going to be all right   by Derek Mahon
December 24th 2018

http://www.suehepworth.com/2018/12/hope-and-love.html

Printed in Great Britain
by Amazon